Compliance and the Future of Arms Control

Authors
Gloria Duffy, Project Director
Gregory Dalton
Matthew State
Leo Sartori

Working Group Signatories
John H. Barton, Professor, School of Law, Stanford
David M. Bernstein, Assistant to the Director, Center
Coit D. Blacker, Associate Director, Center
George Bunn, Visiting Scholar, Center and School of Law, Stanford; former General Counsel, U.S. Arms Control and Disarmament Agency
Alexander Dallin, Professor of History and Political Science, Stanford
Hugh DeWitt, Physicist, Lawrence Livermore National Laboratory
Sidney D. Drell, Co-Director, Center; Professor and Deputy Director, Stanford Linear Accelerator Center
Gloria Duffy, President, Global Outlook
Philip J. Farley, Senior Research Associate, Center; former Deputy Director, U.S. Arms Control and Disarmament Agency; Alternate Chairman, U.S. SALT I delegation
Alexander L. George, Professor of Political Science, Stanford
David Holloway, Professor of Political Science, Stanford
Steven Kull, Arms Control Fellow, Center
John W. Lewis, Co-Director, Center; Professor of Political Science, Stanford
Wolfgang K. H. Panofsky, Professor and Director Emeritus, Stanford Linear Accelerator Center
Leo Sartori, Professor of Physics and Political Science, University of Nebraska

Other Signatories
Robert Buchheim, U.S. Commissioner, Standing Consultative Commission, 1977–81
Raymond L. Garthoff, Senior Fellow, Brookings Institution
Sidney N. Graybeal, Vice President, System Planning Corporation; U.S. Commissioner, Standing Consultative Commission, 1973–76
Gerald W. Johnson, Adjunct Professor, Institute on Global Conflict and Cooperation, University of California, San Diego; member, SALT II delegation
Michael Krepon, Senior Associate, Carnegie Endowment for International Peace
William Perry, President, H & Q Technology Partners; former Under Secretary of Defense for Research and Engineering
Theodore J. Ralston, Representative, International Liaison Office, Microelectronics and Computer Technology Corporation

Compliance and the Future of Arms Control

Report of a project sponsored by the
Center for International Security and Arms Control,
Stanford University,
and Global Outlook

Gloria Duffy, Project Director

The Center for International Security and Arms Control at Stanford University brings together Stanford faculty members from several scholarly disciplines with senior specialists from around the world for research projects, seminars and conferences, and international scholarly exchange. The Center sponsors undergraduate and graduate courses, fellowship programs at the predoctoral, postdoctoral, and midcareer levels, and publications series, including Occasional Papers, Special Reports, and, through Stanford University Press, ISIS Studies in International Security and Arms Control. The opinions expressed in *Compliance and the Future of Arms Control* are those of the authors and do not represent positions of the Center, its supporters, or Stanford University.

Global Outlook does research on U.S.-Soviet relations and security in the nuclear age. Its findings and recommendations are disseminated through books, articles, congressional testimony, briefings for journalists and elected officials, and presentations for the public. Global Outlook advocates no party position or political viewpoint, but favors measures to decrease conflict and improve the security of the United States in the process of strengthening world security.

Library of Congress Cataloging-in-Publication Data

Compliance and the future of arms control : report of a project sponsored by the Center for International Security and Arms Control, Stanford University, and Global Outlook : Gloria Duffy, project director.
    p.   cm.
    Bibliography: p.
    Includes index.
    ISBN 0-88730-277-7.   ISBN 0-88730-280-7 (pbk.)
    1. Nuclear arms control—Verification.   2. United States—Foreign relations—Soviet Union.   3. Soviet Union—Foreign relations—United States.   4. Security, International.   I. Stanford University. Center for International Security and Arms Control.   II. Global Outlook (Think Tank)
JX1974.7.C573   1988
327.1'74—dc19   88-6218
                                                                    CIP

Contents

Preface

For twenty years after the first arms control agreement of the nuclear age—
the Antarctic Treaty—was signed in 1959, neither the United States nor
the Soviet Union expressed major dissatisfactions about compliance with
the terms of arms control accords. Disputes and complaints regarding compliance periodically arose, but the two parties were eventually able to
resolve all such disagreements.

In 1979 U.S. officials began to question Soviet arms control compliance. By 1983 both the United States and Soviet Union were expressing
grave and generalized dissatisfaction with the state of each other's compliance with arms control agreements. By 1986 forty separate accusations
of arms control violations had been publicly aired by the two nations,
eighteen by the United States against the Soviet Union and twenty-two
by the Soviet Union against the United States.

By 1986 the process of resolving disputes about treaty interpretation
and compliance, through the Standing Consultative Commission and other
diplomatic avenues used in the past, had broken down. In November 1986
the United States withdrew from the SALT I Interim Agreement and the
unratified but theretofore upheld SALT II Treaty, citing as its reason Soviet
violations of these and other arms control accords. U.S. withdrawal from
the SALT agreements removed the only existing constraints on strategic
offensive nuclear weapons between the superpowers.

Between 1983 and 1986 the United States and Soviet Union became
involved in a debate over the quality and acceptability of one another's
compliance with arms control agreements. This dispute began to take a
real toll on the status of the arms control agreements in force when concerns about Soviet compliance became the basis for U.S. decisions to abandon existing agreements.

Yet, during this same period of time U.S.-Soviet relations in general
were in an extremely disputatious state—over arms control, over regional
conflicts, over human-rights issues, and over the fundamental assumptions on which U.S.-Soviet mutual-security arrangements had been built.
It became increasingly difficult to know whether the concerns expressed
by both governments were an actual signal of trouble in the state of compliance with arms control agreements or simply one more sign of mutual
frustration in U.S.-Soviet relations. Did a real crisis in compliance with

arms control agreements exist? Or did the frustration in U.S.-Soviet relations simply create a crisis of confidence that raised doubt about the
mutual-security agreements put in place by the superpowers since 1959?

In the United States and abroad, the public, the press, and legislative
bodies have had only the statements of U.S. and Soviet officials to rely
on for comprehensive judgments about arms control compliance. The polemical, accusatory nature of U.S. and Soviet government pronouncements
about compliance since 1983 indicates political agendas at work rather
than dispassionate analysis of the situation. In part because of the sensitive nature of data that involve intelligence sources and methods, neither
government has publicly offered detailed information or analysis to back
up its charges and concerns about compliance.

If the impression that the U.S. government sought to convey between
1983 and 1987 — that Soviet compliance with arms control agreements
has been poor and agreements have frequently been violated — is correct,
then obviously the United States should take pause about the wisdom of
entering into further security agreements with the Soviet Union. Because
the question of past compliance with arms control agreements is so crucial to the future of existing accords and to the possibility for any new
U.S.-Soviet arms control measures, an expert working group based at the
Stanford University Center for International Security and Arms Control
undertook a comprehensive review of U.S. and Soviet compliance with
arms control agreements. The review was directed and staffed by Global
Outlook, a research organization specializing in international-security
issues.

The working group was convened in the summer of 1985. Over the
ensuing eighteen months, the group examined in detail the overall record
of U.S. and Soviet compliance and the U.S. and Soviet charges of noncompliance. The working group reviewed the legal, national-security, and
political aspects of U.S. and Soviet behavior bearing on compliance with
agreements. It closely examined Soviet behavior, compared the strategies
successive U.S. administrations have used to handle compliance issues,
and weighed the degree of success with which different U.S. approaches
have been met.

The group examined compliance in the context of overall U.S.-Soviet
relations. It studied the U.S.-Soviet process for resolving compliance disputes as it has functioned since the Standing Consultative Commission
was established in 1972. And the group explored the implications of the
experience to date with arms control compliance for the future of the
dispute-resolution process and the nature of future arms control
agreements.

The working group was chaired by Gloria Duffy. It included several
former U.S. arms control negotiators and officials involved in making arms
control policy, a former member of the president's General Advisory Com-

mittee on Arms Control and Disarmament, a former general counsel and a former deputy director of the Arms Control and Disarmament Agency, former members of the president's Science Advisory Committee, physicists, Soviet specialists, political scientists, international-law specialists, and experts on nuclear weapons and nuclear testing. Staff for the project were Gloria Duffy, Gregory Dalton, Margaret Beernink, Matthew State, and Leo Sartori (consultant).

This report is the result of the working group's efforts and presents the conclusions of its comprehensive review of the compliance situation. Not all working group members or signatories necessarily endorse every statement made in the report, but they find themselves in agreement with its main thrust and conclusions.

The report is divided into nine chapters. Chapter 1, written by Gloria Duffy with assistance from Wolfgang K. H. Panofsky, outlines the key analytic principles that must inform an assessment of arms control compliance. Chapter 2, written by Gloria Duffy, reviews the positive record of arms control compliance. The second part of this chapter examines charges of U.S. and Soviet noncompliance that involve ambiguous treaty provisions or ambiguous behavior by parties to treaties but do not constitute arms control violations.

Chapters 3 and 4 analyze areas that the working group felt to be of some concern regarding U.S. and Soviet compliance. These include two instances of questionable Soviet compliance with the SALT II agreement: the SS-25 ICBM and encryption of ballistic-missile–flight-test telemetry. Leo Sartori wrote both of these case studies. An area of U.S. questionable compliance with the ABM Treaty involves U.S. modernization or construction of new large phased-array radars. The analysis of the U.S. Thule, Fylingdales, and PAVE PAWS programs was written by Greg Dalton.

The working group found one clear instance of an arms control violation: the Soviet large phased-array radar at Abalakovo in Siberia. The case study on Abalakovo, chapter 5, was written by Greg Dalton. Finally, the working group found that U.S. statements about early deployment of a strategic-defense and reinterpretation of the ABM Treaty raise concerns regarding future U.S. ABM Treaty compliance, in light of robust U.S. strategic-defense research through the Strategic Defense Initiative. Matthew State wrote chapter 6, an analysis of U.S. strategic-defense efforts and ABM Treaty compliance.

Chapter 7 of the report, written by Gloria Duffy, reviews Soviet compliance behavior in its political context and sketches a portrait of the internal and external factors that may shape Soviet compliance behavior and decision making. Chapter 8, written by Greg Dalton, evaluates the operation of the Standing Consultative Commission from 1972 to the present.

Finally, chapter 9, written by Gloria Duffy, details the working group's conclusions about the state of arms control compliance and recommendations for steps to resolve the current compliance disputes and to improve the functioning of arms control agreements in the future. Four appendixes summarize U.S. and Soviet charges of noncompliance, detail the methodology for measuring the yield of underground nuclear tests, and provide a chronology of Standing Consultative Commission operations and a list of U.S.-Soviet agreements reached through that body.

Acknowledgments

This report would not have been possible without the assistance of many people and institutions. Sidney Drell and John Lewis of the Stanford Center for International Security and Arms Control encouraged the project from the start. Chip Blacker skillfully coordinated editing of the manuscript. Fritz Mosher, Wade Greene, Enid Schoettle, and Hal Harvey were instrumental on behalf of the foundations that provided financial assistance: the Carnegie Corporation of New York, Rockefeller Family Associates, the Ford Foundation, and the New Land Foundation. The Ravenal Foundation and an anonymous donor also provided funding. Gerry Bowman and other staff at the Center were indispensable to the smooth running of the study.

The members of the working group were unselfish with their contributions of time and thought, fitting meetings and other activities into already overwhelmed schedules. In a very literal sense, this report represents the combined intellectual resources of the entire group.

Individuals outside the regular working group also contributed importantly. Chief among these was Michael Krepon, head of the Verification Project at the Carnegie Endowment for International Peace. Krepon was indefatigably generous with his knowledge, sources, contacts, and advice, and he organized an extremely useful meeting of his Verification Project working group to critique part of the draft report. Individuals who made presentations to the working group or provided advice and information, other than those listed as contributors and signatories to this report, were Barry Blechman, Paul Brown, Dan Caldwell, William Colby, Tom Connolly, David Perlman, Robert Einhorn, Rob Elder, Jack Evernden, Mark Garrison, Jim Goldsborough, Charles Gellner, Willard J. Hannon, John Harvey, Warren Heckrotte, Gail Lapidus, Matthew Meselson, Jack Matlock, Roger Molander, Janne Nolan, Dmitri Ponamareff, William Potter, John Rhinelander, Harry Rowen, Condoleezza Rice, James Rubin, Walter Slocombe, Gerard Smith, and Phillip Trimble.

Gregory Dalton and Matthew State provided extensive assistance with the project in general, in addition to their role as coauthors of the report. Margaret Beernink provided assistance at an earlier stage.

Finally, the report itself was much improved through the comments of Sid Drell, Pief Panofsky, Dave Bernstein, Ray Garthoff, Bob Buchheim,

Sid Graybeal, Jim Hannon, Paul Brown, Chip Blacker, George Bunn, John Barton, Steve Kull, Alex George, Leo Sartori, and David Holloway.

To these individuals, institutions, and foundations, who provided the material, operational, and intellectual wherewithal to undertake a study of this magnitude, I am deeply grateful.

Gloria Duffy

Chapter One
Introduction: Thinking About Compliance

Arms control is the process by which nations with adversary interests agree that their individual national security is better served if the arms competition between them is managed under agreed covenants. There is a reasonable consensus that the security of the United States and Soviet Union is improved by accords constraining their nuclear arms competition.[1] Alternatives to arms control — an unlimited nuclear arms race, on the one hand, and unilateral disarmament on the other — are not acceptable. A technological solution achieved by effectively defending against nuclear attack is a quite remote possibility, pursuit of which simply encourages a competition for technological countermeasures.

In the United States we tend to focus primarily on the first of two aspects of arms control: the negotiation of agreements. Arms control negotiations are seen as something akin to a sporting event. The U.S. public and press follow the plays and maneuvers on both sides. When an agreement is signed, there is a sense of success, as though the goal has been reached.

But the end of the negotiations is, in fact, only the beginning of the arms control process. The test of arms control's success is whether the parties to an agreement abide by its terms over time, and whether each side recognizes and credits the other side's compliance. If the signatories do not comply with their obligations to reduce weapons or forces or to change their behavior, or if compliance is not recognized, then the agreement becomes little more than a meaningless scrap of paper. Compliance is the actual practice of arms control.

In domestic law, courts uphold compliance with agreements through their authority to interpret the law where its application to a specific situation is in question, and through their power to order enforcement of their findings. In the international sphere, the task of balancing conflicting interpretations of agreements is more difficult, because it involves the most intense national-security interests of the countries involved; yet there are no courts to which the behavior of the parties is subject. The resolution of compliance issues must be left to the limited authority and enforcement powers of provisions or institutions established by the agreements. Compliance is thus voluntary and depends on the political climate and the political will of the parties to make the arms control regime function. This political will must be based on the continuing resolve of the parties that their national security is better served if the arms control regime continues to prevail than if it lapses. The parties must base such resolve, in turn, on a net assessment weighing the accomplishments of agreements against concerns about compliance.

Because compliance is voluntary, a responsibility rests with each of the parties to an agreement to make accurate judgments about whether its own behavior accords with the obligations embodied in a treaty, and whether the activities of the other party are consistent with treaty requirements. In making such judgments, it makes little sense for either the United States or Soviet Union to look at one another's compliance-related behavior in a vacuum. A number of fundamental considerations—related to the nature and status of agreements, the political and technological context of agreements, and the means for pursuit of redress when compliance is in question—must be taken into account in performing a balanced assessment of arms control compliance.

A net assessment must include considerations such as the following: How are concerns about compliance related to the legal status of agreements? What are the national-security implications of instances of suspected noncompliance? Keeping in mind the inherent ambiguities of agreements, and the necessity that the parties maintain the will to work out interpretations of treaty provisions, what political, military, and technological factors have influenced the quality of compliance and the will to resolve compliance disputes?

In much of the recent dialogue challenging the record of compliance with arms control agreements, standards have been invoked that are not consistent with these basic considerations. The remainder of this chapter outlines the key concepts that should inform a responsible assessment of arms control compliance, which is, in turn, an important element in the net assessment of the value of arms control agreements.

The Nature and Status of Agreements

Treaty Ambiguities

Perhaps the single most important consideration to keep in mind when approaching the question of arms control compliance is that all agreements are to some extent ambiguous. Even in the best of circumstances, when the parties to an agreement earnestly seek to make it work, compliance issues will inevitably arise. Between countries with conflicting interests, it is simply not possible to construct a perfect agreement that will never be subject to divergent interpretations. On the contrary, each side will naturally try to interpret agreements in a way that accrues to its own benefit.

The emergence of compliance issues and some difficulty in resolving them should therefore not be surprising and should not be taken to discredit arms control agreements. After all, at least as much dispute and controversy can accompany the carrying out domestically of labor-relations agreements, environmental regulations, or even real-estate or marriage contracts. Yet no one would seriously suggest that, for example, because it requires some effort to define precisely what constitutes fraud, all statutes restraining fraud should be judged to have failed and should be abandoned.

The temptation is always great to accuse past agreements of excessive ambiguity that has fostered divergent interpretations. Yet, drafting an arms control agreement involves making a judgment about whether excessive precision would lead to sufficiently better compliance to justify the risk of compromise of U.S. intelligence values, or even to better compliance per se than would a degree of ambiguity.

For example, the dispute between the United States and Soviet Union over whether Soviet encryption practices "impede" verification of compliance with SALT II concerns a provision that is admittedly and deliberately vague.[2] Yet the United States has judged that, because of the implied compromise of sources and methods of intelligence collection, provisions precisely specifying which telemetry channels can or cannot legally be encrypted would endanger security more seriously than would the ambiguity resulting from such broad terminology.

It is also not necessarily the case that increased precision improves the prospects for compliance with an agreement. Nothing could be more precise than the provision of the Threshold Test Ban Treaty that sets 150 kilotons as the upper limit for the permissible yield of an underground nuclear explosion. Yet, as we know, this precision has not prevented dispute. In this case, the controversy does not arise from ambiguity of drafting but rather from the uncertainty of the natural world, from deficiencies in physical measurement, and from poorly defined methodologies for evaluating compliance. The designer of a nuclear weapon cannot precisely predict the yield at which his device will detonate, and the technician measuring yield can perform such measurement only subject to some uncertainty.

Advancing technology is making the drafting of precise definitions of the boundary between allowed and forbidden activities progressively more difficult. The number of multiple-function systems is increasing. Defensive technologies, such as those evolving under the aegis of the Strategic Defense Initiative (SDI), have potential offensive applications. "Tactical" military systems can perform "strategic" missions, depending on their geographic locations.

Although these technological developments should give a greater sense of urgency to arms control, they also contribute to the obsolescence of arms control provisions that are too narrowly drawn. Moreover, some level of ambiguity can often bridge differences in point of view and interests both within each negotiating side and between or among the negotiating parties, and can help to avert confrontation on the smallest detail. Indeed, the drafting of provisions of an arms control agreement frequently demands what is known in the legal profession as "creative ambiguity," a level of ambiguity optimally adapted to the situation on a case-by-case basis.

Standards that have been invoked to judge compliance in recent years have not taken into account the ambiguity inherent in international agreements. Some people demand a level of compliance with international constraints that would be impossible to apply in domestic law. Others seem unrealistically to expect that international constraints should be much freer from ambiguity and diversity of interpretation than domestic law has ever been.

Verification Constraints

A second set of considerations to keep in mind involves the inherent limitations of verification capabilities. Verification is the means by which one party determines whether or not another party to an agreement is complying with its terms. Verification measures include four primary types of procedures: (1) national technical means (NTM), such as satellite surveillance, radar surveillance from locations outside the boundaries of the country monitored, radioactive air sampling, teleseismic geophysical observations, and communications intercepts; (2) cooperative means of verification, such as the deliberate opening of certain features of military systems to surveillance, specific channeling of military products through agreed check points, and noninterference with means of verification; (3) on-site inspection; and (4) "soft" methods of verification, such as using agents, interviewing émigrés, and analyzing information leaks.

It is a truism that good verification capabilities serve as a deterrent to noncompliance. By providing early detection of suspicious activity, such capabilities may also enhance the prospects for resolving compliance disputes before a questionable program is completed and the difficulty of backing away from it has thus increased for the suspect party.

Although there has been much debate about the standards that verification capabilities must meet, most people would agree that verification should be "effective" in the sense that, as a minimum, (1) no violation that endangers national security should remain undetected and unidentified and (2) no violation that interferes in a basic way with the purpose of an agreement should remain undetected and unidentified. Critics of this approach to verification have demanded higher standards, frequently not in a constructive spirit with regard to arms control, at times even demanding that *no* violations of an arms control agreement should escape observation. Such a standard of "perfect" verification is probably impossible to attain and may in fact not contribute to improving determinations about compliance.

More intrusive measures of verification, especially on-site inspection, are often demanded as a way of improving confidence in compliance. But the effectiveness of on-site inspection is limited. Neither the United States nor Soviet Union could agree to an arrangement under which either side would initiate an on-site inspection at a time and place of its own choosing. On-site inspection involving sovereign nations would require some mechanism to trigger permission to conduct an inspection, most likely the mutual consent of the parties. External political pressures would certainly influence, and potentially constrain, the parties' willingness to authorize an inspection.

In attempting to improve the certainty and reach of verification, policymakers face a series of trade-offs. Both the United States and the Soviet Union, for instance, value their national sovereignty and privacy. The Soviet Union is traditionally more secretive about information it considers to be of importance for national security, although the United States is certainly sensitive about military secrets as well. There is necessarily overlap between the collection of information relevant to an arms control agreement and the collection of military intelligence of broader value. Given their penchant for secrecy, the Soviets tend to press for verification activities restricted only to the agreement at hand. As a more open society competing with one that is more closed, the United States has a natural interest in using verification of arms control agreements to increase its general knowledge of Soviet military assets and practices. The tension between these differing priorities of the two sides limits the available verification means.

Another constraint on more extensive means of verification is cost. Intelligence collection in general, including the part of information gathering associated with arms control verification, is subject to budgetary and resource priorities.

In choosing standards of verification, the liability of intrusiveness must be balanced against the value of higher-quality verification, and the cost and resources dedicated to verification must be weighed against the value of the information gathered. Verification methods and technologies to support various agreements can certainly be improved, but, given the compromises inherent in their design, they will likely never render agreements perfectly verifiable.

In addition, questions about whether or not an activity is in compliance with an agreement quite often do not turn on the simple availability of information through verification means. Even with good information about military behavior, evaluations of one party's compliance may depend on a broader legal and political analysis, including interpretation of the provisions of agreements and the obligations of the parties. For instance, the United States is not unclear about the level of telemetry encryption currently practiced by the Soviet Union. The doubt arises, rather, in determining whether the existing degree of encryption exceeds the level permitted by the SALT II agreement.

Enhanced verification procedures alone thus would not be a panacea for the challenges involved in performing a balanced evaluation of compliance. The process of evaluating intelligence information — including such tasks as defining what constitutes a significant violation — may in fact be a much weaker link in the verification process than monitoring or data-collection capabilities. The task of evaluation is particularly complicated in the United States because it is subject to interagency politics and competition.

Status of Agreements

A third key consideration that must inform judgments about compliance is the fact that various agreements have differing status under international law and customary international behavior. The expected standards of compliance should clearly be related to the particular status of each agreement.

Arms control agreements, by and large, were originally designed to be pacts under international law. Only four arms control agreements out of the twenty involving the United States and Soviet Union were not structured as treaties. The SALT I Interim Agreement, designed to be quickly superseded by SALT II, was an executive agreement, but even it was subject to a resolution of approval by the U.S. Congress.

But, because of political circumstances and consequent U.S. nonratification, the reality today is that several agreements represent less than full legal commitments. In terms of their legal status, arms control agreements today fall into several categories: (1) agreements in force, that is, signed and ratified; (2) agreements that are signed, but not ratified, with ratification pending; (3) agreements that are signed, but not ratified, with the ratification process discontinued; (4) agreements that are "declaratory," that is, based on declarations of intent by national leaders; and (5) agreements, such as moratoriums or declaratory acts, that are announced as being in force for fixed terms. From a legal standpoint, the agreements in each of these distinct categories entail different obligations by the parties.

Treaties in force obviously involve the strictest obligations for compliance. The purpose of a treaty is to build, over time, a set of norms for international conduct. Unlike less formal agreements, treaties are supported by a large weight of customary international behavior and principles such as Grotius's law, *pacta sunt servanda,* or "promises given must be kept." The treaty-ratification process subjects treaties to "publicity and consensus-building around the international norm and symbolizes the domestic political blessing of the legal commitment."[3] A treaty in force has legal status under the U.S. Constitution, and compliance with it is a legal obligation.

Among the treaties in this category are the ABM Treaty and its protocols, the Geneva Protocol, the Antarctic Treaty, the Limited Test Ban Treaty, the Outer Space Treaty, the Latin American Nuclear-Free Zone Treaty, the Non-Proliferation Treaty, the Seabed Arms Control Treaty, the Biological

Weapons Convention, the Convention on Physical Protection of Nuclear Material, and the Environmental Modification Convention. Other legally binding agreements are the "Hot Line" agreements, the Prevention of Nuclear War Agreement, the "Accidents Measures" Agreement, the Incidents at Sea Agreement, and the SALT I Interim Agreement (from which the United States withdrew in November 1986).

The Vienna Convention on the Law of Treaties, embodying customary international norms, holds that, when parties have signed a treaty, as long as they intend to complete ratification, they should refrain from steps that are inconsistent with the treaty.[4] This is generally understood to mean that compliance with every provision of an agreement is not required. Rather, neither side should take significant, active steps that would frustrate the purpose of the treaty or its operation once it is ratified. For example, if a treaty calls for weapon dismantlements, the parties need not take steps to dismantle while ratification is pending, but at the same time they should not add systems to those that existed at the time the treaty was signed.

The major agreement in this second category was SALT II, until it was withdrawn from Senate consideration in 1981.[5] The Soviet Union was thus in compliance with the SALT II Treaty when it held static its strategic launcher total at 2,504, the number that existed when the agreement was signed. Had the treaty been ratified, the Soviet Union would have been required to reduce its strategic launchers to 2,400, then to 2,250 by January 1981.

Finally, the obligation of the parties to comply with agreements that are signed, but for which the ratification process has been discontinued, is a political commitment, subject to interpretation by their national leaderships. In terms of the strength of expectations about compliance, these agreements merge with declaratory agreements or those based on reciprocal unilateral statements, generating weaker obligations for compliance than the agreements in the first two categories. Agreements in this third category include the 1974 Threshold Test Ban Treaty, the Peaceful Nuclear Explosions Treaty, and SALT II after 1981.[6]

Some international-law specialists contend that parties to agreements can only be held to strict standards of compliance when the agreements are ratified, if ratification is required to bring them into full force. Thus, Phillip Trimble argues that the United States cannot legitimately charge the Soviet Union with noncompliance with either the Threshold Test Ban Treaty or SALT II, since they have not been fully in force.[7] Politically binding declarations to uphold an agreement place clear obligations upon the parties. But by declining to ratify and bring several agreements into full legal force, the United States has sent signals about the status of these agreements. The United States must temper with realism its expectations for high standards of compliance with these agreements that the United States has consigned to a state of legal limbo.

The Context of Arms Control

Arms control agreements are imbedded in a political and technological context that affects incentives for compliance, perceptions about compliance, and the prospects for resolving disputes related to compliance. National decision makers concerned with making judgments about compliance often seem to be unaware of the extent to which overall political and technological trends affect compliance. Certain characteristics of the environment can foster compliance, and others can degrade compliance. Among the contextual factors that may undercut compliance are (1) signatories' unilateral advocacy of reinterpretations of an agreement, seeking to weaken its limitations; (2) brinksmanship on the part of the signatories pushing at the limit of conduct permissible under the treaty; (3) parties' public promotion of military programs that, although their current conduct conforms to the provisions of the agreement, have goals that conflict with the stated objectives of the agreement; (4) deterioration of relations among or between the parties that makes civil discourse in a problem-solving spirit difficult; (5) the evolution of technology that threatens obsolescence of the provisions of the agreement.

Among those forces that strengthen compliance with agreements are (1) a good record of compliance with past agreements, recognized by parties to the agreements; (2) a demonstrable economic savings and increased stability attributable to past agreements; (3) an improving international climate involving the signatories; (4) evident progress toward future, more incisive arms control agreements; and (5) resolution of ambiguities related to the provisions of arms control treaties through a joint problem-solving approach between the parties.

Two detailed observations about the effects of these contextual factors on compliance should be kept in mind. First, the more ambitious and complex an arms control agreement is, the greater is the potential for questions regarding compliance to arise if the political environment is not supportive. The SALT II Treaty was the most comprehensive attempt by the United States and Soviet Union to impose constraints on their strategic arsenals. SALT II incorporated more qualitative provisions than the predecessor SALT I Interim Agreement, in an attempt to limit the modernization of strategic offensive weapons. Qualitative arms control provisions may be more prone to give rise to questions about compliance than quantitative ones, because judgments about whether a certain design fulfills qualitative treaty obligations may be more subjective than simply determining whether the forces of one side or the other meet numerical restrictions.

The general atmosphere of political relations between countries that are parties to treaties affects their interpretations of treaty obligations. In periods when political tensions are high and the prospects for expanding the arms control regime are poor, parties see greater advantage to permissive interpretations of agreements in pursuit of their military programs. Compliance disputes are also more difficult to resolve by civil and private means when political tension is high.

Thus, in the 1970s the United States and Soviet Union agreed to more-restrictive strategic arms limits than ever before. But these agreements—especially SALT II, which contained stronger qualitative restraints than previous agreements, requiring substantial interpretation in relation to compliance—were expected to perform in the 1980s in a more difficult environment than previous agreements had encountered in the 1970s, an environment in which consultative mechanisms were not functioning well. Such a situation could not help but put stresses on compliance.

The second observation about the effects of the context upon compliance relates to new technological developments. Changes in the military and strategic situation, some caused by new technological developments, also place strains on treaty compliance if not integrated into the arms control framework through new accords. In particular, some of the elements in the strategic situation that had made possible the strategic arms control regime constructed in the early 1970s had changed significantly by the early 1980s.

The strategic arms control regime had been based on a number of factors that made the SALT I and SALT II limits seem both palatable and advantageous to the United States and Soviet Union. Primarily, rough parity in strategic forces had brought about a broad strategic stability. The existence of strategic sufficiency on both sides meant that increments to forces would not result in instability. Any potentially destabilizing developments could be redressed through arms control measures aimed at maintaining the balance of forces. And reconnaissance and intelligence capabilities had developed sufficiently on both sides to provide confidence in the verifiability of arms control agreements.

But developments in weapons technology in the 1970s served both to upset the perception that parity existed and to decrease confidence in the verifiability of agreements. Unconstrained by any ban on warhead fractionation in SALT I, the Soviet Union had proceeded to place multiple independently targetable reentry vehicles (MIRVs) on its force of heavy missiles in the 1970s, causing some people to question the survivability of the U.S. land-based intercontinental ballistic missile (ICBM) force. The United States had deployed the Minuteman III with counterforce potential, placing at risk a substantial portion of the Soviet land-based force. The United States continued to deploy a new class of Trident-based submarine-launched ballistic missiles, putting an ever-larger number of strategic targets in the Soviet Union under time-urgent threat of accurate attack. The strategic arms competition proved to be quite dynamic during the 1970s, despite the SALT agreements.

Neither side necessarily saw the potential for obtaining strategic superiority through continued modernization. But increased political tensions fostered worst-case perceptions on each side of the other side's forces. These worst-case perceptions, in turn, drove each nation to pursue programs to offset the other nation's perceived advantage. The possibility for modernization of forces within the limits of the existing agreements was still great enough to permit this sort of competition. The incentives were thus high for both sides to push the limits of the agreements as far as possible, as the Soviet Union did, for instance, in the case of the SS-25 ICBM. After 1979 no new agreements or substantial clarifications of existing treaties were achieved to integrate these new developments into the arms control framework.

Developments in military technology may also render verification, the basis for determining compliance, more difficult. Large phased-array radars, such as the Soviet installation at Abalakovo, as a class represent a case in which the technology of weapons systems has made verification more problematic. It is not possible, using national technical means of verification, to determine the specific application for which such multiuse systems are intended. Lacking progress toward refined ABM Treaty provisions or new cooperative verification procedures, the limited means for verifying the purpose of these installations has left the question of Soviet compliance with the ABM Treaty restrictions on such radars mired in uncertainty and public controversy.

Evaluating Compliance

Given the ambiguity that may characterize some provisions of agreements and the varying status of agreements with regard to expectations of compliance, the parties have a significant degree of latitude in evaluating one another's compliance. In addition, the periodic tensions to which U.S.-Soviet relations are subject can affect the judgments each side makes about compliance. Insulating compliance from shifts in the political situation is possible only if certain important distinctions are kept in mind.

The first distinction is between activities of an adversary that present security threats but do not affect compliance with agreements and activities that do affect treaty compliance. The national-security implications of an arms control violation, whether the violation is strongly suspected or definitely determined, are arguably the most important criteria for determining a response. But not all activities that cause national-security concern are arms control compliance issues.

In recent years this distinction has become blurred. Thus, in periodic "noncompliance" statements, the United States and Soviet Union have accused one another of activities that, though perhaps regrettable, do not relate to obligations assumed in agreements. Soviet allegations in 1984 that the United States was striving for military superiority and violating a SALT II protocol that would have expired in 1981 even had SALT II been ratified, exemplify this lack of differentiation, as does the U.S. complaint that through building the SS-19 the Soviet Union exceeded the size of the largest permitted light missile under the SALT I Interim Agreement. This last complaint is based on a unilateral U.S. understanding not accepted by the Soviet Union.

For the purpose of evaluating compliance, the threat to U.S. or Soviet security cannot be judged to have increased simply because more-threatening military activities are evident on one side or the other. A realistic assessment of the national-security impact of a violation or an instance of questionable compliance requires an evaluation of the *marginal* threat of the action at issue, that is, the net effect on national security of the particular characteristics of the activity that raise compliance concerns.

The remedy for concerns about military security caused by activities of a party that are unconstrained by arms control agreements is to seek more comprehensive arms control restrictions so that these activities will be restrained. But one side's concerns about the other's military behavior in general are not compliance issues, and including them in discussions of compliance simply contributes to an argumentative atmosphere in which real compliance concerns are impossible to address.

In addition to being precise about the military threat represented by compliance concerns, each party to an agreement must keep a clear separation between its evaluation of the other party's compliance and its own desires to pursue new military programs that may conflict with treaty obligations. When one party to an agreement cites the other side's noncompliance as justification for pursuing a noncompliant program, suspicion arises about the motivation for the concern about compliance and undercuts the credibility of the concern. In announcing its decision in May 1986 to withdraw from the SALT II Treaty by exceeding the agreement's MIRVed-launcher ceilings, the United States cited Soviet SALT II violations. But some administration officials had publicly made the argument that U.S. security would be improved if the United States could pursue strategic modernization programs free from the obligation to adhere to SALT II constraints. The administration charged that the Soviet Union was violating provisions of the agreement related to the SS-25 and encryption, not the SALT II MIRVed-launcher limits, which raised further suspicions about the real connection of the U.S. action to Soviet behavior.

An equally important requirement is that standards for judging compliance must be applied equally to both parties. In times when political relations are poor, the United States and Soviet Union may tend to make judgments about compliance in which each country is permissive about its own behavior but interprets its adversary's arms control obligations in a restrictive fashion. The United States thus has accused the Soviet Union of moving in a general way toward a strategic defense of its territory in violation of the ABM Treaty, when announced U.S. policy is to pursue this same goal through the Strategic Defense Initiative.[8] By contributing to a general climate of accusation, double standards of this sort increase the difficulty of resolving valid compliance problems.

Some consideration must also be given to determining whether a violation is intentional or unintentional. Escape of radioactivity from U.S. and Soviet underground nuclear tests since 1963 may have violated limits of the Limited Test Ban Treaty. But such emissions by both countries were clearly unintentional and must be evaluated in that light.

Finally, a sense of perspective about the compliance questions at issue must underlie evaluations of compliance. How significant are the military activities about which compliance concerns have been raised? How do the areas of compliance concern weigh in the balance with provisions that have generated no controversy? What is the overall pattern — one of compliance or one of noncompliance?

In the long run, the success of arms control will be judged on the basis of whether it has demonstrably advanced the national security of the United States and has lessened the likelihood and severity of potential conflict. Such a judgment must be based on a net assessment of the parties' compliance with the provisions of arms control agreements. It is misleading and damaging to publicize only alleged or real noncompliance with agreements, while ignoring the complete record of actual arms control, that is, limitations and reductions of armaments flowing from compliance with the agreements.

Yet, during the last few years, U.S. public attention has been focused by the executive branch and stemming from that, by Congress, on charges of violations, whereas the record of destruction or deactivation of weapons systems in compliance with agreements has been given scant public attention. This unbalanced public coverage has given a highly unjustified black eye to the arms control process. For instance, the General Advisory Committee on Arms Control and Disarmament (GAC), advising the president, the secretary of state, and the director of the Arms Control and Disarmament Agency (ACDA), was charged at the beginning of the Reagan administration with examining the record of noncompliance with the arms control agreements. But neither that committee nor other bodies of the government have ever apparently been tasked with performing a net assessment of compliance, including U.S. and Soviet compliance and noncompliance with agreements.

The Pursuit of Compliance

Once the verification process has revealed conduct that raises concerns about arms control compliance, some action should be taken in response, to promote compliance. Various options are available for response to suspected noncompliance. At one extreme, the party having uncovered a suspicious activity can go public and confront the other party with a charge of violation. At the other extreme, the suspecting party might choose not to respond at all, hoping the activity either is not what it seems, is trivial, or will not recur.

A balance of values is clearly involved in deciding how to respond to suspected violations. If suspicious events result immediately in public confrontation involving accusations and denial, the parties will find it difficult to retreat from such positions. In consequence, resolution will become difficult, public confidence in the arms control process will erode, and the relationship among the parties will suffer. At the other extreme, disregard of suspected violations will also lead to erosion of confidence in the arms control process, since the events of concern will become public knowledge sooner or later. Disregard could also weaken deterrence of more significant violations.

Using consultative bodies to deal with activities that generate concern about compliance is the best way to avoid either of these two extremes. The Standing Consultative Commission (SCC), established by the SALT I Treaty, is such a body. Other arms control agreements contain provisions for consultation and mediation, some involving the United Nations.

In order to give the problem-solving process a maximum opportunity for success, it is essential that the process proceed out of the limelight and with as much privacy as possible. When the SCC was proceeding in such a manner in the past, its record in problem solving was good. During the Reagan administration, once the SCC process was paralleled, or even replaced, with public confrontation, its effectiveness deteriorated.

Yet, total privacy in evaluating evidence and resolving conflict related to suspected treaty violations is also not acceptable. The democratic process in the United States demands an informed electorate and legislature. Deliberations about ratification of arms control agreements are necessarily influenced by the compliance record of the past. This, in turn, leads to demands for information about the past record of success in resolving charges of noncompliance.

The detailed negotiating record of most arms control agreements and the ensuing consultations in the SCC continue to be classified by mutual agreement between the parties. Yet frequently, as we know from the analogous domestic-court procedure, interpretation of apparently ambiguous law is facilitated if the interpreters can refer to legislative history in order to document the intent of the parties. To quote a passage from a letter, of December 1, 1986, from Senator Carl Levin to Secretary of State George Shultz regarding interpretation of the ABM Treaty:

And as Tsune-Chi Yu points out in his *The Interpretation of Treaties,*
" . . . It is the function of the interpreter to ascertain the genuine sense

in which the negotiators have employed the words rather than to ascertain the bare meaning of the words themselves."

Treaty interpretation, then, is designed to allow us to discover intent and one of the ways to discover intent is to determine what the negotiators themselves believed they were agreeing to. Indeed, in one celebrated case involving the Jay Treaty between the United States and Great Britain, efforts to resolve an ambiguous point involved taking depositions from John Adams and John Jay, members of the negotiating team. In theory and practice, then, interpreters of treaties are bound to discover the understanding and intent of the parties to an agreement which is arguably ambiguous and, in the process, they may be guided by the understandings and intentions of the negotiators.

Thus, the value of keeping the negotiating history of an arms control treaty and subsequent SCC deliberations and agreements private has to be balanced against the value of using that very history in interpreting ambiguous events or evaluating contested interpretations of a treaty. A possible compromise would be to reveal the negotiating history, still on a classified basis, to legislative bodies that are attempting to review the merit of charges of noncompliance but to deny full public access to the negotiating record.

Private problem-solving activities should be given all possible opportunity to succeed before either party resorts to more overt measures; public confrontation should be a last resort. Unfortunately, in recent years this prescription has rarely been followed, with a resulting negative impact on the arms control process. It appears easier for the Reagan administration to denounce alleged Soviet violations than to negotiate solutions in the interest of increased security.

Once problem solving in a productive spirit has failed, more substantive response must be contemplated. What response is chosen will, of course, depend on the overall political context, and no general prescriptions can be given. It is essential, however, that an effort be made to prevent such a response from leading to a mutual escalation of violations of arms control agreements, thereby destroying the fruits of past achievements.

Thus, a response to a suspected violation should be carefully tailored to avoid overreaction. In other words, responsive noncompliance should not have a perceived military impact higher than that reasonably associated with the alleged noncompliance by the other party. Once the stage of public confrontation has been reached, it is again of greatest importance not to overgeneralize alleged transgressions by the other party. There is a great deal of difference between charging the Soviet Union with constructing a radar with a permitted function at a location judged illegal under the ABM Treaty and a charge that the Soviets have a general policy of violating arms control agreements.

Response to compliance problems involves a difficult balance of values that must be worked out in a political context. A sensible policy should not be publicly interpretable as one that condones violations; yet overreaction is clearly incompatible with a viable arms control process.

This report examines the record of U.S. and Soviet compliance with arms control agreements. It employs an approach that takes into account factors including the inherent ambiguity of international agreements, the differing legal status of agreements, the limitations of verification, the political and strategic environment that surrounds compliance, the marginal strategic significance of the compliance behavior of both parties, the need to avoid double standards, and the requirements for effectively pursuing resolution of compliance disputes. In making an evaluation of compliance with past arms control accords, we hope to provide a basis for a net assessment of the extent to which these agreements have served U.S. national security.

Chapter Two

The Compliance Record

The Overall Record

Coming to a judgment about overall U.S. and Soviet compliance with arms control agreements requires weighing those areas in which compliance has been good against those areas in which compliance has been questionable or poor. In the process of performing such a net assessment, important questions must be asked about U.S. and Soviet compliance: Have the most central provisions of the agreements been upheld? What is the balance between concerns about noncompliance and the national-security benefits of agreements? The answers to questions such as these must be taken into account in evaluating whether the net effect of arms control agreements is positive or negative for U.S. national security.

This chapter evaluates the record of compliance with arms control agreements in relation to concerns that have been raised about compliance. This review leads to the conclusion that both the United States and Soviet Union have adhered to the overwhelming majority of their existing arms control obligations. Most of the charges of noncompliance made in recent years actually relate to areas of ambiguity and disagreement about behavior or treaty provisions. With sufficient will and cooperative spirit, the United States and Soviet Union could resolve these disputes through diplomatic means.

Twenty arms control agreements involving the United States and Soviet Union exist today. Of these, eleven have not been the subject of significant, unresolved complaints regarding compliance:

Antarctic Treaty, 1959
"Hot Line" Agreements, 1963 and 1971
Outer Space Treaty, 1967
Latin American Nuclear-Free Zone Treaty, 1967
Seabed Arms Control Treaty, 1971
"Accident Measures" Agreement, 1971
Incidents at Sea Agreement, 1972
Prevention of Nuclear War Agreement, 1973

Peaceful Nuclear Explosions Treaty, 1976
Environmental Modification Convention, 1977
Nuclear Material Convention, 1980

These eleven agreements, compliance with which has been generally acceptable to both sides, have contributed importantly to the security of the United States, the Soviet Union, and indeed every country on earth. These agreements have proscribed nuclear weapons from several physical areas: outer space, the seabed, and most of Latin America. The Antarctic Treaty demilitarized and internationalized the continent of Antarctica, ensuring the scientists of all nations access to its resources for the purpose of study.

These agreements have also made important strides in establishing procedures to moderate crises between the United States and Soviet Union, including direct communications links and agreed measures in case of an accident involving nuclear weapons. The Incidents at Sea Agreement established "rules of the road" for U.S. and Soviet military ships at sea. These rules have decreased the type of naval confrontations that occurred frequently prior to the agreement's existence.[1]

The agreements have also lessened the likelihood of nuclear proliferation by safeguarding nuclear materials against diversion during shipment, limited the size of peaceful nuclear explosions, and barred countries from experimenting with techniques for conducting warfare by modifying the weather or other aspects of the environment.

Eight agreements have been the target of U.S. and Soviet reciprocal charges of noncompliance since 1983:

Geneva Protocol, 1925
Limited Test Ban Treaty, 1963
Biological Weapons Convention, 1972
ABM Treaty, 1972
SALT I Interim Agreement, 1972
Threshold Test Ban Treaty, 1974
Confidence-Building Measures of the Helsinki Final Act, 1975
SALT II Treaty, 1979

The Soviet Union has expressed concern, in addition, about U.S. adherence to the 1968 Non-Proliferation Treaty; there is no analogous U.S. charge against the Soviet Union.

Among these agreements, only the ABM Treaty, the Biological Weapons Convention, the Geneva Protocol, the Non-Proliferation Treaty, and the Limited Test Ban Treaty are ratified treaties fully in force. The Helsinki Final Act is, and the SALT I Interim Agreement was until November 1986, an executive agreement in force. The Threshold Test Ban Treaty and the SALT II Treaty had, until late 1986, the status of treaties for which the ratification process had been discontinued. Expectations for compliance with these last two agreements have been based upon the declaratory political commitment of the parties.

A detailed examination of compliance with the nine agreements about which compliance concerns have been voiced leads to the conclusion that, despite the complaints about adherence, the central provisions of the agreements have been upheld.

SALT I Interim Agreement

The SALT I Interim Agreement set forth three key limits: (1) a ban on new fixed ICBM launchers, (2) a qualitative limit on ICBM modernization through a restriction on conversion of "light" ICBMs to "heavy" ICBMs, and (3) numerical ceilings on submarine-launched ballistic missile (SLBM) launchers and ballistic-missile submarines. Neither the United States nor the Soviet Union has violated these constraints.[2]

When SALT I was signed in 1972, Soviet fixed ICBM launchers totaled 1,607. In 1986 the U.S. Defense Department publication *Soviet Military Power* cited the Soviet ICBM launcher total as 1,398. To accommodate deployment of new generations of ICBMs—SS-17s, SS-19s, SS-18s, and SS-25s—the Soviet Union has retired SS-11s and SS-9s. In 1972 U.S. fixed ICBM launchers totaled 1,054; and in 1986 the total was 1,012. (See figures 1 and 2 for a summary of Soviet and U.S. deactivations.)

Article II of the Interim Agreement prohibits the parties from converting launchers for light ICBMs into launchers for modern, heavy ICBMs. No definition of a heavy missile was included in the agreement. But Agreed Statement C and Common Understanding A of the agreement prohibited a significant increase in the size of ICBM silo launchers, defined as an increase greater than 10–15 percent of the dimensions of ICBM silos at the time the agreement was signed.

Even though Common Understanding A was not formally initialed by both parties, it was included in the SALT I negotiating record, and both parties have abided by the precise letter of its terms. Despite a program of hardening and modernizing silos during the transition from Minuteman II to Minuteman III, the United States has not deployed ICBM launchers with dimensions more than 10–15 percent greater than those of the launchers existing at the time the Interim Agreement was signed. Even though the United States questioned in 1975 whether the Soviet SS-19 ICBM silo launcher adhered to the SALT I size limitation on launchers, deployment of the SS-19 did not require silo-dimension increases that violated the letter of the Interim Agreement. Although the Soviet Union has consistently modernized its ICBM force since 1972, no Soviet launcher has exceeded the Interim Agreement limits on silo dimensions.

Neither the United States nor the Soviet Union has exceeded the limit set in 1972 on the number of strategic SLBM launchers: 950 for the Soviet

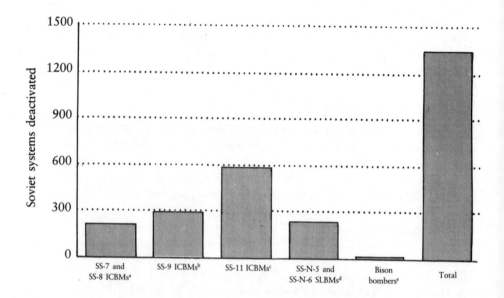

Fig. 1. **Soviet SALT deactivations, 1972–86** (adapted from "The U.S. and Soviet Positive SALT Compliance Record," *Arms Control Today* 16 [May–June 1986]: 7; data updated January 1987)

[a]Between 1975 and 1978 the Soviet Union removed 209 SS-7 and SS-8 ICBM launchers to allow for permitted increases in SLBMs.

[b]Between 1973 and 1980 the Soviet Union removed 288 SS-9 ICBMs as it deployed SS-18 ICBMs.

[c]Between 1974 and 1986 the Soviet Union withdrew 582 SS-11 ICBMs as it deployed newer SS-17, SS-18, and SS-25 ICBMs.

[d]Between 1977 and 1985 the Soviet Union removed 21 SS-N-5 and 224 SS-N-6 SLBMs as it deployed SS-N-18 and SS-N-20 SLBMs.

[e]In 1985–86 the Soviet Union dismantled 21 Bison bombers.

Also, between 1972 and 1985 the Soviet Union dismantled or converted 14 Yankee-class submarines and 7 Hotel-class SSBNs as it added new Delta- and Typhoon-class submarines.

Total deactivations, 1972–86: 1,079 ICBMs, 245 SLBMs, 21 bombers, and 21 nuclear missile–carrying submarines.

Between 1986 and 1990 SALT II would require the Soviet Union to remove older ICBMs, SLBMs, and heavy bombers as it deployed new ones. Approximately 500–600 systems would have to be removed.

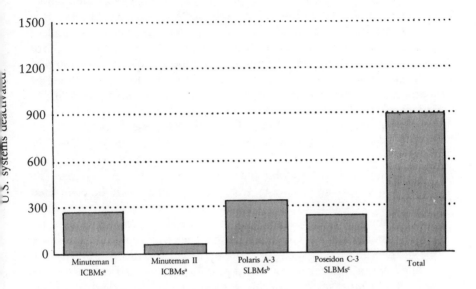

Fig. 2. **U.S. SALT deactivations, 1972–86** (adapted from "The U.S. and Soviet Positive SALT Compliance Record," *Arms Control Today* 16 [May–June 1986]: 7; data updated January 1987)

ᵃBetween 1972 and 1975 the United States replaced 260 Minuteman I ICBMs and 60 Minuteman II ICBMs with Minuteman III ICBMs. (U.S. dismantling of 42 Titan II ICBMs is omitted from the graph because no SALT limits would have been violated if the missiles had remained. U.S. withdrawal of B-52 strategic bombers is also omitted since no limit would have been violated had they remained and since they have been reintroduced as cruise-missile carriers.)

ᵇBetween 1972 and 1986 the United States replaced 176 Polaris A-3 SLBMs on 11 submarines with Poseidon C-3 SLBMs; between 1980 and 1986 the United States dismantled or converted 10 Polaris submarines carrying 160 A-3 SLBMs in preparation for the deployment of Trident submarines.

ᶜBetween 1979 and 1986 the United States replaced 192 Poseidon C-3 SLBMs with Trident C-4 SLBMs on 12 submarines; in 1985–86 the United States dismantled 3 Poseidon submarines carrying 48 C-3 SLBMs.

Total deactivations, 1972–86: 320 ICBMs, 576 SLBMs, and 13 nuclear missile–carrying submarines.

Between 1986 and 1990 SALT II would require the United States to remove older ICBMs, SLBMs, or ALCM-carrying bombers as it deployed new ones. Approximately 200–300 systems would have to be removed.

Union and 710 for the United States. The 1986 edition of the U.S. Defense Department publication *Soviet Military Power* cited 944 as the number of deployed Soviet SALT I–accountable SLBM launchers. In 1986 U.S. SLBMs totaled 648. Both sides have also respected ceilings set for modern strategic-ballistic-missile submarines: 62 for the Soviet Union and 44 for the United States. In 1986 the Soviet Union fielded 62 such submarines, and the United States had a fleet of 37. Both sides have also abided by a provision requiring them to dismantle an ICBM launcher for each SLBM launcher added to a base level of 656 for the United States and 740 for the Soviet Union, up to ceilings of 710 and 950, respectively.

In 1976 the Soviet Union notified the United States through the SCC that, because of technical difficulties, it did not expect to meet an SLBM-dismantling requirement within the time limit set by SCC procedures. The Soviet Union specified a date by which dismantling would be completed and agreed not to perform sea trials of additional submarines with SLBMs, which would place the Soviet Union above the SLBM ceiling, until the required dismantling was completed. The Soviet Union proceeded to meet the dismantling requirement by the date it had specified.[3]

The Interim Agreement contained prohibitions on interference by each side with the other's national technical means of verification and on deliberate concealment to impede verification. Both sides have in general complied with these prohibitions. The Soviet Union objected through the SCC to shelters placed by the United States over Minuteman silos during the conversion to Minuteman III. The United States decreased the size of these shelters and eventually removed them.[4]

SALT II

The central limitations of the unratified SALT II Treaty consist of (1) a ceiling on the aggregate number of strategic nuclear delivery vehicles (SNDVs); (2) subceilings on the number of MIRVed systems; (3) restrictions on fractionation of missiles; (4) a ban on additional fixed ICBM launchers and constraints on launcher modification; (5) restrictions on new systems and on modernization and replacement of existing strategic systems; (6) restrictions on the Backfire bomber; and (7) a ban on interference with NTM and on deliberate concealment, including a restriction on encryption of ballistic-missile–flight-test telemetry.

1. **SNDV ceiling.** The United States has adhered to the SALT II ceiling on the aggregate number of SNDVs, deploying no more than the 1,935 launchers in existence in 1982, at the time the United States announced its policy of not undercutting the SALT II limits. In November 1986 the United States renounced its obligation to stay under the ceiling but has remained under it. The Soviet Union has not exceeded the 2,504 launchers that were operational in 1982, when it announced its policy of not

undercutting the ceilings. The Soviet Union did not reduce to 2,400 launchers, nor further reduce to 2,250 by January 1, 1981, as the treaty would have required had it been ratified and come into force. The Vienna Convention on the Law of Treaties supports this approach, taken by both countries in their policies regarding SALT II compliance after the treaty was signed in 1979. Signing the treaty required both to refrain from steps that would actively undercut the unratified treaty. But, because the treaty remained unratified, neither side was required to dismantle forces that exceeded the treaty's limits.

2. **Subceilings on MIRVed systems.** Until the United States withdrew from SALT II, neither country had exceeded the ceiling of 1,320 on MIRVed systems. Neither had built MIRVed missiles in excess of the 1,200 permitted by SALT II nor gone above the sublimit, within that number, of 820 ICBMs. In November 1986 the United States breached the limit of 1,320 on MIRVed launchers through deployment of an additional B-52 cruise-missile carrier.

3. **Fractionation limits.** SALT II constrained the proliferation of warheads by limiting each system, in tests and deployments, to the maximum number of warheads with which the system had been flight-tested prior to the conclusion of the treaty. The one new type of ICBM allowed by the treaty was limited to no more than 10 warheads, and new SLBMs were restricted to no more than 14 reentry vehicles. Heavy bombers equipped for long-range cruise missiles were to carry on the average no more than 28 cruise missiles. Neither side is known to have tested or deployed systems with greater than the permitted number of warheads.

4. **Ban on additional fixed ICBM launchers and limits on launcher modification.** When SALT II was signed, the Soviet Union had 1,398 fixed ICBM launchers, a number that has remained constant since that time. The number of U.S. launchers has remained constant at 1,024. The number of Soviet heavy ICBMs has remained constant at 308, in line with SALT II limits on modification of ICBMs. Neither have U.S. ICBMs been modified in prohibited ways. The available evidence indicates that both sides have respected all other SALT II restrictions on launcher modification.

5. **Restrictions on new systems and on modernization and replacement of existing systems.** The United States has not deployed strategic ballistic missiles modified in ways prohibited by SALT II. The U.S. MX missile conforms to the restrictions for the one new type of ICBM. The Soviet Union has deployed four new strategic ballistic missiles since SALT II was signed. Three of these have been clearly within the parameters set out by SALT II. One of these—the SS-24—is the one new type allowed by the treaty. The fourth—the SS-25—is the subject of a Reagan administration charge that the Soviet Union has tested and deployed more than one new type of ICBM. The status of the SS-25 is questionable (see chapter 4 of this

report). The Soviet Union has also modified the SS-17 and SS-19 ICBMs, within the limits set by SALT II.

6. Restrictions on the Backfire bomber. The Soviet Union has removed probes on the Backfire bomber to make it unsuitable for aerial refueling, in line with SALT II obligations. The Reagan administration charges that the Soviets have staged the bomber in a manner giving it the prohibited capability of striking targets on U.S. territory and that they have produced it at a rate inconsistent with SALT II requirements. In 1985, though, the Soviet Union took steps to ensure that the Backfire program would be more clearly consistent with SALT II obligations.

7. Ban on interference with verification. Both countries have in general adhered to the requirements for noninterference with NTM and against deliberate concealment. The United States has charged the Soviet Union with a prohibited degree of encryption of ballistic-missile–flight-test telemetry. Chapter 4 examines this allegation in detail.

ABM Treaty

The central provisions of the ABM Treaty and its 1974 protocol are (1) a limit for each side of one deployed antiballistic missile (ABM) system within a permitted configuration; destruction and dismantlement of other existing ABM systems or components; and (2) a prohibition for each side on laying a base for a nationwide ABM system or defense of an individual region. The treaty specifies that these central provisions are to be carried out through adherence to a number of more specific restrictions: (a) not to develop, test, or deploy ABM systems or components that are air-based, space-based, sea-based, or mobile land-based; (b) not to develop, test, or deploy MIRVed, semiautomatic, or rapidly reloadable ABM launchers; (c) not to give missiles, launchers, or radar, other than those that pertain to ABM systems, the capability to counter strategic ballistic missiles and not to test them in an ABM mode; (d) not to transfer ABM systems or components to other countries or to deploy them outside the national territory; (e) not to deploy large phased-array radars, other than on the periphery of the national territory and oriented outward, except for verification or space tracking; and (f) if ABM systems based on "other physical principles" become practicable, to discuss specific limitations on these technologies.

Neither the United States nor the Soviet Union has deployed more than a single ABM system as stipulated by the treaty. Both sides have dismantled components of other ABM systems. Neither side has, as yet, laid a base for a strategic defense of its national territory. Compliance by both the United States and Soviet Union with some of the more specific provisions designed to uphold the overall objectives of the treaty has become the subject of debate.

Limited Test Ban Treaty

The multilateral Limited Test Ban Treaty (LTBT) prohibits nuclear-weapon tests in the atmosphere, in outer space, and under water. None of the parties to the treaty, including the United States and Soviet Union, have conducted nuclear tests in the restricted environments since the LTBT went into effect in 1963.[5] Questions have been raised about U.S. and Soviet compliance with an LTBT prohibition on venting, from permitted nuclear tests, that causes "radioactive debris to be present outside the territorial limits of the State under whose jurisdiction or control such explosion is conducted." The United States has taken steps in the design of its nuclear-weapon tests since the 1970s to prevent the venting of radioactivity.

Threshold Test Ban Treaty

Although the 1974 Threshold Test Ban Treaty (TTBT) has not been ratified by the United States, both the United States and Soviet Union have stated their political commitment to adhere to its primary provision: a 150-kiloton yield limit for underground nuclear tests. Both the United States and Soviet Union have decreased the yield of their nuclear-test explosions, in a manner consistent with adherence to such a limit. Whether both sides have precisely respected the 150-kiloton limit is a matter of debate. But the questions about compliance likely arise from difficulties in accurately verifying the yield of underground nuclear tests and from the unreliability of designed yield of test explosions rather than from yields by either party that are intentionally over the 150-kiloton limit. Chapter 3 of this report discusses the TTBT verification issue.

Biological Weapons Convention

The multilateral Biological Weapons Convention (BWC) prohibits the development or use and production, stockpiling, or other acquisition of biological weapons. The agreement allows parties to retain amounts of biological agents or toxins suitable for "prophylactic, protective, or other peaceful purposes." There has been no verified use, development, production, stockpiling, or acquisition of biological weapons by the United States or Soviet Union, although U.S. charges that the Soviet Union has been engaging in these activities have raised serious questions.

Geneva Protocol

The 113-nation 1925 Geneva Protocol prohibits the use in war of asphyxiating, poisonous, or other gases or analogous materials and of bacteriological methods of warfare. The agreement was ratified by the United States in 1975, fifty years after it was negotiated. There has been no verified use of such materials or methods in war by the United States or the Soviet Union, although the United States has charged the Soviet Union with using such weapons or transferring them to parties involved in conflicts in Afghanistan and elsewhere.

Confidence-Building Measures of the Helsinki Final Act

The Final Act of the 1975 Conference on Security and Cooperation in Europe, signed by the United States and Soviet Union as well as 32 European nations and Canada, calls for confidence-building measures to lessen tension in Europe. These include required prior notification of major military maneuvers, voluntary notification of smaller-scale maneuvers, voluntary exchange of observers to attend maneuvers, and voluntary notification for large-scale movements of troops. Only the notification of major maneuvers is obligatory.

Since 1975 both the United States and Soviet Union have provided not only the obligatory notification of maneuvers but also a fluctuating amount of additional information and access for observers in the voluntary categories. The United States has complained about one Soviet maneuver, which took place in 1981, for which notification was provided later than required by the Final Act. Since 1981 the Soviets have punctually provided the required notice of large-scale maneuvers.

Non-Proliferation Treaty

The 1968, multilateral Non-Proliferation Treaty (NPT) is designed to prohibit the spread of nuclear weapons. Both the United States and Soviet Union have upheld the treaty's prohibitions on transferring nuclear weapons, or the capability to manufacture nuclear weapons, to nonnuclear-weapon states. Both have, in fact, strengthened their commitment to the NPT regime through additional safeguards and export restrictions. The Soviet Union has charged the United States with violating a general provision of the agreement that calls upon the nuclear-weapon states to pursue nuclear disarmament. But this provision is generally regarded as exhortatory, and it contains no standards for judging progress other than a directive to seek general and complete disarmament.

Benefits of the Agreements

In summary, the majority of the twenty arms control agreements that have been achieved have not been subject to any public complaints regarding U.S. or Soviet compliance. Of the minority of agreements about which compliance concerns have recently been raised, compliance with some but by no means all of the key provisions of the agreements has been questioned. In spite of the concerns that have been raised about compliance, the net effect of the arms control agreements in force has been strongly positive.

As a result of these agreements, U.S. security and well-being has been improved in three ways: (1) the Soviet nuclear threat has been constrained and rendered more predictable; (2) the danger of nuclear war has been lessened in significant ways; and (3) the environmental consequences of nuclear testing have been markedly reduced.

The Limited Test Ban Treaty, the Threshold Test Ban Treaty, SALT I, and SALT II have constrained the yield of nuclear weapons, the numbers of warheads deployed, and the types of launchers on which warheads are deployed in a manner that has contributed to security and stability. Before the LTBT the United States and the Soviet Union frequently tested nuclear weapons in the tens-of-megatons range. The largest test ever conducted was a 1961 atmospheric test, at the Soviet Arctic test site, registering 58 megatons. By restricting nuclear testing to the underground environment, the LTBT has limited the yields that can be produced.

The TTBT further restrains the size of warheads the two countries can test underground. (The largest underground test before the TTBT was the 5,000-kiloton U.S. Cannikin test in 1971 in the Aleutian Islands; several Soviet tests have been in the same range.) Soviet nuclear weapons are generally believed to have a lower yield-to-weight ratio than the comparable U.S. systems. Together with the SALT II fractionation limits, the 150-kiloton limit has prevented the Soviet Union from emplacing more weapons with a higher yield-to-weight ratio on their large intercontinental missiles. To ensure the reliability of warheads with higher yield-to-weight ratios than those of their present weapons, the Soviet Union would need to conduct weapon testing to the full yield of lighter-weight weapons of 500, 1,000, or 2,000 kilotons.[6] The TTBT has prevented the Soviet Union from doing so.

The SALT I and SALT II ceilings have placed an effective cap on the number of strategic offensive weapons. In particular, the limits have required the Soviet Union to dismantle older systems in the process of strategic modernization. Prior to the SALT limits the Soviets simply retained their older systems as they added new weapons. The SALT II fractionation limits have prevented the placement of a greater number of warheads on individual launchers, limiting the vulnerability of each side's forces. By restricting the number of warheads on accurate land-based launchers in particular, SALT II has helped to preserve the survivability of each country's deterrent.

The qualitative provisions of SALT II have prevented the unconstrained modernization of ICBMs in terms of throw-weight and other parameters. The MIRVed-launcher subceilings have further limited numbers of warheads on deployed systems.

The ABM Treaty has constrained the ability of either country to mount quickly an antiballistic-missile defense, thus undercutting the deterrent relationship. The restriction on construction of large phased-array radars in the interior of each country has extended the lead time required for deployment of a nationwide ABM system to the point that neither side needs to fear unanticipated emergence of a strategic defense on the other side.

The immediate environmental consequences of nuclear weapons have been greatly diminished through limits on testing. The small amounts of radioactivity vented by both parties since the LTBT went into effect in 1963 pale in comparison to the large-scale radioactive contamination caused by atmospheric testing from 1945 to 1963; overall atmospheric contamination has been reduced by two orders of magnitude.

The biological- and chemical-weapons agreements have established important norms against the production and use of such weapons, even though some question exists about Soviet compliance with the intent of the accords. The agreements have also set desirable standards for cooperation by parties with investigation into concerns about compliance, for consultation, and for dispute resolution.

The confidence-building measures of the 1975 Helsinki Final Act have served to diminish the danger of misperception and miscalculation in U.S.-Soviet military relations, decreasing the likelihood of an engagement between conventional forces that could lead to war and possibly to a nuclear exchange. These measures have operated well in practice, diminishing the element of surprise and misperception that can result from large, unexpected movements of troops. In addition, these measures served as the basis for a more extensive agreement on confidence-building measures — the Stockholm Document, negotiated in 1986.

All of these agreements have established important norms such as noninterference with national technical means of verification; and several have provided important procedures for consultation and dispute resolution.

Patterns of Compliance

The overall pattern on the part of both the United States and Soviet Union has been one in which compliance with agreements has clearly far outweighed noncompliance. A secondary pattern in the past was one of accommodation and correction of activities about which compliance concerns had been raised. There are many examples of this pattern on both sides: Soviet SLBM dismantling in 1976, ultimate removal of U.S. Minuteman shelters, the U.S. effort to prevent venting from nuclear tests, and Soviet steps in 1985 to make the Backfire production rate clearly consistent with SALT II requirements.

Although both sides could certainly improve their compliance, most of the concerns about compliance that have been expressed recently by the

United States and the Soviet Union are an expression of mutual frustration with the state of U.S.-Soviet relations and the arms control process.
The concerns are a bellwether of the poor state of superpower relations
in recent years rather than an indication of widespread compliance
problems.

In particular, most of the recent assertions of noncompliance have to
do with gray areas in agreements or behavior that could have been clarified
and subjected to agreed interpretations had the U.S.-Soviet process of consultation and dispute resolution been functioning adequately during the
past six years. Chapter 3 presents an analysis of recent charges of noncompliance that involve ambiguous activities or treaty provisions. These
charges represent cases in which, despite repeated U.S. or Soviet accusations, neither party is clearly violating the terms of an agreement.

Chapter Three

Gray-Area Disputes

Overview of Unresolved U.S. and Soviet Charges

In four formal White House reports on Soviet noncompliance with arms control agreements, issued since 1983, the Reagan administration has charged the Soviet Union with eighteen separate violations of eight agreements.[1] Two other reports with less official status, one compiled in 1983 by the president's General Advisory Committee on Arms Control and Disarmament and the other issued in 1985 by the secretary of defense, advanced additional charges.[2] (Appendix A of this report lists the charges contained in the White House and GAC reports.)

The primary source for Soviet allegations of U.S. noncompliance is an aide-mémoire released by the Soviet Foreign Ministry in January 1984, in response to the first White House report.[3] In the fall of 1985 the Soviets added one charge — that U.S. modernization of radars at Thule, Greenland, and Fylingdales Moor, England, violates the ABM Treaty. Numerous official Soviet statements about U.S. compliance since 1984 have simply reiterated the allegations made in the January 1984 aide-mémoire. (Appendix B of this report lists the Soviet charges.)

The hallmark of most of these charges is gray areas of ambiguity, rather than black and white instances of arms control violations. In the December 1985 White House report on Soviet noncompliance, several categories among the U.S. gray-area charges are apparent: cases in which the administration itself admits the evidence to be insufficient or ambiguous; cases in which Soviet behavior has improved after a period of questionable compliance; charges retained by the Reagan administration despite a burden of evidence to the contrary; charges based upon a worst-case interpretation of Soviet behavior that differs little from U.S. behavior; and relatively minor disputes over treaty interpretation in which the United States bases a charge of Soviet noncompliance upon its own unilateral treaty interpretation, without seeking a new common understanding with the Soviets through the SCC.

The analogous Soviet charges about U.S. behavior demonstrate a great deal more about the frustrations in U.S.-Soviet relations during the early 1980s than they do about U.S. noncompliance with arms control agreements. These charges separate into a number of categories: those that exhibit a worst-case interpretation of U.S. behavior not dissimilar from Soviet activities; cases involving ambiguities in treaty provisions that could have been successfully addressed in the SCC; charges that reopen issues formerly addressed in the SCC; and charges that seem exclusively calculated to even the score of U.S. charges against the Soviet Union.

This chapter examines some thirty charges made by the United States and the Soviet Union that do not involve clear arms control violations. All of these disputes could likely be resolved with the proper will and approach in the Standing Consultative Commission or through other consultative means.

ABM Treaty: U.S. Charges

Territorial Defense

The administration combines five Soviet activities to judge "that the aggregate of the Soviet Union's ABM and ABM-related actions (e.g. radar construction, concurrent testing, SA-5 upgrade, ABM rapid reload and ABM mobility) suggests that the U.S.S.R. may be preparing an ABM defense of its national territory." It makes little sense on either technical or legal grounds to take one or several activities that could have ABM potential and make a determination on that basis alone that a country may be preparing an ABM defense of its national territory. To make an accurate judgment about whether any single component or even several components have a potential nationwide ABM mission, their technical characteristics must be evaluated in the context of other necessary elements of a total system providing area defense.

ABM systems based on currently available technology can be understood in terms of four functions, each of which can be performed by different components. These functions are (1) detection of distant objects, (2) battle management, (3) engagement, and (4) interception. Before discussing the specific compliance issues pertaining to a possible Soviet territorial defense, it is useful to review briefly the four functions.

1. Detection of distant objects. Fast-approaching missiles and warheads must be detected at a range great enough to allow time for the different elements of an ABM defense to function effectively. ABM systems using present technology employ large, specialized search radars to accomplish this task. Such radars must have very large antennas that can radiate and collect enormous amounts of power.

2. Battle management. In ABM systems like the Soviet system at Moscow and the now-deactivated U.S. Safeguard-Sentinel system at Grand Forks, large, powerful phased-array radars are also used to track incoming warheads after receiving early warning from the distant early-warning search radars. These are referred to as battle-management radars; their tasks include target identification, tracking, queuing, impact-point prediction, and hand-over to local defense units. Battle-management radars operate at higher frequencies than do the early-warning ones since they need not acquire the incoming warheads at such large distances. But their beams must not be bent or absorbed (that is, they must not be blinded) by regions of high ionization caused by high-altitude nuclear explosions. Tracking data are then used by the ABM system to predict the future locations of objects and the points at which they will impact—making it possible for local defenses to launch and guide interceptors to approaching warheads.

3. **Engagement.** The engagement function is often performed by radars that are considerably smaller and less powerful than their battle-management counterparts. Only if they are provided with tracking data from the much larger radars can these radars acquire approaching warheads at long-enough range to allow time for interceptors to be launched. If the engagement radars are sufficiently sophisticated, they can be used to track both interceptors and targets.

In modern ABM systems of the type the United States and Soviet Union are capable of deploying today, single-engagement radars can perform the multiple functions of target acquisition, tracking, and interceptor guidance. However, these more modern radars can still only search small areas of sky for objects approaching at long range. The performance of modern ABM systems therefore remains greatly dependent on timely and accurate tracking data from battle-management radars.

4. **Interception.** The ability to guide interceptors to hit incoming warheads is largely dependent upon detection and tracking data provided by other ABM components.

In addition to the technical characteristics of these four types of components, other factors should be considered in evaluating the threat of the evolution of a Soviet nationwide ABM defense. One question worth considering is whether the Soviet Union has a technology base capable of supporting these components in order to provide an effective territorial defense. The Strategic Defense Initiative represents the current U.S. effort to establish such a base, which does not now exist. In a comparison of U.S. and Soviet standing in the twenty basic technologies most important for defense, most of them key for strategic defense, the Joint Chiefs of Staff (JCS) in their 1987 posture statement found the United States to be superior in fourteen, the Soviet Union to be superior in none, and the two countries to be equal in six.[4]

Another question is whether data-processing capabilities and the individual components have developed to the point that an ABM system could be effectively internetted. A nationwide ABM defense would be a major challenge to large-scale, real-time data-acquisition and -processing capabilities. The requirement of internetting sophisticated data-processing equipment with ABM components should be considered when evaluating the adaptability of those individual components to a nationwide ABM defense. Although such internetting and computer capabilities do not involve clear signatures observable by national technical means, the absence of intelligence information on such activities weighs against the near-term potential for Soviet territorial defense.

Finally, mounting an ABM system would require widespread deployments of systems and components, and extensive site preparation. These activities would be detectable through U.S. intelligence means. The absence of such indicators also argues against the possibility that in the near future the Soviet Union will be able to mount an effective, nationwide ABM defense.

Mobility of ABM-System Components

The U.S. charge dealing with mobility of ABM-system components relates to the capability of the Soviet Flat Twin and Pawn Shop ABM radars to be deployed relatively quickly. The U.S. concern is that, assuming the existence of long–lead-time ABM-system components such as large phased-array radars (LPARs), the Soviet Union could rapidly deploy numerous mobile engagement radars and interceptors to constitute a ground-based ABM system.

The development and testing of mobile ABM radars would violate Article V.1 of the ABM Treaty: "Each Party undertakes not to develop, test, or deploy ABM systems or components which are sea-based, air-based, space-based, or mobile land-based." Common Understanding C states that this prohibition "would rule out the deployment of ABM launchers and radars which were not of permanent fixed types." The treaty lacks a clear definition of what constitutes permanently fixed radars or launchers, in other words, how much time must be required to disassemble and move them before they are considered to be fixed land-based systems and therefore legal. According to one study at the time the treaty was drafted, the U.S. interpretation of transportable as it applied to the SA-2 air-defense system was "that if such activity [i.e. the disassembly and relocation of a radar] occurred in a week or less, it would be considered inconsistent with the treaty."[5]

The Soviets have tested prototype Pawn Shop radars at their ABM test range at Sary Shagan and at their test area on the Kamchatka Peninsula. The treaty permits ABM components such as these radars to be located at ABM test ranges as well as at the one operational Soviet ABM site around Moscow. Flat Twin radars are under construction as part of the upgrade of the Moscow ABM system.[6]

This case, by the administration's own judgment, falls into the category of concerns based on ambiguous evidence. At issue is the question of what constitutes a mobile system, as opposed to one that is transportable. It is not clear that a radar that can only be deployed within a number of weeks, requiring substantial site preparation as does Flat Twin, is what the ABM Treaty intended to prevent through its prohibition on mobile components.[7] Flat Twin is clearly not mobile in the sense of being able to be moved about easily or hidden. Radars of these types tested at Sary Shagan do not appear to have wheels, tracks, specialized transport vehicles, or any other capabilities associated with mobility. A nationwide Soviet ABM system based on the deployment of such components would require years to deploy and would provide dubious coverage.

The ABM Treaty lacks a clear definition of exactly what constitutes mobility. It should be the responsibility of the SCC to arrive at a more precise, agreed-upon U.S.-Soviet definition and appropriate safeguards against breakout. But at present a conflict exists between the U.S. interest in obtaining such an agreement to constrain Soviet breakout potential and the current administration's attempt, stemming from the U.S. pursuit of a nationwide, space-based ballistic-missile defense, to avoid analogous restraints on the Strategic Defense Initiative. The Reagan administration seeks to preserve as much U.S. flexibility as possible with regard to component mobility. Even if the SDI were to produce only a terminal ABM defense, the system employed might involve mobile radars and other mobile components.

Concurrent Testing of ABM and Non-ABM Components

The Soviets have periodically operated surface-to-air missile (SAM) radars at the Sary Shagan test range during ABM test flights. The operation of the SA-5 radar, a conventional air-defense radar deployed throughout the Soviet Union, concurrently with testing of ballistic missiles, ABM systems, and their components has raised U.S. concern that the Soviets could be testing the potential for using air-defense radars for ABM defense.

Article VI(a) of the ABM Treaty states that both parties agree "not to give missiles, launchers, or radars, other than ABM interceptor missiles, ABM launchers, or ABM radars, capabilities to counter strategic ballistic missiles or their elements in flight trajectory, and not to test them in an ABM mode." Radars used for purposes such as range safety and instrumentation are exempt from this ban.

U.S. concern dates back to 1974, when the Soviet Union used the SA-5 radar to track ballistic missiles during test flights. The Soviet activity ceased for a period of time after the United States raised the issue in the SCC. The Soviets later explained that the radars had been used for range-instrumentation purposes. They stated that they had not used the SA-5 radar to control an interceptor but only to track the incoming reentry vehicle (RV) during the test, a use that, they contended, did not constitute testing in an ABM mode. The United States considered this argument to be weak, since other radars located at the test range obviated the need to use the SA-5 radar specifically for instrumentation purposes.

The Soviets resumed operation of the SA-5 radar during tests after 1974, causing the United States once again to raise the issue in the SCC. An agreement in the SCC in 1978 further refined the phrase "in an ABM mode" to ban any concurrent testing of ABM and air-defense components at the same test range. Air-defense radars used for instrumentation were prohibited from making measurements on strategic ballistic missiles.

Between 1978 and 1982 the SCC worked out elements of a common understanding that simply banned all concurrent operation of ABM and non-ABM components, except for detection of potentially hostile aircraft that are clearly demonstrable to be in the area.[8] The understanding requires a party seeking an exception to provide justification for the exception within a period of thirty days or at the next SCC meeting, whichever occurs first.

This understanding languished in the SCC from 1982 until 1985 because of interagency disputes in the United States over the appropriate U.S. approach in the SCC. Finally, at the spring 1985 SCC session, the United States and Soviet Union signed this common understanding. In its December 1985 noncompliance report, the U.S. administration classified this charge as based on evidence "insufficient fully to assess compliance with Soviet obligations under the ABM Treaty."

The U.S. concern about the SA-5 was debatable from the start. The SA-5 system is marginal for intercepting ballistic missiles with a high weight-to-drag ratio. Since the 1985 common understanding was reached, the United States has provided no new public information to indicate that Soviet behavior has been unsatisfactory. Because the charge does not refer to Soviet behavior since the understanding clarifying Soviet obligations was reached, this charge should not be included in U.S. noncompliance reports.

ABM Capabilities of Modern Surface-to-Air Missile Systems

The ABM Treaty prohibits the parties from giving systems other than ABM systems the capability to counter strategic ballistic missiles, and from testing them in an ABM mode (Article VI[a]). The U.S. concern is that the mobile SA-X-12, a SAM now being tested for the upgrade of the permitted Soviet ABM defense of Moscow, has an antitactical ballistic missile (ATBM) intercept capability that could equip the system, if deployed with a nuclear warhead, to attack some SLBMs.

The SA-X-12 was observed in 1983 and 1984 in tests against a missile similar to the SS-12 tactical ballistic missile, raising the question of whether the Soviets are testing the SA-X-12 in an ABM mode. In its Unilateral Statement B at the time of the ABM Treaty, the United States stated that it would consider a missile, launcher, or radar to be tested in an ABM mode if "an interceptor missile is flight tested against a target vehicle which has a flight trajectory with characteristics of a strategic ballistic missile flight trajectory." However, both sides are permitted to develop, test, and deploy interceptors to attack incoming tactical ballistic missiles.

The administration's conclusion is that the evidence about this charge is "insufficient fully to assess compliance." Such a charge, based on insufficient evidence, does not belong in reports on Soviet noncompliance. The SCC has never reached a common definition of what constitutes a flight trajectory with characteristics of a strategic-ballistic-missile flight trajectory. The United States could appropriately pursue such a definition through the SCC if it is concerned about further attempting to distinguish permitted ATBM developments from prohibited ABM developments.

It is important to note the limitations of interceptors when considering the possible upgrade of defenses relying on SAM or ATBM interceptors to give them the capability to intercept strategic ballistic missiles. Although such an upgrade could enable the interceptor to hit strategic ballistic missiles under limited engagement conditions and geometries, one must recognize that the offense has a fair amount of control over the attack signature and geometry.

Rapid Reload of ABM Launchers

Article V.2 of the ABM Treaty states: "Each party undertakes not to develop, test, or deploy ABM launchers for launching more than one ABM interceptor missile at a time from each launcher, not to modify deployed launchers to provide them with such a capability, not to develop, test, or deploy automatic or semi-automatic or other similar systems for rapid reload of ABM launchers." The United States charges that the Soviet Galosh ABM interceptor missiles around Moscow, when tested at Sary Shagan, demonstrated a reload and refire time of much less than a day. The United States also alleges that a separate Soviet ABM interceptor at Sary Shagan has been reloaded in less than a day.

Once again, the Reagan administration finds the evidence to be ambiguous but of serious concern. The intent of the treaty provision is to circumscribe the ability of the one hundred permitted launchers at the one permitted ABM site to exceed, through multiplying the number of interceptors they could launch during a brief period of time, their otherwise limited capacity to defend against a ballistic-missile attack. Within this definition of the treaty's intent, it is not clear that "less than a day" constitutes a rapid-reload capability for an ABM launcher. If it does, the Soviet Union could have legitimately made a similar case with regard to the U.S. Safeguard ABM system. In addition, in the ABM Treaty negotiations the United States did not regard the reload capability of the Soviet interceptors for the Galosh system, at that time demonstrated to be several hours, to constitute a rapid-reload capacity.

The lack of a definition of a rapid-reload capability creates another ambiguity in the treaty provisions that should be the subject of an SCC attempt to reach a common understanding. But U.S. enthusiasm for jointly pursuing such an agreement with the Soviet Union has again been hampered by its pursuit of an effective ballistic-missile intercept capability.

Analysis

If the Soviet Union could assemble even a rudimentary territorial defense from existing components, this should be a matter of some concern to the United States. But a system whose successful operation is contingent on so many conditionals could hardly represent a reliable enough defense against nuclear attack to threaten the U.S. deterrent.

From a legal standpoint, the U.S. charge that the Soviet Union may be laying the base for a territorial defense is no better than the sum of its parts. As a 1985 report on ABM Treaty compliance pointed out: "Legally, the argument would be that the Soviets could violate Article I(2) [the general prohibition on territorial defense] even though they did not violate any of the specific articles, such as Articles III, V, and VI. A more logical interpretation would be that a violation of either Article III, Article V or Article VI would have to be demonstrated before any conclusion that the activities constitute a base for a nationwide ABM system."[9] In light of the JCS assessment of supporting technology, the administration's concern that the Soviets may be laying the base for an effective strategic defense seems to present a weaker case than do its charges regarding individual Soviet programs.

The U.S. charge exemplifies a double standard by the United States in recent years in dealing with the issue of Soviet compliance. The United States is accusing the Soviet Union of possibly moving clandestinely toward deploying a nationwide ABM system, the same goal that the administration has publicly embraced through the Strategic Defense Initiative. There is only a stylistic difference from the standpoint of ABM Treaty compliance between what the United States seeks to do publicly and what the Soviets are accused of doing secretively, if both countries were to construct territorial defenses.

It also bears noting that this U.S. charge appeared first in the December 1985 White House report, as the administration was pushing forward with its own interpretation of the ABM Treaty, which would permit U.S. development of an ABM territorial defense based on new, exotic technologies. The timing of the U.S. charge raises a concern that the present administration is attempting to justify its public SDI program with accusations of a clandestine Soviet strategic-defense effort.

The appropriate response for the United States, if it is indeed concerned about a nationwide Soviet ABM defense program, is to seek to tighten the ABM Treaty to create stronger barriers against the potential of either side to break out of its provisions. The United States could take such an approach either through ongoing arms control negotiations, through the SCC, or through the ABM Treaty review conference scheduled for 1987. However, the recent U.S. approach has been to seek a loosening rather than a strengthening of ABM Treaty restrictions.

ABM Treaty: Soviet Charges

Shemya Radar

The Soviet Union has questioned whether the U.S. Cobra Dane LPAR in the Aleutian Islands could be used for ABM purposes, in contravention of Article VI(a) of the ABM Treaty, in which the parties agree not to give non-ABM radars the capability to "counter strategic ballistic missiles or their elements in flight trajectory, and not to test them in an ABM mode." The Soviet Union has alleged that "the United States has deployed a big radar station on Shemya Island, the construction of which entailed the utilization of radar system elements tested for ABM purposes." The Soviets apparently believe that components previously tested for use in ABM systems were incorporated into the Shemya installation rather than that the Shemya radar itself has been tested in an ABM mode.

The Soviet Union first raised the Shemya issue in the SCC in 1975, in apparent response to U.S. questions in 1974 about the Soviet radar at Pechora. The Soviets dropped the issue after some discussion, seemingly satisfied that, if no U.S. system of ABM interceptors was in place, any ABM potential of the radar was unimportant. The Soviets raised the issue again in 1984 as a tit for tat to the U.S. charges on Abalakovo and other alleged ABM Treaty violations.

The ABM Treaty permits LPARs for space-tracking and verification purposes to be located anywhere in a country. It permits early-warning LPARs to be located on the periphery, oriented outward. It prohibits LPARs for ABM purposes outside the one permitted ABM site and agreed test sites. The Shemya radar, unlike the Abalakovo radar, is clearly located on the country's periphery and oriented outward. Because of its orientation and location, Shemya is much less suited to ABM purposes than Abalakovo, which is in closer proximity to ICBM fields.

However, because functions may be changed quickly and internally through the software operating the radars, NTM cannot necessarily distinguish which function an LPAR serves. LPARs by nature can be capable of more than a single function, even though they are not optimally suited for more than one. One of the few ways to determine the purpose of an LPAR through NTM is through verifying whether it has been tested in an ABM mode, and, as discussed, ambiguity surrounds the definition of "in an ABM mode."

To the extent that it goes beyond a tit-for-tat response, Soviet concern about Shemya has probably been reawakened by the announced U.S.

intent to pursue a strategic defense. Within the framework of a nation-wide strategic-defense program, any residual ABM capability of a radar such as Shemya—to provide initial warning of attack, to support battle management, to distinguish RVs from decoys, or to guide interceptors to their targets—would likely cause greater Soviet consternation.

Although the U.S. State Department held a press conference on January 30, 1984, to discuss the Soviet charges, the United States did not directly address the Soviet allegation that the Shemya installation made use of "radar system elements" that had been tested for ABM purposes. The U.S. spokesman merely stated, "The Shemya Island radar in the Aleutians is for national technical means of verification."[10]

Like a number of U.S. charges, this Soviet allegation is reopening an issue that appeared to have been addressed effectively in the SCC. This issue does, however, point up the need for the SCC to reach a more effective agreement on what constitutes "testing in an ABM mode" and on measures to distinguish permitted LPARs from those that are restricted.

ABM Interceptors with Multiple Warheads

Agreed Statement D of the ABM Treaty prohibits the development, testing, or deployment of MIRVed ABM interceptors. A Soviet charge related to the U.S. Homing Overlay Experiment (HOE) presumably refers to the fact that the program was originally designed to investigate placing multiple kill vehicles on each interceptor launcher (see chapter 6). No such vehicles were tested during the life of the program, which ended in mid-1984.

The Soviet Union has also raised the question of testing in an ABM mode in the case of HOE tests in 1983–84, because two stages of the Minuteman I were employed. The need is again evident for a more precise definition of testing in an ABM mode.

Nonconfidentiality of SCC

The SALT I negotiators who wrote the SCC regulations designed the SCC as a confidential forum to refine treaty language as a means of resolving compliance disputes. SCC deliberations, as well as their outcome, are intended to remain private. The thinking behind the confidentiality of the SCC was that such a forum could operate more effectively if compliance did not become a matter of public accusation. The Soviet side, in particular, seemed to exhibit much greater comfort about sharing the sensitive military information sometimes required to clarify compliance if they could be assured that the information would not be used for public criticism of the Soviet Union.

The Soviet Union charges that the United States "systematically violates the agreed-upon principle of observing the confidentiality of the discussion of questions connected with the fulfillment of commitments on the limitation of strategic arms, and this is detrimental to the normal activity of the Soviet-American Standing Consultative Commission."

The United States has resorted to public statements about Soviet noncompliance since 1983. The Reagan administration contends that it has been forced to go public with charges of Soviet violations because of Soviet intransigence in the SCC. There is some truth in both the U.S. and Soviet positions in this case. However, the SCC regulations state that it is the SCC *proceedings* that must not be made public without the express consent of the two countries' commissioners. Although the United States has made its charges of Soviet violations in public, it has not made public the proceedings of the SCC, that is, the record of the actual exchanges in SCC sessions.

SALT II Treaty: U.S. Charges

Limits on Strategic Nuclear Delivery Vehicles

The Reagan administration has cited the Soviet Union for exceeding by as many as 36 systems the limit of 2,504 SNDVs to which it has been held since its pledge in 1982 not to undercut SALT II limits. According to the administration's December 1985 noncompliance report, the Soviets had 2,520 SNDVs near the end of 1985, or 16 over the limit.

This U.S. charge revolves around the inability of the SCC to reach a U.S.-Soviet agreement on bomber-dismantling and -destruction procedures for the SALT II Treaty, a matter that has been before the consultative body since the conclusion of the SALT II agreement. Robert Buchheim, U.S. SCC commissioner from 1977 to 1981, reports: "The bomber procedures are almost complete and would have been done had I not refused to complete them on the basis of instructions. It was inherent in those procedures that you could take a bomber out of the count merely by putting fuselage skin over the bomb-bay opening. Bomb bays have been built for many years to make it easy to take those doors on and off, making it possible to take a bomber out of the count and return it to the bomb-carrying mode in half an hour. That was not my idea of a verifiable procedure, but those procedures certainly can be finished. They are just sitting there." In the view of a more recent U.S. SCC delegation member, the reason the bomber-dismantling procedures were not completed as of 1986 was that the Reagan administration had not decided how to regard its obligations under the SALT II Treaty. According to Buchheim, "The Soviets rejected completing the procedures for the same reason." He adds that "they didn't want to waste their time" working out procedures for an agreement that might soon be discarded.[11]

The SALT II agreement permits the conversion of bombers to tankers. Because Soviet aircraft of one type, the Bison, are tankers as well as bombers, the issue of dismantling/conversion is more complex for the

Bison than for other bombers. In the face of the incomplete provisions for bomber dismantling, the Soviet Union stalled on dismantling Bison bombers, failing to satisfy the United States that a number of Bisons were actually being used as tankers in such a way that they could not quickly be returned to service as bombers. The Bisons that the Soviets claimed to have converted to tankers accounted for the U.S. charge that the Soviets exceeded the limit of 2,504 SNDVs.

Reportedly, the Office of the Secretary of Defense alone within the U.S. government was eager to pursue this charge and to raise it in the SCC. After the United States raised the issue in 1985, according to an SCC source, the Soviets began to cut up the fuselages of some of the disputed Bisons. This action presumably accounts for the drop in the number, as cited by the administration, of Soviet launchers accountable to SALT II from a high of 2,540 early in 1985 to 2,520 at the end of the year. By February 1986, according to the Joint Chiefs of Staff posture statement for fiscal year 1987, which was based on Defense Intelligence Agency data, the Soviets had 2,477 SALT II–accountable launchers.[12]

With the downward trend continuing, there was little reason for concern about compliance with the SNDV limits until the United States decided to withdraw from SALT II and thus open the door to both U.S. and Soviet abrogation of the ceilings. The United States and Soviet Union failed to use the SCC effectively in this case to implement a treaty. In the absence of agreed-upon SCC procedures, the United States has been relying on its own unilateral interpretations of bomber-dismantlement/conversion requirements to charge that Soviet behavior is inadequate.

Deployment of SS-16 ICBMs

The SALT II Treaty (Article IV[8], Common Understanding) bans production, testing, or deployment of the light, mobile SS-16 ICBM. The United States charges that what it believed to be SS-16 missiles at the Soviet Plesetsk missile test site violated the provision against SS-16 deployment, because these missiles could potentially be launched from rail-mobile launchers or other means at the site. U.S. surveillance satellites reportedly have never actually observed SS-16 missiles at the site.[13] However, modification and expansion since 1979 of the sites associated with the SS-16 and lack of Soviet willingness to provide any evidence for U.S. NTM to observe that the SS-16 has been dismantled (such as telling the United States where to observe the discarded motors for the missiles) have prompted the U.S. charge. The charge hinges on the view that, without evidence of the SS-16's destruction, the United States must consider it to still be deployed.

The Reagan administration judges that the evidence on the SS-16 is somewhat ambiguous, but that it points to a probable violation of the Soviets' political commitment to SALT II. But this is a case in which the Soviet

Union may have changed its behavior to improve compliance with an agreement. In late 1985 U.S. intelligence observed the Soviets moving warhead transporters and other support equipment for mobile missiles onto railcars at Plesetsk. Much of the intelligence community drew the conclusion that the Soviets were removing the SS-16s from Plesetsk, sending them into storage.[14] This charge, therefore, does not currently represent Soviet noncompliance, if ever it did.

Intercontinental Operating Capability of the Backfire Bomber

In a letter from General Secretary Leonid Brezhnev to President Jimmy Carter at the time of the SALT II Treaty signing, the Soviet Union agreed that the "radius of action" of the Backfire bomber (Tu-22M) would not be increased "in such a way as to enable it to strike targets on the territory of the U.S.A." The Soviet Union was to forgo giving the Backfire an in-flight refueling capability, to ensure that its range could not be extended to an intercontinental level, which would allow the Soviet Union to strike the United States on a round-trip mission.

The Reagan administration has cited the Soviets for temporary staging of the Backfire at bases in the Soviet Arctic, for periods of a few days, which could be construed, according to the administration, "as training for operational use of such bases. If so staged, such bombers, under certain conditions, could attack some areas in the United States even without aerial refueling." The administration rates the Soviet behavior as "a cause for concern and continued careful monitoring." It calls this activity inconsistent with the Soviet Backfire statement of 1979.

The validity of this charge depends upon whether the United States is correctly estimating the range of the Backfire bomber, as well as upon correctly identifying current Soviet operational practices. Since 1979 the Central Intelligence Agency (CIA) has questioned the definition of the Backfire as a potential strategic bomber. In September 1985 the Defense Intelligence Agency lowered its estimate of the Backfire's range when fully loaded by about 20 percent, to a figure more consistent with the CIA's longtime position.[15] The change was due, in part, to an increased estimate of the bomber's fuel consumption. The Backfire's present lack of a midair refueling capability raises considerable doubt about its ability to carry out a round-trip mission against the continental United States even from bases in the Arctic and thus about the validity of the U.S. charge. Despite this new intelligence assessment, the administration retained the charge of Soviet noncompliance in its report issued in December 1985. As currently configured, the Backfire bomber does not seem to be a violation of the Soviet commitment.

Fig. 3. **Soviet Backfire bomber** (reprinted from U.S. Defense Department, *Soviet Military Power*, 5th ed. [Washington, March 1986], 119)

Backfire Production Rate

The SALT II Backfire letter also contained a restriction on the production rate of the Backfire. The letter did not contain the production figure, commonly cited in the United States, of thirty per year. The belief that it did is a misconception. It would have been uncharacteristic for the Soviets to offer such data about their military programs, and they in fact did not in this case. Rather, Brezhnev committed the Soviet Union not to increase "the production rate of this airplane as compared to the present rate." The United States expressed its understanding that the production rate of Backfire at that time was thirty per year, and, according to Secretary of State Cyrus Vance, Secretary Brezhnev verbally assented to the U.S. figure at the Vienna summit.[16]

The United States has charged that the Soviet production rate "slightly" exceeded thirty per year from 1979 to the end of 1983. After 1983 the Soviet production rate dropped to "slightly less" than thirty aircraft per year. The administration notes that its charge is based on ambiguous data. The concern is that, by producing at above the permitted level for several years, the Soviets might have been able to obtain a few more Backfire aircraft than they were technically permitted by SALT II.

By the Reagan administration's own account, the Soviet Union now appears to be in compliance with the production restriction. The Soviets should be considered to have fulfilled the provisions of the Backfire letter if their Backfire production rate continues to fall just short of thirty per year. Within a short period of time that rate will compensate for any slightly higher production in earlier years, if indeed such higher production ever occurred, and the Soviet Backfire inventory will reflect the average of thirty aircraft per year implicitly required by SALT II.

Concealment of Association Between Missiles and Launchers

SALT II (Article XV, First Common Understanding) obligates the parties not to impede verification by concealing the association between ICBMs and their launchers during testing. Observation of this association is important to the determination of whether a launcher should be counted as a MIRVed or non-MIRVed launcher toward the subtotals on MIRVed launchers and whether it is a launcher accountable to SALT II.

The United States charges the Soviet Union with failing to allow the United States adequately to observe the mobile SS-25 launchers loaded with SS-25 missiles during the testing period, causing the United States to be unsure about whether missiles launched in tests are indeed the SS-25s or, for instance, mobile SS-20 intermediate-range ballistic missiles, which are not accountable to SALT II. The Soviets have reportedly placed nets over the SS-25 transporter-erector-launchers (TELs), concealing the features that would identify the launchers. If the United States is unable to distinguish

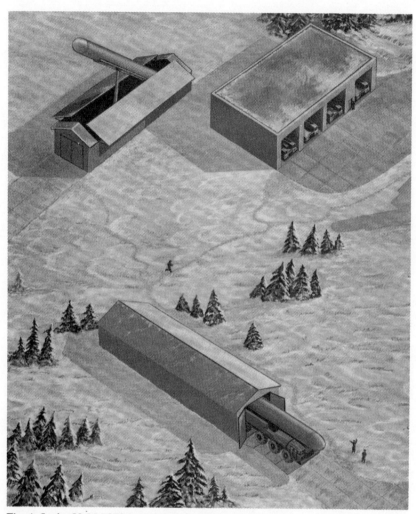

Fig. 4. **Soviet SS-25 ICBMs and their launchers** (reprinted from U.S. Defense Department, *Soviet Military Power*, 5th ed. [Washington, March 1986], 24)

the SS-25 from the SS-20, the possibility exists that the Soviet Union could hide SS-25s in fields among unrestricted SS-20s, launch SS-25s from SS-20 TELs, and thus exceed the limits on strategic-missile launchers.

The Soviets apparently do remove the nets from the TELs during test launches, in accordance with their interpretation of the treaty provision. Their position is that the missile-launcher association should be observable by U.S. NTM at the time of test launch. The U.S. position is that, since U.S. NTM are not always available at the time the Soviets test, the Soviets should reveal the missile-launcher association at times other than during test launches.

Article XV by itself does not provide a determination about what measures are required to ensure that each country can ascertain the other's missile-launcher associations. The United States raised the issue in both 1984 and 1985 in the SCC, arguing that the U.S. interpretation of what is required by Article XV is correct and that the Soviet Union should comply with that interpretation. The Soviets predictably responded that they have no way to distinguish whether a Minuteman silo contains a single-warhead Minuteman II ICBM or a MIRVed Minuteman III ICBM. Clearly, the job of the SCC should be to define more precisely what measures are required to ensure that the missile-launcher association can be verified. The SCC's failure to act is an instance of its paralysis in recent years in clarifying treaty provisions.

Salt II Treaty: Soviet Charges

Midgetman ICBM

The United States is developing a small (19-ton), potentially mobile missile commonly referred to as Midgetman. Such a missile was recommended by the President's Commission on Strategic Forces (Scowcroft Commission) in April 1983. The commission took the position that the missile should be small, mobile, and have a single warhead, to add survivability to the U.S. land-based deterrent. This missile is still in the stage of research and development.

In Article IV.9 of the SALT II Treaty, the United States and Soviet Union agreed not to flight-test or deploy more than one new type of ICBM for the duration of the treaty.[17] In October 1982 the United States informed the Soviet Union in the SCC that the MX missile would be its one new type. Since May 1982, when the United States pledged not to undercut the terms of SALT II, the Soviet Union has accused the United States of activities that do "not accord with the tasks of limiting strategic arms that have found reflection in the attained agreements," through pursuing a second new type of ICBM.[18]

The Midgetman issue differs substantially from the question of Soviet compliance with the restriction on new types of ICBMs. In one sense, Midgetman is potentially a more clear-cut compliance issue; but the Soviets have been premature in pointing out its compliance implications. The Soviets are correct in asserting that Midgetman would violate the terms of the SALT II restriction on new types at the point it was flight-tested. There is no ambiguity as there is related to the question of whether the SS-25 is a permitted modernization of an existing ICBM. Midgetman does not remotely resemble the U.S. Minuteman series of ICBMs, and has even less in common with the MX missile. All the possible configurations of Midgetman that have been discussed are substantially smaller in length, diameter, weight, range, and throw-weight than predecessor U.S. ICBMs. The United States would have no basis for claiming that Midgetman was a permitted modernization of any existing ICBM.

But Midgetman is not an immediate compliance concern, unlike the SS-25, which is already deployed and functional. SALT II expressly prohibited additional new types only when they are flight-tested or deployed. Midgetman remains a considerable distance from flight testing or deployment, although the president moved closer to this point in May 1986. When President Reagan announced the U.S. decision not to abide by the terms of SALT II after the end of 1986, he accelerated movement toward the Midgetman by directing the Defense Department to submit a report by November 1986 on alternative configurations for the small ICBM.[19]

In recommending a small, mobile ICBM, the Scowcroft Commission noted in 1983 that such an ICBM would not be inconsistent with SALT II, because the treaty would have expired by the time the missile was flight-tested. The commission endorsed an approach to follow-on arms control agreements that would permit the deployment of such survivable, non-MIRVed ICBMs.[20]

Had the United States not announced in May 1986 that it was withdrawing from the SALT II agreement, it would have drawn closer to violating SALT II as the Midgetman program proceeded. Technically, the president's May 1986 statement relieved the United States of any obligation to abide by the SALT II restriction on new types of ICBMs.

Deployments of Ground-Launched and Sea-Launched Cruise Missiles

The SALT II Protocol contains a ban on deployment of land- or sea-based cruise missiles with a range in excess of 600 kilometers (Article II.1). The SALT II Protocol was an agreement of limited duration, which would have expired on December 31, 1981, even had SALT II been ratified. Because the United States deployed the ground-launched and sea-launched cruise missiles (GLCMs and SLCMs) cited by the Soviets only after the protocol would have expired, there is little basis for this Soviet charge.

It was anticipated at the time SALT II was negotiated that the difficult issues provisionally dealt with in the protocol would be addressed in a subsequent negotiation. Because of U.S. nonratification of SALT II, the process never moved forward. The question of GLCMs and SLCMs was among the unresolved issues that were regarded by the two countries as potentially destabilizing enough to be flagged for future attention by negotiators.

Deployment of Pershing II

A Soviet charge similar to that involving GLCMs and SLCMs concerns the Pershing II. The Soviet Union has charged that U.S./NATO deployment of the Pershing II, a land-mobile intermediate-range ballistic missile, in Europe at the end of 1983 violated the noncircumvention clause of SALT II, which states that neither party shall "circumvent the provisions of this Treaty, through any other state or states, or in any other manner" (Article XII). The charge is based upon the concern that the Pershing II increases the number of U.S. warheads potentially deliverable against targets in the Soviet Union, to a number above the level set by the SALT II ceilings. But the noncircumvention clause is a general provision, and determinations about violations of such a provision are extremely subjective.

SALT I Interim Agreement

U.S. Charge: Use of Remaining Facilities

The Reagan administration charges the Soviet Union with using missile-support facilities at former SS-7 sites for the new SS-25 missiles, in violation of the SALT I Interim Agreement. According to the administration, the Interim Agreement and its procedures prohibit both countries from using certain storage, support, or launch facilities remaining at sites of destroyed ICBMs for new ICBMs.

The U.S.-Soviet agreement regarding facilities at former sites is part of the dismantling and destruction procedures worked out in the SCC for implementation of the Interim Agreement. These procedures specify that launchers and their associated equipment must be dismantled, but support and other facilities may be used for purposes not inconsistent with the agreement. At issue is whether the use being made of facilities remaining at the SS-7 sites in the process of deploying the SS-25 is consistent with the Interim Agreement. The issue is complicated by the interim use of these facilities as part of sites for the SS-20 intermediate-range missiles, which are not covered by any arms control agreement.

The purpose of the SCC procedures was to prevent rapid reactivation of the sites of dismantled missiles. In this light, there is a real question about the meaningfulness of the distinction the U.S. administration makes between use for purposes consistent and inconsistent with the Interim Agreement. The SS-7 launch facilities were destroyed by the Soviets in compliance with the Interim Agreement. Other structures, whose dismantling was not required by the SCC, were left at the SS-7 sites. The Soviet Union is clearly using these support facilities to avoid the cost of constructing similar new facilities for the SS-25.

If the SCC procedures allow such structures to remain, it seems questionable whether the Soviet Union should be expected not to use them. If, in the process of deploying a new missile that is of a substantially different type than one that was dismantled, structures would need to be built that are nearly identical to those used for the old missile, what is the point of requiring a country to duplicate the structures? It is highly unlikely that the SS-7 site is being reactivated for launch of the dismantled SS-7s or any other fixed-site ICBMs, since the SS-7 was silo-launched and its launch facilities have been destroyed. The SS-25 now being deployed at the site is mobile, launched from TELs above the ground.

This issue seems to be a technical concern rather than a substantive concern about reactivation of dismantled missile launchers. Through the SCC the United States and the Soviet Union should be able to reach a common understanding either to require dismantling of the facilities in question or to allow their use if similar structures would be permitted for a newly deployed system.

Soviet Charge: Minuteman II and Titan II ICBM Shelters

The Soviet Union, through diplomatic and political channels since 1973 and since 1975 in the SCC, has repeatedly raised an issue concerning the SALT I Interim Agreement's prohibition on deliberate concealment to impede verification of compliance with the agreement's limits (Article V.3).

In 1973, while conducting silo-modification and -hardening work, the United States erected 2,700–square-foot prefabricated construction shelters covering Minuteman silos and their launch and control facilities. The Soviet Union objected that such large shelters made it impossible for their satellites to determine whether the United States was making illegal changes in the silos.

In particular, the size of the shelters may have impeded Soviet ability to monitor materials entering or leaving the silo area. The Soviets have maintained that it is difficult to distinguish non-MIRVed–Minuteman II launchers from MIRVed–Minuteman III launchers, and that the shelters exacerbated the problem. In their January 1984 aide-mémoire, the Soviet Union charged that, because of their inability during the 1970s adequately to distinguish between the two missiles, they would have to assume that Minuteman IIs had been converted into Minuteman IIIs, a conversion that might violate the SALT II limit on MIRVed ICBMs.

The United States claimed that it erected the shelters to protect workers against the weather and to aid in the curing of concrete at Midwestern bases subject to heavy winter snows. In 1977, four years after the Soviet

Union initially raised the matter in the SCC, the United States cut the size of the shelters in half. The Soviets continued to object in the SCC. The United States insisted that the shelters were not for deliberate concealment and stalled on making further changes. In May 1979, at the end of the SALT II negotiations, the United States finally removed the shelters in question. The United States and Soviet Union agreed to a common understanding in SALT II (Article XV.3) that prohibits the placement over ICBM silo launchers of shelters that inhibit verification by national technical means.

Although the United States did not meet the Soviet concern until the silo-modernization program was complete, the current Soviet charge relates to U.S. behavior that has ceased, just as a number of the U.S. charges deal with past Soviet activities. Today it is a specious charge.

Biological and Toxin Weapons Convention and Geneva Protocol: U.S. Charges

Concern that the Soviet Union has violated the multilateral Biological Weapons Convention and Geneva Protocol dates from the latter part of the Carter administration. Allegations contained in the December 1985 noncompliance report include the charge that the Soviets have maintained an active biological-weapons research and stockpiling program, as demonstrated by an alleged release of anthrax spores from a biological-weapons production facility in Sverdlovsk in 1979 causing an outbreak of pulmonary anthrax. The report accuses the Soviets of providing trichothecene mycotoxins to the governments of Vietnam and Laos, the so-called yellow rain reported to have been used in attacks on guerrilla forces and civilian populations in Laos and Kampuchea. Finally, the United States accuses the Soviet Union of directly using chemical and toxin weapons in Afghanistan and of providing them to the Afghan government for use against guerrilla insurgents.

The 1972 Biological and Toxin Weapons Convention prohibits the development, production, stockpiling, and transfer to any other parties of biological and toxin weapons. The 1925 Geneva Protocol prohibits the first use in war of chemical or bacteriological agents. The Soviet Union is a party to both agreements.

A sharp debate has raged between government and nongovernment scientists in the United States on Soviet compliance with these two agreements. An extensive exploration of the evidence on the U.S. charges is beyond the scope of this report and, in truth, would add little to the already vigorous debate under way.[21] Soviet use or transfer of biological or toxin weapons, as has been charged by the United States, would be inexcusable. Yet the evidence presented on either side of the debate is unconvincing. Unfortunately, no effective means of verification support the chemical- and biological-weapons agreements.

The inadequate nature of the verification provisions of these agreements makes the mechanisms that do exist for consultation and dispute resolution exceedingly important. Article V of the BWC stipulates: "The States Parties to this Convention undertake to consult one another and to cooperate in solving any problems which may arise in relation to the objective of, or in the application of the provisions of, the Convention. Consultation and cooperation pursuant to this article may also be undertaken through appropriate international procedures within the framework of the United Nations and in accordance with its Charter."

Following the Sverdlovsk incident, the United States asked the Soviet Union to cooperate in providing data related to the alleged accident. The Soviet Union refused, holding that the incident involved an epidemic of intestinal anthrax caused by tainted meat and was unrelated to the obligations contained in the BWC. If this explanation is correct, the Soviet Union should have had no reason, other than habitual secrecy, to deny information to the United States about the anthrax epidemic. The Soviet Union did not comply with the consultation provisions of the BWC, and its lack of compliance fueled suspicion about a possible Soviet biological- and toxin-weapons program.

However, in 1986 the Soviet Union took steps to redress its poor compliance with the consultation requirements of the BWC. At the September 1986 review conference for the BWC, Soviet delegate Nikolai Antonov presented a detailed description of the events surrounding the 1979 anthrax outbreak.[22] Western delegates received the opportunity to question Antonov, an official of the Soviet Ministry of Public Health, and U.S. scientists were invited to visit Sverdlovsk. The information presented by the Soviets in 1986 gave some credibility to their position that the 1979 outbreak was caused by contaminated animal feed.

The Reagan administration has noted in its noncompliance reports that no confirmed use of suspected chemical and toxin weapons has occurred in Afghanistan or Southeast Asia since 1983.[23] If such use did occur in the past, the U.S. reports would support the conclusion that the Soviet Union did take steps to improve its compliance behavior, or the behavior of its allies, beginning in 1984.

Limited Test Ban Treaty: U.S. and Soviet Charges

The United States and the Soviet Union have charged one another with venting radioactivity beyond their respective borders from underground nuclear tests, in contravention of the 1963 LTBT ban on causing "radioactive debris to be present outside the territorial limits of the State under whose jurisdiction or control" nuclear explosions are conducted. This provision represents an environmental concern rather than an attempt to prevent behavior that would allow one country to obtain unilateral military advantage.

In its nuclear tests at the Semipalatinsk test area in Siberia (200 miles north of the Chinese border), the Soviet Union has not been sufficiently careful to select sites with the geological stability required to fully contain the radioactivity released during underground blasts; nor has the Soviet Union buried nuclear charges deeply enough during testing. The Soviets have apparently been unwilling to bear the financial and other costs of burying test charges deeply enough, of carefully selecting the test sites, and of properly constructing and stemming the emplacement holes.

As a result, many Soviet tests since 1963 have inadvertently released radioactivity. In some cases the radioactive emissions have crossed national borders. Such radioactivity has been detected by U.S. "sniffer" aircraft in the Arctic and by radiation detectors in northern Europe and the Far East, where prevailing winds have carried emissions.

Since the LTBT was signed, the United States has also, although less frequently in more recent years, inadvertently released radioactivity from underground tests.[24] The United States was apparently the first country to violate the LTBT by releasing radioactivity that crossed international borders. After the U.S. Pike test on March 13, 1964, radioactive debris crossed the Mexican border. A test on April 14, 1965, released radioactivity that reached Canada. A December 1968 cratering blast, Project Schooner, caused radiation to be detected at four Canadian ground stations, as well as in Mexico, and resulted in several exchanges of information between the U.S. and Canadian governments.

The most significant U.S. venting incident occurred during the 1970 Baneberry test at the Nevada test site, when the earth above the explosion cracked. A cloud of radioactive debris, which shot up into the air many thousands of feet, contained radioactive particles and radioactive gas. The U.S. Air Force followed this cloud across the western United States into Canada. The Canadians chose not to make an issue of this inadvertent LTBT violation by the United States.

The Baneberry test caused the United States to inaugurate steps to prevent venting from its nuclear tests. After Baneberry the United States shut down its nuclear-test program for six months to evaluate the situation and to allow implementation of those steps. No further U.S. ventings have occurred.

It is important to distinguish between a venting and a seepage. All releases of radioactivity are not ventings. Ventings are prompt, sometimes spectacular, and more dangerous than seepages. Seepages occur some time after an event and involve slow releases of small amounts of radioactive material. Seepages do not usually pose a hazard beyond the test site. Some radioactive material seeped after the U.S. Riola test in 1981, and a small amount of radiation was detected at a location just outside the test-site boundary. Another seepage occurred after the Agrini blast in 1984, but no radioactivity was detected away from the test site.

Since Baneberry the U.S. record on inadvertent releases has improved substantially. The United States has been more willing than the Soviet Union to bear the costs of ensuring better containment of tests and has instituted a review process within the U.S. Department of Energy. A containment evaluation panel reviews each planned explosion by applying criteria for successful containment, which is defined as "containment such that a test results in no radioactivity detected off-site as measured by normal monitoring equipment and no unanticipated release of radioactivity on-site." Only upon the panel's approval and recommendation to proceed does the United States perform a test. Tests have reportedly been delayed or changed because of concerns expressed during the review process.

The U.S. and Soviet instances of release of radioactivity have been the subject of numerous diplomatic notes and tit-for-tat charges over the years. The issue is further complicated by the difference between the Soviet and U.S. understandings of the LTBT ban on releasing radioactivity. The Soviet Union holds that the ban applies only to particulate matter, whereas the United States holds that it includes gases as well. It is clear that neither the United States nor Soviet Union has intentionally violated the ban, nor is either gaining any military advantage whatsoever from the releases that do occur. The appropriate concern is that, although amounts of radioactivity traveling across borders are relatively small, the Soviet Union is not interpreting its obligation not to release radioactivity across national boundaries as conservatively as is the United States. The Soviet Union is unintentionally subjecting its citizens and the citizens of neighboring countries to radioactive fallout, which the LTBT was designed to prevent.

Threshold Test Ban Treaty

U.S. Charges

The Reagan administration has charged the Soviet Union with a "likely violation" of exceeding the 150-kiloton limit on underground tests set by the 1974 Threshold Test Ban Treaty. The TTBT is one of the three nuclear–arms control treaties concluded in the 1970s that the United States did not ratify. But in 1976 both the United States and Soviet Union announced their intention to abide by the central provision of the TTBT—the 150-kiloton yield limit set by the agreement.

The United States determines the yields of Soviet tests primarily by measuring seismic waves produced by Soviet nuclear explosions and monitored at seismic stations outside the Soviet Union. Seismologists have cautioned that the seismic method of calculating yields could result in an uncertainty factor of plus or minus a factor of two in estimating yields. Thus, a Soviet test at 150 kilotons could give rise to a seismic signal that could be interpreted as coming, at one extreme, from a 300-kiloton blast or, at the opposite extreme, from a 75-kiloton blast.

The genesis of the Reagan administration's concern about Soviet test yields was a review of U.S. and Soviet test yields from 1976 to 1981 conducted in 1983 by the Defense Advanced Research Projects Agency (DARPA).[25] DARPA found that two U.S. tests and nine Soviet tests during this period had seismic signals larger than would be expected from a 150-kiloton test. The methodology used by the DARPA analysts extrapolated experience gained from measuring U.S. tests at the Nevada test site to measure explosions for the Soviet test site at Semipalatinsk in central Siberia.

The U.S. Nevada test site is geologically younger and thus more active than the Soviet test site at Semipalatinsk. As a result, absorption of seismic waves as they pass through the underlying geologic media is greater in Nevada than at the Soviet test site. Thus, an explosion in Nevada will produce a smaller signal at distant recording stations than will a Soviet test with the same yield. Because the United States does not have access to the yields of past Soviet explosions to determine the extent of the difference between signals, it must estimate the difference by indirect means.

Two expert review panels, one commissioned by DARPA and the other by the Air Force Technical Applications Center, reported by October of 1985 that the official U.S. methodology for estimating Soviet test yields was faulty and resulted in overestimates of Soviet yields. These panels reportedly endorsed a change in the U.S. methodology for estimating Soviet yields.

The consensus of opinion today is that the traditional extrapolation did not adequately reflect the geologic differences between the Nevada test site and the Soviet test area.[26] Adding to the uncertainty caused by the statistical spread in yield estimates, the methodology used by DARPA analysts introduced a systematic overestimation of Soviet yields, based on the assumption that the seismic signal-to-yield formula obtained from U.S. tests in Nevada would also apply to Soviet tests at Semipalatinsk. The consensus among seismologists in general is that, because of the geological differences between the Nevada test site and the Soviet test area, the formula should be corrected by using a magnitude bias of 0.4 rather than 0.2. (Appendix C of this report discusses technical aspects of the estimation of Soviet test yields.)

In January 1986 Director of Central Intelligence William Casey reportedly changed the CIA procedures for estimating the yields of large Soviet tests to conform to the recommendations of the review panels.[27] The CIA is formally the lead U.S. agency for estimating Soviet test yields. This change in procedure has had the effect of significantly reducing the estimates of Soviet yields.

In December 1985 President Reagan signed National Security Decision Directive 202, requesting a review of how the methodological changes would affect the past U.S. charges of Soviet violations. The review remained uncompleted during 1986. However, Roger Batzel, director of the Lawrence Livermore National Laboratory, testified before Congress in January 1987: "Based on our own assessment of the relationship between yields and seismic magnitude for the Soviet test sites and the patterns of Soviet testing, we have concluded that the Soviets appear to be observing some yield limit. Livermore's best estimate of this yield limit, based on a probabilistic assessment, is that it is consistent with TTBT compliance."[28] The director of the Los Alamos National Laboratory, Siegfried Hecker, joined Batzel in this judgment in subsequent congressional testimony. Other experts predict that the changes in yield calculation will reduce the assessments of Soviet test yields to the point that few, if any past tests will be shown to have exceeded the 150-kiloton limit.[29]

In addition to the uncertainties of measurement, a second uncertainty affects the estimation of nuclear test yields. The nuclear-weapon designer cannot always be certain that a test will produce the yield for which it is designed. Because of the difficulty of predicting the exact yield of an explosion designed near the 150-kiloton level, the United States and Soviet Union agreed during the negotiation of the TTBT that one or two slight breaches per year of the limit would not be considered a violation of the treaty. This understanding was contained in the transmittal documents that accompanied the submission of the TTBT to the U.S. Senate. It is possible that, after a review applying the new bias factor, Soviet tests previously found to be above the 150-kiloton level will fit within the confines of this understanding.

In response to the burden of data contradicting the charges of Soviet violations, the U.S. Department of Defense and ACDA have claimed that other sources of data besides seismic data, including human intelligence and communications intercepts, indicate that the Soviets are substantially exceeding the 150-kiloton limit. Yet, when interviewed in public, Richard Perle, former assistant secretary of defense, and Manfred Eimer, chief of ACDA's Bureau of Verification and Intelligence, have been unable to substantiate the existence of such data.[30] The expert community still regards seismic data as the only reliable measure of Soviet test yields.

Because of the uncertainties inherent in estimating the yields of Soviet nuclear tests and the revised methodology developed by seismologists for estimating yields, there is no persuasive basis for charging the Soviet Union with significant violations of the 150-kiloton ceiling of the TTBT. This dispute has persisted in part because, since the United States did not ratify the accord, the consultative procedures called for by the agreement have never come into use.

The Threshold Test Ban Treaty Protocol stipulated that the United States and Soviet Union would exchange "yield, date, time, depth and coordinates for two nuclear weapon tests for calibration purposes from each geophysically distinct testing area where underground nuclear weapon tests have been and are to be conducted." Comparing such Soviet test data with remotely measured yields could assist the United States in calibrating its seismometers to account for bias, if the Soviet data could be validated. But the data exchange never took place, because the United States never ratified the TTBT.

The TTBT Protocol also obligates the parties to consult, make inquiries, and furnish information to resolve questions regarding yield, a process that has been characterized in the past six years by accusations rather than exchange of data. In this regard, a joint program recently initiated by the U.S. Natural Resources Defense Council, the U.S. Geological Survey, and the Soviet Academy of Sciences could play an important role. The U.S. organizations and the Soviet government have agreed to place seismometers at test sites in both countries. The United States may be able to gain some information about the geology of the Soviet test site from the seismometers in the Soviet Union. With validation, such data could assist the United States in determining the proper magnitude bias factor to incorporate in its yield calculations.

Soviet Charges

The Soviet Union criticizes the United States for not ratifying the TTBT and the Peaceful Nuclear Explosions Treaty, charging that the United States is "thereby blocking the entry into effect of a number of important measures directed at raising confidence in the strict fulfillment of agreements." In addition, according to the Soviet government: "There have been repeated instances of the American side exceeding the imposed ceiling on the yield of the tested nuclear devices. Despite assurances that the United States intends to observe the 150-kiloton limitation, the practice of exceeding the permitted limit of yield of the nuclear devices that are being tested appears to be continuing."

The methodological limitations that have caused the United States to overestimate the Soviet yields do not apply to Soviet estimates of U.S. yields. The public availability of studies on the geology of the Nevada test site provides the Soviets with direct seismic data reflecting the greater attenuation of seismic waves at the Nevada site than at the Soviet test location. Soviet seismologists are probably able to correct their seismic measurements of U.S. tests in Nevada with an accurate bias factor.

Some of the Soviet charges of U.S. violations of the 150-kiloton limit have been made for tit-for-tat reasons. Other Soviet charges may reflect uncertainty in their measurements of U.S. test yields. Two sources of error are associated with any yield measurement: systematic error, which is corrected by a bias factor, and random error, which reflects the statistical nature of the measurement process. For any given number of explosions with true yields at 150 kilotons, half will appear to be above 150 kilotons and half below 150 kilotons. It is this random error that has probably caused the Soviets to claim U.S. noncompliance with the 150-kiloton limit. The charges may also reflect a few instances in which the United States has slightly exceeded the threshold because of the unreliability of designed yields. But these U.S. tests have represented unintentional U.S. violations of the limit, in which weapons designed for a permitted explosive yield have actually exceeded that yield by 10 percent or more. These U.S. tests, like the few Soviet tests over the limit, are probably within the allowance, provided in the TTBT negotiating record, of one or two tests per year slightly in excess of 150 kilotons.

Non-Proliferation Treaty: Soviet Charge

Article VI of the 1968 Non-Proliferation Treaty calls on both superpowers to "pursue negotiations in good faith on effective measures relating to cessation of the nuclear arms race at an early date and to nuclear disarmament, and on a treaty on general and complete disarmament under strict and effective international control." This pledge was one quid pro quo of the NPT, in return for which nonnuclear-weapon signatories agreed to forgo steps to procure their own nuclear weapons. At the NPT review conferences, held every five years, nonnuclear-weapon states traditionally criticize both the United States and Soviet Union for failing to meet their Article VI obligations. The Soviet Union has charged that the United States has not sought to constrain the nuclear-arms competition and is seeking military superiority.

Whether the United States is striving for military superiority and whether it lacks good faith in pursuing arms control are questions of very subjective judgment. There is ample reason for concern about both U.S. and Soviet performance toward their NPT obligation. No nuclear–arms control agreement has been ratified and come fully into force between the superpowers for fourteen years. The Soviet Union has violated an agreement in one instance and has trod close to noncompliance with agreements in other cases, and the United States has decided to withdraw from the two existing agreements constraining offensive strategic weapons. Both the Soviet Union and United States are currently engaged in programs to further develop a number of nuclear-weapon systems.

But Article VI of the NPT is exhortatory rather than specific in nature. It does not bind the nuclear-weapon states to any definite action during any specified time period. Therefore, U.S. and Soviet nonperformance in relation to the clause, even though it causes general concern, does not belong in a reasoned discussion of arms control compliance.

Helsinki Final Act

U.S. Charge

Confidence-building measures contained in the 1975 Helsinki Final Act obligate the parties to provide 21-days advance notification ("or in the case of a maneuver arranged at shorter notice at the earliest possible opportunity prior to its starting date") to one another of military maneuvers of over 25,000 troops. Parties are requested to state the designation of the exercise, its general purpose, the countries involved, the types of forces involved, their numerical strength, the area of the maneuvers, and the time within which the exercise will take place. If possible, the information should include additional data on the components of the forces engaged and the period of involvement of these forces. The signatories of the Helsinki pact agreed to invite other signatories voluntarily and on a bilateral basis to send observers to attend military maneuvers.

The Reagan administration has accused the Soviet Union of violating some of these provisions in connection with its Zapad-81 military exercise. On August 14, 21 days before the beginning of Zapad-81, the Soviet Union notified the Helsinki signatories that it would conduct exercises from September 4 to 12 in the Baltic and Byelorussian military regions. The Soviets provided data on the general area, purpose, and duration of the maneuvers. However, they neglected to state prior to the exercise the number of troops or the number of countries involved. On September 5 the Soviet Union announced through the news agency TASS that the number of troops would be about 100,000. The Reagan administration also charges that, although the Zapad-81 exercise is the only instance of Soviet failure to provide required data on a military exercise, the Warsaw Pact countries have provided a bare minimum of the information required and have invited NATO observers to less than half of their major military maneuvers.

It should be noted that the preamble to the Helsinki accord states that compliance with all provisions except those for notification of large-scale maneuvers "rests upon a voluntary basis." Zapad-81 was an isolated instance of Soviet noncooperation with the voluntary measures set forth by the Helsinki agreement. The Soviet Union has provided the requisite notification of all other major military maneuvers before and since that time. The Soviet pattern has been one of compliance with the prior-notification provisions of the Helsinki accord.

Soviet Charges

As a riposte to the U.S. charge on notification, the Soviets more vaguely cite the United States for annually staging "in Europe military exercises on a tremendous scale, and it is becoming increasingly more difficult to distinguish them from an actual deployment of armed forces for waging war." The Soviet charge concerns general language of the Helsinki accord relating to fostering stability on the European continent. The Helsinki accord does not prohibit large military exercises. The fact that there has been a pattern of such exercises by both the United States and Soviet Union is precisely the reason for the prior-notification provisions and other confidence-building measures contained in the Helsinki agreement.

The Soviet Union has also made a number of indirect and irrelevant responses to U.S. charges of Soviet violations of chemical- and biological-weapons accords, citing the Helsinki Final Act. The Soviets charge that U.S. movement toward production of the Redeye binary-chemical munitions and their stockpiling in the United States and deployment in Europe constitutes an increase in the military danger in Europe. The Soviets claim that these measures, like the military exercises, contravene the U.S. obligation under the Helsinki Final Act to lessen military tension and promote disarmament in Europe. Nonetheless, the Soviets are not charging the United States with specific violations of provisions of the Helsinki agreement.

Other Soviet Complaints

Soviet charges also include a number of general criticisms of U.S. behavior, most of which have to do with the effect of U.S. policies on the environment for negotiations rather than with U.S. compliance with specific terms of agreements. The Soviets argue, for example, that the United States "disorganized" the arms control process by abandoning negotiations on a comprehensive test-ban treaty, antisatellite systems, and forces in the Indian Ocean. By striving for military superiority through a strategic modernization program, the United States, according to the Soviets, undermined the basis of treaties like SALT I, which were premised on principles of "equality and equal security."

Though atmospherics are clearly important to the arms control process, these additional Soviet complaints are in the nature of frustrations about the state of U.S.-Soviet relations. They have little to do with treaty compliance, and their inclusion in documents on that subject has simply contributed to the negative tone of the compliance debate.

Chapter Four

Questionable Compliance

Although most of the charges of noncompliance with arms control treaties involve gray areas of interpretation, the working group found three categories of concern about U.S. and Soviet compliance that must be considered: questionable compliance, violation, and threat of breach of a treaty.

The category of questionable compliance represents activities that, because of ambiguities surrounding the permissibility of behavior under treaties, cannot at this time be determined to be violations of arms control obligations. But neither are the activities unequivocally in compliance, and they do thus raise serious questions regarding compliance.

Two Soviet activities, the testing and deployment of the SS-25 ICBM and the current high level of encryption of missile–flight-test telemetry, are instances of questionable Soviet compliance, raising doubts about the Soviet Union's adherence to its pledge not to undercut the SALT II Treaty. One area of U.S. activity—the modernization/replacement of large phased-array radars at Thule, Greenland, and Fylingdales Moors, England, and the configuration of two PAVE PAWS radars in the United States—constitutes questionable compliance with the ABM Treaty.

A treaty violation, the second category, is an action that is clearly contrary to an arms control obligation taken on in an agreement. The Soviet Abalakovo radar is a violation of the Soviet Union's legal undertaking embodied in the ABM Treaty.

Concerning threat of breach of a treaty, the third category, both domestic law and international law recognize a category of behavior short of violation ("anticipatory breach of contract in domestic law" and *rebus sic stantibus* in international law) in which a party to an agreement behaves in a fashion that changes the conditions forming the basis for an agreement.[1] It is the widely recognized right of a party, whose national security is threatened through the behavior of another party, to take reasonable steps to safeguard its national security. Breakout from an agreement binding an aggrieved party could be justified if the breakout were necessary for the party to safeguard its national interests. The right to take such response is specifically recognized in the withdrawal clauses of the ABM Treaty and other arms control agreements.

U.S. statements regarding early deployment of a strategic defense of U.S. territory and the U.S. attempt to justify a new, more permissive interpretation of its obligations under the ABM Treaty, to allow development and testing of exotic, space-based ABM components, raise concerns about U.S. intent with regard to ABM Treaty compliance. U.S. behavior could possibly change the basis on which consent of the parties to the ABM Treaty rests and could certainly give the Soviet Union a rationale for breakout from the treaty.

Chapters 4, 5, and 6 present detailed studies of each of five concerns regarding U.S. and Soviet arms control compliance. The studies provide the basis for the working group's findings and the evaluation of the military significance of the activities in question.

The Soviet SS-25 ICBM

Treaty Provisions

SALT II allows the United States and Soviet Union each to flight-test or deploy only one new type of light ICBM. Article IV.9, First Agreed Statement, defines "new type" as any ICBM "different from those ICBMs flight-tested as of May 1, 1979, in any one or more of the following respects: (a) the number of stages, the length, the largest diameter, the launch-weight, or the throw-weight of the missile; (b) the type of propellant (that is, liquid or solid) of any of its stages." The term "different," as applied to the final four parameters listed in (a), means a difference, either an increase or decrease, greater than 5 percent. The one new type allowed may be either MIRVed or unMIRVed. If MIRVed, it may carry no more than ten reentry vehicles.

In another provision relative to ICBM modernization, Article IV.10, Third Agreed Statement (c), the parties agree "not to flight-test or deploy ICBMs equipped with a single reentry vehicle and with an appropriate device for targeting a reentry vehicle, of a type flight-tested as of May 1, 1979, with a reentry vehicle the weight of which is less than fifty percent of the throw-weight of that ICBM."

Finally, Article X states, "Subject to the provisions of this Treaty, modernization and replacement of strategic offensive arms may be carried out."

Background

The possibility of imposing limitations on new types of ICBMs was first discussed at the 1974 Vladivostok summit between President Ford and General Secretary Brezhnev. The Vladivostok aide-mémoire, which set forth the outline of a new agreement to follow SALT I, included the statement that the agreement "could also provide for additional limitations on deployment of new types of strategic arms during the period of its effectiveness." No specific provisions were proposed until 1977, however, and final agreement was reached only late in the SALT II negotiations.

The limitation on new types was considered a significant conceptual advance in arms control. Whereas SALT I had simply set ceilings on numbers of launchers, SALT II for the first time imposed restrictions on the types of missiles that could be deployed. The intent was to forestall the development of new, possibly destabilizing kinds of ICBMs.[2] The United States had seen the Soviets deploy generation after generation of improved ICBMs. The SS-17, SS-18, and SS-19, being deployed in the late 1970s, were the fourth generation, and a fifth was known to be on the drawing boards. By limiting each side to a single new type, the Carter administration hoped that SALT II would constrain the capabilities of that fifth generation. A total ban on new types would have been more constraining but was unacceptable to the United States because of the perceived need to protect the planned development of the MX missile.[3] Inasmuch as the MX program was the only major ICBM program planned by the United States, whereas the Soviets were engaged in modernizing several of their missiles, it was apparent that any limitations adopted would have greater impact, at least in the short term, on Soviet programs than on American ones. The Soviets' acceptance of any restrictions on new types was generally regarded as a concession on their part.

The negotiation of the provision was drawn out and contentious. The major difficulty concerned how to define a new type of ICBM. The initial U.S. proposal, presented in fall 1977, was quite ambitious; it classified as a new type any ICBM that had a propulsion system, guidance system, reentry vehicles, penetration aids, and/or postboost vehicles of a type different from similar components on existing ICBMs.[4] If adopted, such a definition would have drastically constrained missile development by both countries. In particular, the Carter administration hoped that a ban on changes in missile guidance would head off improvements in the accuracy of Soviet ICBMs, improvements that could increase the vulnerability of the U.S. Minuteman force.

It was soon obvious, however, that much of the U.S. proposal would have been practically impossible to verify by national technical means. Besides, the Soviets were unwilling to accept so broad a definition of a new type. In April 1978 the U.S. delegation tabled a new, scaled-down proposal. Except for a few parameters that were dropped at the insistence of the Soviets, this proposal formed the basis for the new-type definition as it eventually took shape.[5]

The framers of the treaty were under no illusion that the new-type provision as finally adopted would effectively close off all improvements in Soviet ICBMs. A missile could be modified in a variety of significant ways without being classified as a new type. The SALT II provision permitted changes in the guidance, improvements in the nuclear warhead, and more efficient propellants. In Walter Slocombe's words: "We shouldn't kid ourselves into thinking we're going to stop the entire fifth generation. What we are going to do is to allow the Soviets to make endless, elegant modifications within a strict set of parameters."[6]

It is essential to recognize that a new type is defined strictly by the criteria listed in Article IV.9. As long as the launch-weight, throw-weight, length, and largest diameter of a missile tested are within 5 percent of those of any missile of an existing type (and the kind of propellant and number of stages are the same), the new missile is for treaty purposes to be considered a modification of that existing type, even if it is not actually a derivative of the older missile. The new missile could even be the product of a different design bureau. The definition thus contains an obvious loophole: An entirely new missile could be designed around the basic parameters of an existing type and thereby escape being classified as a new type. The framers of the treaty recognized the existence of this loophole but could find no satisfactory way to plug it. They hoped that the constraints contained in the new-type provision as finally adopted would at least inhibit the development of the fifth-generation Soviet missiles.[7]

The 5 percent criterion in the new-type definition was the subject of considerable debate, both within the Carter administration and with the Soviets at Geneva. The Soviets at first argued for a greater permitted deviation. Later they proposed that only increases in launch-weight or throw-weight should be restricted. For the United States the problem was one of verification. It was doubtful that changes in launch-weight or throw-weight as low as 5 percent could be detected with any confidence by NTM. In the end, however, the administration decided that limiting allowed changes to 5 percent would hold the Soviets to a stricter standard, even though it was unlikely that so small a violation could be confirmed or would ever be charged.

The requirement that the weight of the reentry vehicle must be at least half the throw-weight was intended to limit the capability of either side to break out from the treaty's ceilings on MIRVed launchers. The reasoning was that, if the weight of the RV were only a small fraction of a missile's throw-weight, the missile would be capable of carrying several such RVs and could rapidly be converted to a MIRVed configuration. There is no legitimate reason to design a missile in which most of the payload capability goes unused, unless, perhaps, the designer envisions a large decoy load to overcome an ABM defense on the other side.

U.S. Charges

In October 1982 the Soviet Union flight-tested a MIRVed ICBM, the SS-24, and informed the United States that the missile was its one allowed new type. In February 1983 a flight test was observed at Plesetsk of a single-RV missile that was assigned the designation PL-5, later changed to SS-25. Rumors quickly surfaced that this missile was judged to be a second Soviet new type and therefore represented a treaty violation. The Reagan administration's first noncompliance report, issued in January 1984, characterized the evidence as somewhat ambiguous and concluded that flight testing of the SS-25 was a probable violation. In the next report (February 1985) the administration assessed the flight testing to be a definite violation. The December 1985 noncompliance report described the evidence as convincing and cited deployment of the SS-25, which began in 1985, as an additional violation. The first two noncompliance reports did not specify in what way the SS-25 allegedly violated the new-type provision, but the third one identified the throw-weight as the parameter whose value was outside the permitted range.

The Reagan administration further charges that, even if the SS-25 were not a new type, it would violate the treaty because the weight of its re-entry vehicle is less than half the ICBM's throw-weight. No precise figure for the ratio of RV weight to throw-weight for the SS-25 has been officially cited, but according to press reports the fraction is assessed to be between 40 percent and 50 percent.[8]

Finally, the administration has charged that encryption of telemetry in the flight tests of the SS-25 violates the deliberate concealment provision of the treaty. The next section of this chapter reviews in detail the encryption issue.

The Soviet Union flatly denies all of the accusations, maintaining that the missile the United States calls the SS-25 is an allowed modification of the SS-13, an old, single-RV ICBM first flight-tested in the middle 1960s. (The Soviet designations for the SS-13 and SS-25 are RS-12 and RS-12M, respectively.) The SS-13 is notable for being the first solid-fueled Soviet ICBM, but it was considered unsuccessful and the deployment was cut short at sixty missiles.[9]

The administration rejects the Soviet claim that the SS-25 is a modification of the SS-13. According to Secretary of Defense Weinberger, the throw-weight of the SS-25 is nearly twice that of the SS-13.[10] The Soviets contend that the United States is underestimating the throw-weight of the SS-13 as well as overestimating that of the SS-25, thereby greatly overestimating the difference between the two. In fact, according to the Soviets, the SS-13 actually has the greater throw-weight.

Analysis

Estimating the throw-weight of a Soviet missile from flight-test data is a difficult and painstaking task for U.S. analysts. After observing a series of flight tests, the analysts, by utilizing a variety of intelligence data, arrive at a "best value" for the throw-weight, with a range of uncertainty that is typically quite broad. The uncertainty decreases gradually as more tests are observed. Even though the current best-value estimates for the throw-weights of the SS-13 and SS-25 differ by nearly a factor of two, there apparently is still some overlap in the distributions. That is, there is some chance that the quantities being compared are actually within 5 percent of each other and that the apparent difference is due to measurement or statistical errors. That chance is, however, very small. Use of the term "convincing" in the 1985 noncompliance report suggests that the administration is now confident the difference is real.

The Soviet Union contends that the administration's values for the throw-weights of the two missiles are wrong, not because of measurement errors but because certain components have been inappropriately included in U.S. estimates of the SS-25's throw-weight and other components have been excluded in estimates of the SS-13's throw-weight. The Soviet case rests on a literal reading of the treaty definition of missile throw-weight. According to Article II.7, Second Agreed Statement, "The throw-weight of an ICBM is the sum of the weight of (a) its reentry vehicle or reentry vehicles; (b) any self-contained dispensing mechanisms or other appropriate devices for targeting one reentry vehicle, or for releasing or for dispensing and targeting two or more reentry vehicles; and (c) its penetration aids, including devices for their release."

The term "other appropriate devices" is distressingly vague. The common understanding to Article II.7 says only that the term means any device for targeting a reentry vehicle that cannot provide the reentry vehicle with a velocity of more than 1,000 meters per second. (Without such a restriction the entire last stage could be considered a targeting device; the intent was to include only a device that gives the reentry vehicle a small final velocity adjustment.)

All modern missiles, including the SS-25, contain a postboost vehicle (PBV) that separates from the last stage of the booster, carries the reentry vehicle or vehicles, and acts as a dispensing mechanism. If the missile is MIRVed, the RVs are released from the PBV one by one, each aimed toward its own target. Even if the missile carries only a single RV, a PBV is nonetheless useful because it improves the targeting accuracy.

The SS-13 has no postboost vehicle; its reentry vehicle is released directly from the third stage. Furthermore, there is no indication from U.S. sources that the SS-13 has ever been observed to release any penetration aids. Hence, the U.S. assessment of the missile's throw-weight is based simply on the weight of the (single) RV. The Soviets claim, however, that the missile does have both a targeting device and penetration aids, which should be counted as part of the throw-weight. Marshal Sergei F. Akhromeyev, chief of the Soviet Armed Forces General Staff, stated at a press conference on June 4, 1986: "At variance with [the throw-weight definition] provision, the weight of certain elements which make up the throw-weight of the old missile [SS-13] (means to overcome ABM defense and the warhead guidance device) is not included by the United States."[11] By omitting the weight of those components, the United States would of course calculate a throw-weight smaller than the correct value.

Inasmuch as there is no PBV on the SS-13, the guidance device to which Marshal Akhromeyev refers must be presumed to be attached to the third stage. The "means to overcome ABM defense," if it exists, would have to be some unusual type of penetration aid that U.S. observations have failed to identify. It is noteworthy that the Soviets flight-tested the SS-13 several times in 1984, after a lapse of many years, perhaps with the intent of demonstrating something in support of their contentions. Those recent tests have, however, not brought about any change in the U.S. assessment.

As for the SS-25, Marshal Akhromeyev stated at the same press conference that the weight of "equipment used only in testing" is "illegitimately" included in the U.S. calculation of its throw-weight, leading to an overestimate of that parameter. Instrumentation packages are indeed commonly employed in early flight tests of missiles.[12] Again, the Soviet contention is based on a literal reading of the treaty; because the definition of throw-weight makes no mention of instrumentation, its weight should not count in the calculation. The same interpretation would also resolve the issue of the RV weight–to–throw-weight ratio. If the weight of the instrumentation is subtracted from the throw-weight as calculated by the United States, the throw-weight decreases and the fraction contained in the reentry vehicle increases, presumably to a value above the required 50 percent.[13] Figure 5 contains schematic drawings of the SS-13 and SS-25 configurations, based on the working group's understanding of the Soviet position.

If the SS-13 does carry some kind of targeting device, there appears to be at least a technical basis for the Soviet argument that the weight of that device should be considered part of the throw-weight. The treaty definition of throw-weight places no restriction on where the "other appropriate device" may be located. In particular, say the Soviets, it could be attached to the last stage. On the other hand, if the targeting device is indeed part of the last stage and remains attached to it when the RV is released, there would be no way for the United States to determine the weight of the targeting device by NTM, the standard verification technique specified by the treaty.

In fact, how is the United States to verify that the device exists at all? It seems implausible that the framers of the treaty intended that so unverifiable a component be included in the throw-weight. This implausibility is the basis for the administration's position. The administration in fact claims that the SALT II negotiating record reflects an informal understanding that any targeting device should separate from the booster for identification purposes.[14] There is no doubt that this understanding was what

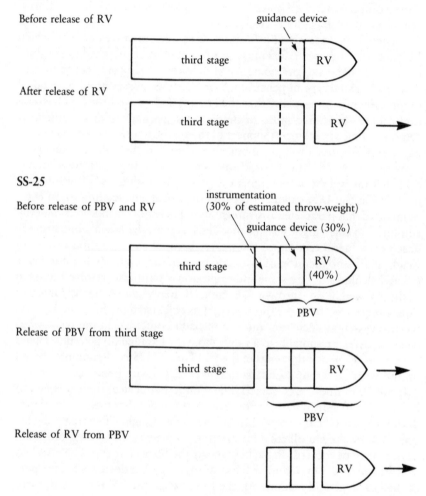

Fig. 5. Configuration of SS-13 and SS-25 ICBMs

the U.S. negotiators intended. Still, the treaty language contains no hint of any such understanding.

The Soviets are likewise technically correct in asserting that the treaty says nothing about instrumentation packages being included in the throw-weight. Again, there is a verification problem: How is the United States to determine the weight of the instrumentation, which is to be subtracted from the PBV weight? The Soviets contend that when the missile is flown in its operational configuration, without any instrumentation, the United States' measurement will reflect the correct lower throw-weight.[15]

The administration rejects the Soviet contention that instrumentation carried on a PBV should not count as part of a missile's throw-weight. The throw-weight, so the counterargument goes, is supposed to measure a missile's payload capability. The flight tests observed to date have demonstrated that the SS-25 is capable of carrying a certain weight, which includes whatever instrumentation is on board. After the instrumentation has been removed, it could be replaced by something else, perhaps by another RV or by penetration aids, either of which would be part of the throw-weight. It is in fact common practice to "off-load" MIRVed missiles during flight testing, replacing one or more RVs with an instrumentation package. But a single-RV missile cannot be so off-loaded, since it would then be left with no RV at all. If the instrumentation is not replaced by anything after it is removed, its weight does not contribute to the missile's useful payload capability. This last point is the basis for the Soviet argument.

The dispute over the SS-13's throw-weight could have been avoided had the throw-weights of existing missile types been included in the agreed data base that accompanies the treaty. Any discrepancy between the throw-weights assigned to the SS-13 by the two sides would have been apparent and would have had to be resolved before the treaty was signed. Unfortunately, the Soviets would not agree to include in the data base any information beyond the numbers of each kind of strategic delivery vehicle limited in the treaty. Some suspect they intentionally limited the data base so as to proceed with questionable programs like the SS-25. Others ascribe the Soviets' attitude simply to their congenital reluctance to disclose any information concerning their weapons.

The SCC has discussed the SS-25 but has made no progress toward resolving the dispute. Apparently, the United States has simply accused the Soviets of a violation and insisted that they terminate the SS-25 program. For their part, the Soviets have not provided any information that might be helpful, such as the nature and weight of the SS-13's "guidance device" or the nature of the penetration aids that they claim it carries and that the United States has not detected. There could be legitimate military reasons for Soviet reluctance to provide information on penetration aids, such as a desire to downplay measures they might be taking to prepare to deal with a potential U.S. strategic defense.

The one conclusion that emerges unequivocally from the preceding analysis is that the SS-25 issue is not an open-and-shut case, as implied by most administration pronouncements on the subject. The administration has been telling the U.S. public and the world that the Soviets have brazenly violated their SALT II commitment by flight-testing and deploying a missile with twice the allowed throw-weight. The actual situation appears to be considerably less clear-cut. It appears that a reasonable though legalistic case can be made for the Soviet position. Secretary of State Shultz in effect conceded as much when he stated in a television interview, "There are questions about whether in a purely technical sense, the SS-25 fits within the treaty language as might be interpreted by a lawyer."[16]

A reasonable case can be made for the administration position as well. The situation appears to be one in which a literal reading of the treaty language and a common-sense interpretation of its intent lead to opposite conclusions. A more forthright presentation of the issue would have at least made it clear that there is a Soviet side to the story, a side not totally devoid of substance.

There is no doubt, incidentally, that the SS-25 is a much more modern missile than the SS-13. It would be astonishing if, after twenty years of progress in missile technology, the Soviets were now deploying a 1960s-vintage ICBM with a few minor modifications. But, as we have already emphasized, such considerations are entirely irrelevant to the question of treaty compliance. A new type is strictly what the treaty says it is. Perhaps the treaty definition is not as comprehensive as it ought to be, but that is not germane to the compliance issue. If the SS-25 is a new missile that technically falls within the box defined by the parameters of the SS-13, it might be proper to reproach the Soviets for exploiting a treaty loophole, but it would not be proper to accuse them of a violation.

There is an interesting footnote to the SS-13–SS-25 controversy. In the classified version of its January 1985 noncompliance report, the administration apparently charged that a new Soviet SLBM, the SS-N-23, is a heavy missile according to the SALT II definition. SALT II does not restrict the number of new types of SLBMs that either side may deploy. But no SLBM may exceed either the throw-weight or the launch-weight of the heaviest light ICBM—the Soviet SS-19. The charge related to the SS-N-23 does not appear in any unclassified administration document, but it was leaked to the press and cited in a 1985 letter to the president from Senator Jesse Helms and several other conservative senators.[17]

The open literature contains little information concerning the SS-N-23. The missile is, however, described briefly in the 1986 edition of *Soviet Military Power.* An illustration shows the dimensions of Soviet and U.S. SLBMs; the SS-N-23 strongly resembles the SS-N-18. The accompanying text states that the SS-N-23 is likely to be deployed on Delta III submarines as a replacement for the SS-N-18 and will have greater throw-weight than the SS-N-18.

The point relevant to the present discussion is that, if the SS-N-23 is more or less the same size as the SS-N-18 (as it must be if it is to replace that missile in existing submarines), it is hard to understand how the SS-N-23's throw-weight could be enough greater than the SS-N-18's to make it a heavy missile, if the throw-weight is calculated in the standard way. Only by counting components not normally included in throw-weight calculations can one reasonably arrive at a throw-weight for the SS-N-23 in the range of the SS-19's. Perhaps administration analysts have constructed an argument by which something besides the weight of the PBV, the RVs, and the penetration aids is included in the throw-weight of the SS-N-23. If so, this is precisely the type of argument that the Soviets have put forward in connection with the SS-13 and that the administration has rejected.

One may speculate that the administration has not publicly raised the SS-N-23 issue because of concern that to do so might weaken the U.S. case in the SS-25 controversy.

Strategic Significance

If one accepts for the sake of argument the administration claim that the SS-25 violates SALT II, what is the strategic significance of that hypothetical violation? According to the December 1985 noncompliance report, the SS-25 has "important political and military implications." First, the relevant question concerns not the strategic significance of the SS-25 but only the significance of the additional throw-weight that constitutes the alleged violation. If the SS-25 had been designed with the throw-weight that the United States assigns to the SS-13, that is, just the weight of the SS-13 reentry vehicle, the SS-25 would unquestionably have had to be considered a modification of the SS-13 under the treaty definition. In that case there would have been no grounds for a charge of noncompliance.

There is no reason that such a hypothetical version of the SS-25 with lower throw-weight could not have been constructed. Its RV would have had to be somewhat lighter than the one carried by the actual SS-25. But, since the SS-25 has throw-weight to spare, the reduction would presumably have been modest.

The nuclear yield of the warhead would perhaps also have been somewhat less than that of the actual SS-25. But, with modern improvements in yield-to-weight ratios of nuclear weapons, there is little doubt that a warhead of sufficient yield for strategic purposes could have been designed. (The high accuracy of present-day missiles has made the yield a much less critical parameter than it was in the past.) In sum, if the SS-25 had been held to what the administration considers to be the throw-weight of the SS-13, instead of that of the actual SS-25, the United States would now be confronting a similar missile carrying a warhead of somewhat smaller yield.

It would be hard to argue that a given number of SS-25s poses a substantially greater threat to U.S. security than would an equal number of those hypothetical missiles. The Soviets did not go to the trouble of developing and deploying the SS-25 for the sake of a few kilograms of extra throw-weight; they have an ample supply of high-throw-weight missiles. The novel feature of the SS-25 is its mobility, which enhances survivability. Mobile missiles are not restricted by the treaty.[18] Whatever the strategic significance of the SS-25, very little of that significance is attributable to the extra throw-weight that constitutes the compliance issue.

The problem of the RV weight–to–throw-weight ratio likewise appears to be of modest strategic significance. The only threat posed by a light reentry vehicle is the potential it poses for breakout to a MIRVed configuration, which could result in a greatly increased number of warheads. If the weight of the SS-25's RV were, say, only 10 percent of its throw-weight, there would indeed be cause for concern; there would be little reason for the Soviets to employ such a light RV unless they were planning to put many more of them on the missile.

But with more than 40 percent of the throw-weight contained in the reentry vehicle, the breakout potential is extremely limited. It is mathematically impossible to load more than two such RVs on the missile, and even that would be technically difficult and perhaps impossible. If the instrumentation package weighs as much as the reentry vehicle, it could perhaps be replaced by a second RV. But only 15–20 percent of the throw-weight would remain for the rest of the PBV. It is doubtful that a satisfactory PBV can be designed with such a small fraction of the throw-weight. Hence, the administration's assertion, in its 1985 noncompliance report, that the SS-25 "could be made more lethal by modifying it to carry more than a single warhead" seems questionable.

The analysis of the SS-25 in the 1985 noncompliance report concludes with the assertion, "Most worrisome is the technical argument by which the Soviets sought to justify the SS-25, for it is likely to be applied to additional prohibited new types of ICBMs in the future."[19] Presumably this statement refers to the Soviet argument that the weight of on-board instrumentation should not be counted as part of a missile's throw-weight. The concern would be that the Soviets might field a follow-on to the SS-19 or SS-18 with extra throw-weight concealed in an instrumentation package, later to be replaced by additional RVs.

It is difficult to understand why this possibility should be so worrisome. If SALT II constraints were still in effect, extra throw-weight could not legally be utilized to add RVs to the missile. Had there been a less confrontational climate, it should have been possible to work out an understanding at the Standing Consultative Commission to resolve the problem. It should still be possible to reach agreement that in the future instrumentation will count as part of the throw-weight.

Concluding Remarks

The Soviets must have recognized at some point that the SS-25 deployment was likely to be challenged. If, as we have argued, the strategic significance of the extra throw-weight is minor, the obvious question is why the Soviets decided to add it. A plausible (though admittedly speculative) explanation emerges from the preceding analysis. The Soviets were obviously eager to deploy a mobile, single-RV ICBM, to enhance the overall survivability of their force. (The same objective motivates U.S. plans to deploy Midgetman.) They also wanted to deploy a MIRVed mobile missile of the MX type: the SS-24. For practical reasons a mobile missile must be solid-fueled. The SS-24, then, had to be a new type, because no baseline solid-fueled missile with the required characteristics was available. The small mobile missile, on the other hand, could be designed around the parameters of the SS-13 and thereby escape being classified as a new type. If the throw-weight of the new small missile had been limited to the weight of the SS-13's reentry vehicle, there would have been no question of its legitimacy. But, because some of the throw-weight had to be used for the PBV, the weight available for the RV would have been reduced. For purely technical reasons, therefore, a somewhat higher throw-weight was attractive to the Soviet weapon designers. Perhaps, for example, it would have allowed them to use off-the-shelf reentry vehicles and warheads rather than new lighter ones that they would have had to design.

The legalistic interpretation of the treaty's throw-weight definition would have provided a tempting rationale for proceeding with the higher–throw-weight design. Although the case for that interpretation was not airtight, it may have been judged good enough to justify going ahead. It is possible that the decision was not made at the highest levels of the Soviet bureaucracy.

It is apparent that Soviet decision makers underestimated the severity of the U.S. reaction to the SS-25. If the scenario sketched bears any resemblance to what actually occurred, in retrospect it represents a serious blunder on their part. Whatever minor technical benefits they have reaped are surely not worth the political fallout that the issue has generated. On the other hand, one could argue that the issue has been exploited by those within the Reagan administration who are more desirous of demonstrating Soviet duplicity than of sustaining existing agreements and achieving further progress in arms control.

Finally, if the Soviets indeed have taken advantage of a legalistic argument to justify a questionable deployment, it is necessary to point out that the United States is not entirely innocent of such practices. Consider, for example, the closely spaced basing mode (Dense Pack) that was at one time proposed for the MX missile. That deployment would have run counter to the Interim Agreement ban on construction of new fixed ICBM launchers. But the Pentagon argued that the proposed deployment was legal because the new silos to be constructed were not launchers but simply shelters. Because the missiles would be encapsulated and the capsule would contain all the equipment necessary to launch the missile, the missiles should, according to the Department of Defense, be considered mobile even though they would be deployed in a fixed mode. This kind of legalistic rationalization is certainly not very different in spirit from the Soviet explanation for the SS-25.

Soviet Telemetry Encryption

Treaty Provisions

The SALT II provision directly relevant to telemetry encryption is Article XV.3, Second Common Understanding: "Each Party is free to use various methods of transmitting telemetric information during testing, including its encryption, except that, in accordance with the provisions of paragraph 3 of Article XV, neither party shall engage in deliberate denial of telemetric information, such as through the use of telemetry encryption, whenever such denial impedes verification of compliance with the provisions of the Treaty." Paragraph 3 of Article XV states: "Each party undertakes not to use deliberate concealment measures which impede verification by national technical means of compliance with the provisions of this Treaty. This obligation shall not require changes in current construction, assembly, conversion, or overhaul practices."

Background

Telemetry, the electronic transmission of information, is routinely used to send data from missiles undergoing flight testing back to collection stations on the ground and occasionally to airborne receivers. Performance data are transmitted for each of the missile stages, the postboost vehicle that carries the reentry vehicles, and for the reentry vehicles themselves after they have been released from the PBV. The data consist of the readings of instruments such as thermometers and fuel flowmeters, recorded onto a number of channels for radio transmission. The data are generally converted into digital form before being transmitted.

The number of sensors for which data are transmitted can run into the hundreds. Sophisticated techniques make it possible to transmit the readings of several instruments over a single channel. The telemetered data

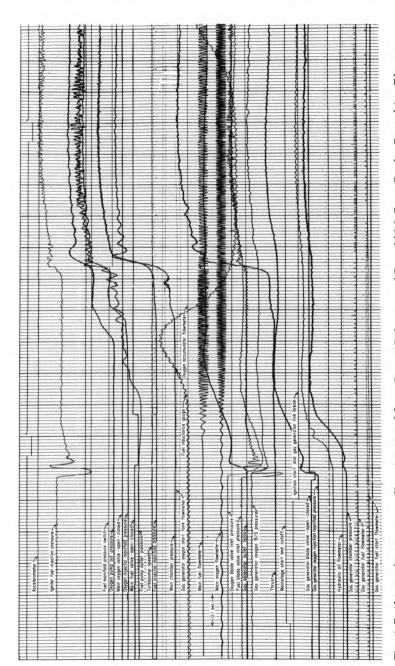

Fig. 6. **Rocket-engine sensor readings** (reprinted from George P. Sutton and Donald M. Ross, *Rocket Propulsion Elements: An Introduction to the Engineering of Rockets*, 4th ed. [New York: John Wiley and Sons, 1976], f. 542 [courtesy Rocketdyne, a division of Rockwell International Corp.])

enable engineers on the ground to monitor the performance of the missile in real time—that is, as the flight progresses. Figure 6 contains a set of rocket-engine sensor readings, demonstrating the complexity found in a typical telemetric transmission.

The United States has for many years monitored the telemetry transmitted during Soviet flight tests, using receivers located at ground stations, on satellites, on ships, and on aircraft. Since Soviet flight tests are conducted over well-known trajectories, the receivers can be located to obtain the best possible access to the transmission. U.S. technicians have had long experience in reading and interpreting Soviet telemetry and identifying individual data channels; but, even when the telemetry is not encoded, the task is far from simple. Soviet technicians similarly monitor and read the telemetry from U.S. missile flight tests.

U.S. intelligence analysts use the telemetric data in assessing the characteristics of the missile being tested. But telemetry is only one of several sources of information employed in the analysis; additional information comes from photoreconnaissance and radar tracking, as well as from nontechnical or "soft" sources. The results of the analysis are used not only to verify treaty compliance but also for other intelligence purposes. In general, only a small fraction of the telemetry refers to properties of the missile limited by any treaty. The remainder contains technical information that, although not relevant to treaty verification, is very useful to the United States in evaluating the capabilities of Soviet weapons.

In 1974 the Soviets began to transmit some of their telemetry in encrypted, or coded, form, thereby making it unreadable to the United States. The SALT II negotiations were by then already in progress. Although the Soviets encrypted only a small fraction of the telemetry at first, the change in their practice troubled the U.S. intelligence community, which would be responsible for verifying compliance with any treaty that was negotiated. The CIA was especially concerned that, if the level of encryption increased, its ability to verify treaty provisions dealing with missile launch-weight and throw-weight could be eroded. The new agreement was likely to include limitations on those parameters, for whose determination telemetric data are particularly useful.

The problem of how to react to Soviet encryption sparked a lively debate within the U.S. government. There was the ever-present risk that bringing up the issue explicitly at the SALT negotiations would result in disclosing to the Soviets sensitive information concerning U.S. capabilities to intercept and read Soviet telemetry, information that the intelligence community was most anxious to protect.[20] On the other hand, the United States could not ignore the potential threat to verification posed by encryption. Accordingly, the United States communicated its concerns to the Soviets in Geneva, albeit circumspectly—the word "encryption" was for a long time not even mentioned.

U.S. negotiators initially sought only Soviet concurrence that telemetry employed in flight testing would be subject to the general ban, carried over from SALT I, on deliberate concealment practices that impede verification. Such concurrence would allow the United States to bring to the SCC as a serious compliance concern any case of encryption that impeded U.S. verification. There could be no question that encryption constitutes deliberate concealment; the only conceivable motive for Soviet encryption could be to prevent the United States from obtaining access to data.

The Soviets at first would not concede that telemetry was covered by the provision on deliberate concealment. They contended that for one country to read the other's telemetry is not a legitimate form of verification but simply eavesdropping. After reluctantly abandoning that position, they argued that no changes in "current test practices" should be required. A grandfather clause exempting current practices would have permitted encryption at least at the level then being employed. (The treaty contains several similar exemptions to protect existing practices.) U.S. negotiators objected that current Soviet test practices were already interfering with verification.

In late 1977 the Carter administration decided to seek an explicit treaty provision dealing with encryption. That decision was reinforced in July 1978, when, in a flight test of their heavy SS-18 ICBM, the Soviets reportedly encrypted more of the telemetry than ever before.[21] Particularly troublesome was the fact that for the first time they encrypted reentry-vehicle telemetry, which is most useful for the determination of missile throw-weight.[22] Since the SS-18 had been flight-tested many times before, the United States already knew its throw-weight. Moreover, the missile in the July 1978 test was a single-RV version of the SS-18. The CIA feared, however, that if telemetry from a future test of a new missile (or even of a MIRVed SS-18) were similarly encrypted, its ability to verify both the throw-weight constraints and the fractionation ceilings of the new treaty could be seriously hampered.[23] It was deemed essential, for political as well as technical reasons, that some resolution of the encryption issue be found. Several influential senators, including, notably, John Glenn, were expressing concern over the verifiability of the treaty; such concern could cost badly needed votes in the battle over ratification that loomed imminent.[24]

Although agreed that the treaty must address encryption, the Carter administration was divided over what sort of provision to seek. The CIA preferred a blanket ban on all encryption; such a ban would have greatly facilitated its monitoring task. But the State Department and ACDA were convinced that the Soviets would never accept a total ban. It would be hard to sustain an argument that the Soviets should not have the right to encrypt data that had nothing to do with any of the treaty's provisions, for example, data dealing with missile accuracy or reliability. Besides, the Pentagon was reported to be anxious to preserve the right to do some encrypting of its own. The United States thus never formally proposed a total ban to the Soviets in Geneva.[25]

The provision finally adopted after much bickering in both Washington and Geneva was an obvious compromise: Encryption would be forbidden, but only when it impeded verification of compliance with the treaty. At Soviet insistence a clause was added to state explicitly that encryption is in general permitted (that is, when it does not impede verification).

The Second Common Understanding to Article XV.3 is largely redundant; it adds little to what is contained in the article itself but simply confirms that telemetric transmission is subject to the article's provisions. Nevertheless, the compliance controversy arises directly from differing interpretations of this common understanding. Everything hinges on the meaning attached to the term "impede," which is not defined in the treaty.

The initial Soviet position was that, so long as the United States is able to verify compliance, by whatever means, it has no cause to complain. In other words, only encryption that *prevents* verification must be avoided. But the treaty clearly goes further. The words "impede" and "prevent" are not synonymous, either in English or in Russian. "To impede" means "to interfere with" or "to make more difficult," and not "to make impossible." The treaty language therefore encompasses the theoretical possibility that encryption can be a violation even though one side is able to verify the other's compliance. But to what extent must the pattern of encryption complicate verification in order to be considered a violation? On this critical question the treaty is silent.

In one sense, practically any encryption can be said to impede verification, for if one side is unable to read the other's encrypted channels, how is it to know whether the content of those channels might be helpful for verification? For that matter, how can one side be sure that the other's unencrypted channels do not contain false data, with the true data concealed in the encrypted channels?

If Soviet telemetry had been encrypted from the outset, these problems could have been serious. But with nearly twenty years of experience in monitoring Soviet missile test firings, U.S. analysts have an extensive data base to draw on. They reportedly know what data are normally telemetered and in what channels each type of data is found. If data needed for verification were missing from a given test, the analysts could presume the data had been encrypted. Administration spokesmen reassured the Senate on this point in 1979.[26]

The possibility that the Soviets could plant false data cannot be ruled out. But, because of the redundancy of U.S. collection assets, it would be a highly risky endeavor for the Soviets to plant false data. Telemetric data can be cross-checked with information obtained from other sources. Inconsistencies are likely to reveal the presence of any false data.

Two more aspects of the encryption provision deserve mention. First, although denial of information must be deliberate in order to constitute a violation, the impeding of verification that results need not be deliberate. In other words, in order to establish a violation, it is not necessary to prove that data were encrypted for the express purpose of impeding verification; the motivation might have been simply to protect military secrets. If, as a result of encryption, verification is impeded, a violation has nonetheless occurred.

Second, the common understanding cites encryption as only one example of how access to telemetric information might be denied. Other techniques could accomplish the same objective: (1) One side could change the frequency of its transmission often and at irregular intervals; the other side would not know at what frequency to set its receivers. (2) One side could transmit telemetry at unusually low power levels or in a highly directional pattern, with only a weak signal emitted in the direction of the other side's receivers. (3) One side could transmit no telemetry at all; it could record data on tape and encapsulate them, then drop the capsule off, just before the missile's impact, for recovery by specially equipped collectors. Although this technique is perhaps the most effective, its major disadvantage is that the information is not received in real time. Furthermore, if a flight should abort, much valuable information could be lost. The data are, however, quite immune from being intercepted, unless the capsule should land in the ocean and be recovered by the other side, a fairly remote possibility.

There can be no doubt that the first technique, frequency switching, is deliberate concealment and would violate the treaty if it impeded verification. Whether the other techniques constitute deliberate concealment is less clear.[27] There are legitimate technical reasons for employing them. The United States, in fact, has often routinely used encapsulation to transmit data from some intelligence satellites and in flight tests of Minuteman II missiles.[28] The United States has apparently also used low-power transmission on occasion. In the case of encapsulation, one could hardly claim that telemetric information had been denied if none was ever transmitted.

This last case raises an interesting question: Is it a violation if one side, for whatever reason, simply does not transmit data that could have helped the other to verify some provision of the treaty? To put the question more broadly: Is each side obligated to make available to the other sufficient data to enable it to verify compliance? Such an obligation would be stronger than one just to abstain from actions that impede verification. The Joint Statement of Principles, which was supposed to guide the negotiation of SALT III, encourages the use of such "cooperative measures," but they were not part of SALT II.

The framers of the treaty have been criticized for drafting a provision so laden with ambiguity as Article XV.3. Since the key term "impede" was left undefined, each side could feel free to assign to it whatever meaning suited that side's purposes. Unless Soviet encryption actually prevented the

United States from verifying compliance, critics warned, it would be hard to prove that verification had been impeded.

Both the Carter administration and Congress fully recognized the potential problems at the time the encryption provision was negotiated. The Senate Foreign Relations Committee report on the treaty noted, "There are no agreed criteria . . . for determining when denial of telemetric information could impede verification."[29] But an outright ban was not acceptable, and a detailed listing of just what encryption would be permitted and what would be forbidden was not a practical possibility. Such a catalog would have led to endless haggling and would have involved the kind of discussion of sources and methods that the U.S. intelligence community was most anxious to avoid.

Acting under instruction, at a meeting with Foreign Secretary Gromyko in 1979, Secretary of State Vance did point to the SS-18 flight test of July 1978 as providing an example of encryption that the United States considered impermissible under the proposed treaty provision.[30] Vance sought Soviet concurrence that similar encryption of telemetry from a new missile would violate the treaty. One objective of his approach was to get the Soviets to admit on the record that there are actual cases in which encryption would impede verification. There was some concern that, even if the treaty were to ban encryption whenever it impeded verification, the Soviets might later argue that such a situation never occurs in practice.

Gromyko's response to Vance was oblique. Gromyko did not contradict Vance but would not explicitly confirm the validity of the U.S. position. He said only that the common understanding would be "adequate" to cover any specific case that might arise. Many in Washington felt that the tactic of citing specific examples of encryption that impeded verification was unwise. The tactic would be of little practical use even if the Soviets assented, because the Soviets could construe the particular examples as giving them carte blanche to encrypt up to the level of those examples, and because no future case was likely to be identical to the ones cited.

The architects of the treaty realized that, in the final analysis, the encryption provision would be successful only if the Soviets cooperated by showing restraint. Secretary Vance's analysis of the treaty notes, "In further discussions . . . the Soviets stated that there must be no encryption of information involving parameters covered by the Treaty, that there was an understanding between the Parties on this issue."[31] With fulfillment of that understanding, there would be no difficulties. After all, the deliberate-concealment provision, including the troublesome, undefined term "impede," had been taken over verbatim from SALT I and had been in effect since 1972 without causing unmanageable problems. The SCC would be available for discussion of ambiguous situations as it had been in the past.[32] The provision adopted seemed better than nothing.

U.S. Charges

Since 1980 the level of Soviet encryption has substantially increased. The first reported case of higher encryption, in January 1980, involved a flight test of a new SLBM, the SS-N-20, in which a "higher proportion of encoding than had been customary with Soviet ICBMs" was detected.[33] Subsequently, telemetry from tests of the SS-24 and SS-25 ICBMs was reported to be heavily encrypted.[34] Administration spokesmen have testified that in some tests, all or nearly all the telemetry was encrypted.[35] President Reagan's first report on Soviet noncompliance, issued in January 1984, found that the Soviets' encryption practices "constitute a violation of a legal obligation prior to 1981 and a violation of their political commitment subsequent to 1981. The nature and extent of encryption of telemetry on new ballistic missiles is an example of deliberate impeding of verification of compliance in violation of this Soviet political commitment." The administration repeated the charge in its two subsequent noncompliance reports.

The technical distinction between the nature of the violations charged before and after 1981 is based on the change in the legal status of SALT II at about that time. Until 1981 the treaty, though unratified, was considered to be awaiting ratification; under international law both signatories were obligated not to take actions that would defeat the object and purpose of the treaty. After the president had indicated that the United States would not ratify SALT II, all legal obligation ceased. However, in May 1982 Reagan announced that the United States would refrain from actions that undercut existing treaties, so long as the Soviets exercised equal restraint. The Soviets' agreement to abide by this policy constitutes the political commitment that they are alleged to have violated in the post-1982 time period.

The noncompliance reports cite only one specific example of Soviet encryption, involving flight testing of the SS-25, that has impeded verification. They do not specify in what way U.S. verification has been impeded. Inasmuch as the SS-25 was first flight-tested in 1983, it cannot account for the pre-1981 violation that has also been charged. The only new missile the Soviets flight-tested between 1979 and 1981 was the SS-N-20; hence the pre-1981 part of the indictment must refer either to the SS-N-20 or to flight tests of missiles of previously existing types.

The Soviets do not deny that they are encrypting; on this one issue the basic facts are not in dispute. The Soviets do deny they are violating the treaty; they contend that encryption has not impeded U.S. verification of their compliance with any treaty provision.

Consistently throughout the course of the controversy, the Soviet response has been to ask the United States to specify just what information it needs. Which are the parameters, the Soviets ask, for which encryption of data is impeding U.S. verification? The U.S. intelligence community is most reluctant to enter into any discussion of this nature, and the United States has never responded positively to the Soviet requests.

Analysis

Before evaluating the charges, it is helpful to identify the specific treaty provisions that potentially relate to telemetry and inquire for each how encryption might affect the verification of compliance. The following outline summarizes major SALT II Treaty provisions governing flight tests of ballistic missiles and discusses their relation to encryption and verification.

A. Provisions affecting ICBMs

1. Fractionation ceiling on the number of reentry vehicles

   The SALT II Treaty limits existing types of ICBMs to the maximum number of RVs with which they were flight-tested prior to May 1979; new types are limited to ten RVs (Articles IV.10 and IV.11). The treaty also stipulates that, if the postboost vehicle carries out all the maneuvers associated with the reentry vehicle, each such procedure counts toward the fractionation ceiling, even if no RV is actually released (Articles IV.10 and IV.11, Second Agreed Statements).

   Radar and optical observations can readily determine the number of RVs released from a missile during a flight test. However, identifying a simulated release is a more demanding task, for which telemetry is a useful, perhaps even necessary, tool. *Encryption could therefore impede verification of fractionation ceilings.*

2. Limitations on the throw-weight and launch-weight of ICBMs

   The new-type limitation (Article IV.9) requires that changes in the launch-weight and throw-weight of ICBMs be limited to 5 percent. In addition, the limitation on heavy ICBMs (Article IV.7) forbids the testing of any ICBM with a launch-weight or throw-weight greater than that of the SS-18.

   Determinations of launch-weight and throw-weight, especially to an accuracy of 5 percent, are demanding tasks. *They are the principal verification tasks for which telemetry is important and which encryption could impede.*

3. Limitations on the weight of reentry vehicles

   There are different limitations on the weight of RVs, depending on whether or not the missile being tested is MIRVed (Article IV.10, Third Agreed Statement). For a single RV with a postboost vehicle, such as the SS-25, the RV must carry at least half of the total throw-weight.

   Verification of RV weight is a task for which telemetry is useful.

B. Provisions affecting SLBMs

1. Ceiling on the number of reentry vehicles

Although the treaty places no restrictions on the number of new types of SLBMs that may be flight-tested or deployed, any new SLBM is subject to a fractionation ceiling of fourteen RVs (Article IV.12). The provision governing simulated releases that applies to ICBMs also applies to SLBMs. *Encryption could impede verification of fractionation ceilings.*

2. Ban on heavy SLBMs

The ban on heavy SLBMs, defined as any whose launch-weight or throw-weight exceeds that of the SS-19 ICBM, is the only limitation on launch-weight of SLBMs (Article IX.9[e]).

Telemetry is, in principle, useful for verifying compliance with the ban on heavy SLBMs. However, because the throw-weight of all Soviet SLBMs tested before 1980 is much less than that of the SS-19, the verification task is considerably less demanding for an SLBM than for an ICBM.[36] Even a relatively crude estimate of throw-weight should suffice, unless there is evidence to suggest that the missile being tested is unusually heavy, with a throw-weight approaching that of the SS-19.

By implication, the administration's position is that the high levels of encryption in recent flight tests constitute a prima facie case for its charge that the Soviets have violated the treaty. In assessing the validity of this claim, it is important to recognize that the fraction of telemetry encrypted in a single flight test or even in a series of tests is by itself a poor measure of whether that encryption is impeding verification. As previously noted, most of the telemetry has nothing to do with treaty-limited parameters. In principle, encryption of even a single critical channel could impede verification; at the opposite extreme, almost all the telemetry could be encrypted without impeding verification, provided a few channels containing the relevant information were transmitted in the open. As General Charles A. Gabriel, U.S. Air Force chief of staff, reportedly told the Senate: "It is misleading to use the level of encryption as a guide for determining how well we can verify what they are doing. More central is the nature of the encryption, that is, what missile-test functions are being encrypted and what functions are being transmitted in the clear."[37] Even total encryption does not necessarily impede; whether it does or not depends on the parameters one is trying to determine and the accuracy with which they must be known in order to verify compliance. If it is possible to obtain the necessary information readily and with sufficient accuracy by other means, it cannot be argued that encryption has impeded verification.

The administration does not contend that encryption has prevented it from verifying Soviet compliance with any specific treaty provision. It would be difficult to sustain such a position. For example, since charges of non-compliance have been leveled in connection with the SS-25, U.S. intelligence must have been able to determine its throw-weight as well as the ratio of RV weight to throw-weight with sufficient accuracy to justify a finding that the treaty has been violated.

In fact, the numbers cited by the administration in the case of the SS-25 suggest a surprisingly high degree of precision. Secretary Weinberger reportedly told the NATO defense ministers in 1985 that the throw-weight of the SS-25 exceeds that of the SS-13 by 92 percent—two significant figures.[38] Moreover, the ratio of RV weight to throw-weight for the SS-25 is reportedly assessed to be somewhat above 40 percent but definitely below 50 percent, the minimum figure allowed by the treaty.[39] These figures imply that the ratio is known within a quite small margin, several percent at most, of uncertainty.

As noted, encryption can violate the treaty even if it does not make verification impossible. It would be helpful to know in just what way, in the view of the administration, U.S. verification has been impeded. Have the Soviets denied through encryption all of the telemetry useful for calculating throw-weights, forcing U.S. intelligence to rely entirely on other, presumably less precise, methods to calculate those parameters? Or have the Soviets encrypted only some of the relevant telemetry, causing a degradation in the quality and perhaps the reliability of the conclusions?

The administration's statements suggest that its throw-weight determinations have been made entirely without telemetric data. "They are giving us nothing of value [from telemetry]," a Pentagon official is quoted as saying.[40] We find it somewhat puzzling that the throw-weight of the SS-25 as well as the ratio of RV weight to throw-weight could have been calculated with such high apparent precision in the absence of any useful telemetric data.

The language employed in the first administration noncompliance report provides a hint of at least a partial possible explanation. The report states that, "based on the one test for which data are available," the SS-25 would be a violation of the provision that requires the RV weight to be at least 50 percent of the throw-weight. This wording suggests that there may have been one early test from which a substantial amount of unencrypted telemetry was obtained. One set of good data could have been sufficient to calculate the ratio of RV weight to throw-weight with fairly high precision.[41]

Determining the throw-weight itself involves a more complex calculation that requires measuring many quantities, each subject to uncertainty; a large number of measurements is necessary in order to reduce the statistical errors. If virtually no useful telemetry were available from all but the earliest flight tests, the uncertainty in the throw-weight determination could remain high. The remark about "giving us nothing of value" might apply only to the more recent tests. The scenario suggested here is speculative but is consistent with the known facts.

What about the pre-1981 violations that the United States has charged? The charge does not refer to a specific missile, but, as noted, it can only be either the SS-N-20 or a missile of an existing type. In the case of the SS-N-20, the only parameters necessary to verify are that the missile carries no more than fourteen RVs and does not exceed the throw-weight of the SS-19. It is hard to see how even total encryption could impede those determinations. The 1986 edition of *Soviet Military Power* lists the SS-N-20 as carrying six to nine RVs and shows it to be about 15 meters long, about two-thirds the length of the SS-19. Other analysts estimate its throw-weight as 5,600 pounds;[42] even a gross error in this estimate would not bring its throw-weight close to that of the SS-19. Shortly after the first encrypted flight test of the SS-N-20, the State Department announced that the missile was not a violation of SALT II.[43] And none of the administration's noncompliance reports cite the SS-N-20 as even a possible violation.

A stronger case can be made that encryption in flight tests of the SS-18/Mod 4 between 1979 and 1981 might have impeded verification of Soviet compliance with the SALT II fractionation ceiling by hampering U.S. identification of possible simulated releases. It was the observation of simulated releases in SS-18 tests in the late 1970s that motivated the United States to insist that the treaty count such simulations as reentry vehicles.[44] If an SS-18 dispensed ten reentry vehicles and carried out any simulated releases, it would be in violation of the fractionation ceiling. Encryption of telemetry could reduce U.S. confidence that no simulated releases had been carried out in any particular test. In 1986 ACDA Director Kenneth Adelman cited encryption of SS-18 telemetry as an example of how verification has been impeded.[45] If encryption of SS-18 telemetry is indeed the basis for the administration charge, it is somewhat strange that the noncompliance reports make absolutely no reference to the SS-18 but, rather, refer specifically to the testing of *new* missiles as the Soviet violation.

Soviet Response

It is difficult to reconcile Soviet pronouncements on the encryption issue with the administration's characterization of the extent of Soviet encryption. Until 1986 the Soviet position seemed to be, in effect, "We do not encrypt anything necessary for verification." This position could be consistent even with total encryption but by itself would be insufficient to establish compliance. However, in a press conference on June 5, 1986, Marshal S. F. Akhromeyev, chief of the Soviet Armed Forces General Staff, and A. A. Bessmertnykh, Soviet deputy foreign minister, asserted: "What are the treaty provisions in question? First and foremost, those relating to the definition of new types of ICBMs: type of propellant, number of stages, length, largest diameter, launch-weight and throw-weight of missiles, and the number of and weight of warheads. They are defined in agreed statements to Article IV of the treaty. We are strictly complying with all *this*" (emphasis added).[46]

It is hard to know what to make of Akhromeyev and Bessmertnykh's statement. Taken literally, the statement is devoid of content. Launch-weight and throw-weight values are not transmitted directly in telemetry, hence cannot be encrypted. That is, there is no channel that says explicitly that the throw-weight of a given missile is so many kilograms. On the other hand, if the Soviet statement is taken to mean that the Soviets do not encrypt any data related to launch-weight or throw-weight (a common-sense interpretation), it runs directly counter to the Pentagon statement that telemetric data have provided nothing of value, as well as to many other statements along similar lines. Although it is conceivable that even with encryption as high as 90 or 95 percent the few unencrypted channels could contain the data required to calculate throw-weight, the administration is plainly saying that this is not the case.

The administration weakens its case by its persistent refusal to discuss any specifics as to how verification has been impeded. The Soviets have repeatedly pressed for specificity, both at the SCC and in public pronouncements. At the press conference on June 4, 1986, Akhromeyev and Bessmertnykh continued: "Since the U.S. side raised the issue of encryption, the Soviet side, in a gesture of constructive approach, expressed readiness to resolve it on a reciprocal basis. We proposed to identify and agree upon the parameters of telemetric information which, in the U.S. side's opinion, must not be encrypted. But the U.S. side has stubbornly evaded solving its own question."[47]

The Soviets are, of course, well aware that, by identifying specific areas where encryption has caused difficulties, the United States would risk exposing details of its intelligence sources and methods. Nevertheless, the Soviet position does not appear completely unreasonable. In domestic law, if one party sues for breach of contract, that party is expected to provide particulars beyond the mere assertion that the contract has been breached.

Critics of the administration's position contend that it should be possible to engage in at least a limited dialogue on encryption without unduly compromising U.S. intelligence sources and methods. The discussion could be terminated at any stage if it appeared that the Soviets were engaged in a fishing expedition. A substantive response by the United States might bring about a reduction in Soviet encryption and would at the very least strengthen the credibility of the charge of noncompliance. Others warn, however, that, if the United States ever got on the slippery slope of discussing particulars concerning encryption, it would be hard to avoid damaging disclosures.

Finally, the unusual status of the treaty during the past five years raises a legal question about compliance. The United States accuses the Soviet Union of violating a political commitment after 1981 not to undercut the treaty. There is no public record of any agreement as to the exact meaning of "undercut" in this context. The Vienna Convention on the Law of Treaties holds that the parties to a treaty should take no action inconsistent with its provisions as long as the parties intend to complete ratification. The convention offers no guidance on the responsibilities of the parties once the ratification process has been abandoned.

Since even the Vienna Convention does not specify that compliance requires active changes in the status quo between signing and ratification of a treaty, it is clear that an agreement for which pursuit of ratification has been discontinued requires something less than total compliance. If their encryption impedes verification without preventing it, the Soviets are clearly not in full compliance with the treaty. But are they undercutting it? The Soviets have not used this line of defense because they insist they are not impeding verification. But precise Soviet— and U.S.— responsibilities under SALT II are a matter of conjecture.

Strategic Significance

The significance of Soviet concealment practices is a function of the marginal effect of the higher Soviet encryption after 1979 on the U.S. ability to verify SALT II provisions, and not of Soviet encryption per se. The United States has means other than telemetry to measure Soviet compliance with the parameters restricted in SALT II. The level of Soviet encryption is a cause for concern about U.S. confidence in the strategic-intelligence data base on which evaluations of Soviet systems tested in the early 1980s might be made in the future. But this deficiency in U.S. strategic intelligence is not a basis for arguing that SALT II verification has been impeded.

If Soviet encryption has actually deprived the United States of the ability to verify compliance with important SALT II provisions, the strategic significance of the encryption could be great, as it might increase the potential for Soviet treaty breakout. Since U.S. verification was not prevented, however, the immediate strategic impact is minimal; the possibility that verification may have been impeded poses no threat to the security of the United States if the United States has nonetheless been able to verify Soviet compliance or noncompliance.[48]

The Soviet increase in the level of encryption during the final phase of the treaty negotiations calls into question Soviet intent with regard to the encryption provision of SALT II. By increasing encryption in 1979, the Soviet Union appears to have sought to establish a basis for later claiming this high level of encryption as the practice at the time SALT II was signed.

The principal threat that the Soviet Union has posed by increasing encryption to the present level is to the viability of future arms control agreements. Unless the encryption issue is satisfactorily resolved, it may not be possible to verify compliance with the more demanding types of limitations that a future agreement may contain. The administration's judgment that encryption and concealment in general "undermine the political confidence necessary for concluding new treaties and underscore the necessity that any new agreement be effectively verifiable" is valid, whether or not current Soviet practices constitute a violation.[49]

In sum, the administration's contention that Soviet encryption is impeding U.S. verification seems plausible; but, because of the ambiguous wording of the treaty and its uncertain status, a Soviet violation cannot be conclusively demonstrated. Soviet performance under the SALT II provision forbidding impeding of verification is a case of questionable compliance. Soviet encryption practices, thus far, have had little effect on U.S. security.

The relatively low impact of Soviet encryption on U.S. security raises an important question: If, indeed, increased encryption has not given the Soviets a significant strategic advantage, why have they resorted to it? Many observers, including Ambassador Ralph Earle, the last SALT negotiator, believe that U.S. failure to ratify SALT II encouraged the Soviet decision to raise the level of their encryption.[50] Earle's view is a reasonable hypothesis about the political calculation underlying Soviet encryption. Knowing that U.S. intelligence exploits telemetry for much more than just verification, the Soviet military and the KGB must have accepted the treaty limitation on encryption only grudgingly. They must have felt especially galled at having to provide the United States with so much "free" intelligence after the Reagan administration had made it clear that the treaty would not be ratified. The fact that telemetry was apparently not required for verification would only have added to their frustration. They may well have concluded that, under the circumstances, the United States was not entitled to more than the minimum information required for verification.

It is worth noting that the Soviet Union could reverse its behavior more readily in the case of encryption than in any other areas where Soviet compliance has been challenged. Relatively little preparation would be required to reduce or even to terminate encryption; surely much greater effort would be needed to resolve the SS-25 or Abalakovo issues. The cost to the Soviet Union would be modest. One can envision circumstances, in the SCC or through some other channel, in which a reduction in encryption might have been rather easily negotiated if the Soviets had had some incentive, such as progress in negotiations toward a new agreement. But with all negotiations stalled since 1981, the Soviets have had little incentive to be so accommodating.

U.S. Thule, Fylingdales Moor, and PAVE PAWS Radars

The United States and Soviet Union are both completing networks of large phased-array radars that are capable of performing a variety of military functions. The declared purpose of the U.S. and Soviet LPAR networks is to provide early warning of possible nuclear attack. Indeed, technical evidence indicates that the Soviet Pechora-type and U.S. PAVE PAWS LPAR networks are generally optimized for early warning of ballistic-missile attack.

However, because even LPARs optimized for early warning could be capable of performing some important tasks in an ABM defense, the U.S. and Soviet governments have each raised concerns regarding the legality under the ABM Treaty of the other's LPAR network. First, the Soviet Union has questioned whether the U.S. PAVE PAWS network violates the ABM Treaty's prohibition on laying the base for an ABM defense. Similarly, the United States has questioned the legality of the Soviet Pechora-type LPAR network. Second, the United States and Soviet Union have questioned the legality of specific radars under specific provisions of the ABM Treaty. The United States has questioned the Soviet LPAR at Abalakovo; and the Soviet Union has questioned U.S. LPARs at Thule, Greenland, at Fylingdales Moor, England, in Georgia, and in Texas. This section addresses the Soviet concerns about U.S. LPARs. Chapter 5 addresses the U.S. concerns about the Soviet radar at Abalakovo.

Before proceeding with an in-depth analysis of the legality and military significance of these specific radars, it is useful to review some of the technical features of LPARs and how they might relate to an ABM defense. For the purposes of ABM Treaty compliance, the pertinent technical distinction is between (1) LPARs that are optimally designed for and used as early-warning facilities and (2) LPARs that may have ABM battle-management capabilities above and beyond the potential ABM capabilities that are inherent in all LPARs. The operating frequency, emitted power, antenna size, and location of LPARs are the critical criteria for making this distinction.

1. Early-warning LPARs. Early-warning radars are designed to operate at the frequencies at which reentry vehicles most efficiently reflect electromagnetic waves. It is at these frequencies that a radar of fixed antenna size and power is able to detect RVs at the longest-possible range.

Radars that operate at these optimal frequencies are very susceptible to the effects of high-altitude nuclear explosions. For instance, a 1-megaton nuclear detonation at an altitude of about 150 kilometers can create a region of high-electron densities over lateral distances of 100–200 kilometers. Radar waves from early-warning radars that pass through parts of such regions would be severely and unpredictably bent and/or absorbed for tens of minutes after a single such detonation. In order to provide early-warning

Fig. 7. Elements of U.S. large phased-array radars (reprinted from Alan S. Krass, *Verification: How Much Is Enough?* [Stockholm: International Peace Research Institute, 1985], 41 [courtesy Eli Brookner, Raytheon Co.])

data quickly, an LPAR must have a very high average power. It must also have very large antennae, so that it can efficiently collect radiation reflected back to it from the objects it is designed to detect. A radar's power-aperture product—the product of its average radiated power and its antennae area—determines the upper limit of its search ability and is an important measure of its potential as an early-warning or ABM battle-management radar.

The power-aperture products, measured in watts times square meters (Wm^2), of the U.S. PAVE PAWS and Ballistic Missile Early Warning System (BMEWS) radars are more than 40 million and 1.8 billion, respectively. If the Soviet LPARs are assumed to use radar technology of the type used by U.S. LPARs like the AN/FPS-85 radars of the 1960s, and if their transmitting and receiving antennae are assumed to have areas of about 50 meters square per side, they would have a radiated average power of about 500,000 watts and a power-aperture product of more than a billion Wm^2.

Essentially all surveillance radars that can perform the function of early warning of ballistic-missile attack therefore have power-aperture products considerably larger than the three million Wm^2 limit set by the ABM Treaty. Radars with power-aperture products below the limit are not capable of reliably performing the long-range search functions required of systems that must operate either in an early-warning or battle-management role. The power-aperture limits in the ABM Treaty thus set severe constraints on the search potential of radars covered by those limits.

2. Battle-management LPARs. ABM battle-management radars must operate at frequencies about ten times higher than those used by radars whose sole purpose is surveillance for early warning of attack. Battle-management radars must be able to function in spite of determined enemy attempts to blind them by using nuclear effects, electronic jamming, or other tactics designed to diminish or eliminate their ability to provide critical surveillance and tracking data for the defense. The effects of high-altitude nuclear detonations on the propagation and absorption of electromagnetic waves are greatly reduced at higher frequencies. Radars that operate at higher frequencies are inherently more resistant to jamming and other electronic countermeasures.

Since the amount of radar energy that is reflected by a reentry vehicle diminishes rapidly as the frequency of a radar increases, the choice of higher frequencies results in a substantially reduced maximum search range. Hence, a large phased-array surveillance radar that is optimized to function as a critical component of an ABM system will not provide maximum warning time of a nuclear attack. Conversely, a radar optimized for maximum warning time will not be able to function as a reliable element of an ABM defense.

In addition to the technical characteristics of particular LPARs, two factors must be considered in an assessment of their potential value for an ABM system. First, unless LPARs are heavily defended by large numbers of interceptors, they are vulnerable to direct attack. Thus, an undefended LPAR that has a frequency and power-aperture product optimized to perform certain ABM functions may be of little value to an ABM system under actual battle conditions.

Second, the battle-management LPARs in an ABM territorial defense must themselves be widely deployed and also given the capability of guiding the interceptors and managing the engagement, or they must be capable of "handing over" that information to interceptors and engagement radars located more closely to the areas to be defended. Thus, the utility of LPARs for ABM defense depends on their ability to provide reliable surveillance information to other elements of a territorial defense or to fully manage the engagements themselves.

Treaty Provisions

Several ABM Treaty provisions are relevant to the new U.S. and Soviet LPARs. Article I prohibits each side from deploying a territorial defense or providing the base for such a defense. Articles III and IV prohibit the deployment of ABM systems or components except at agreed deployment and test sites. Article VI(b) prohibits deployment by each side of LPARs "in the future" for early-warning of strategic-missile attack, except "at locations along the periphery of its national territory and oriented outward." Article VII permits each side to conduct, subject to the provisions of the treaty, "modernization and replacement of ABM systems or their components." Article IX requires each side not to "transfer to other states, and not to deploy outside its national territory, ABM systems or their components limited by this Treaty." Agreed Statement F prohibits deployment of "phased-array radars having a potential (the product of mean emitted power in watts and antenna area in square meters) exceeding three million," except those located at the one permitted ABM site, those at agreed ABM test ranges, those on the periphery of the country and oriented outward, and those for space tracking or national technical means of verification.

Background

When the ABM Treaty negotiations began in 1969, the United States and Soviet Union had each deployed radar systems to warn of ballistic-missile attack. Both sides were also developing a second generation of phased-array radars that were much larger and more capable than any previous system deployed by either side. In the early 1960s the United States deployed installations of its Ballistic Missile Early Warning System in Greenland, England, and Alaska. Those facilities consisted of mechanically steered FPS-49 and electronically scanned FPS-50 fixed-array radars.[51] At the time the ABM Treaty was signed, these BMEWS radars were recognized as early-warning facilities with very "little ABM tracking capability."[52] In 1965 the Soviets began deploying a series of Hen House radars to serve as their early-warning network.[53] Although the Hen House radars were large, vulnerable, and operated at a frequency unsuitable to a nuclear environment, they were of the phased-array type and were capable of long-range target acquisition, a capability that might be useful should they ever be used as part of an ABM system.[54]

Concern about the Hen House systems and the new generation of Soviet large phased-array radars under development caused the United States to seek precise restrictions on LPARs in the ABM Treaty negotiations. The Soviets, on the other hand, argued that all systems, such as the Hen House, that were not overtly related to ABM systems were outside the framework of the negotiations as the framework had been agreed upon on May 20, 1971.[55] Despite this fundamental difference about the extent to which the ABM Treaty should constrain the deployment of phased-array radars, both sides wanted to preserve their right to deploy for early warning their own LPARs that were under development.

The problem the ABM Treaty negotiators faced was how to permit deployment of multiple-use radars for early warning while minimizing their potential ABM applications.[56] Because power-aperture product is one of several determinants of an LPAR's ABM potential that can be verified by NTM, it was incorporated into Agreed Statement F as a means of identifying those LPARs used for early warning that might also have significant ABM potential. The restrictions contained in Agreed Statement F reinforce the more general geographic restrictions that Article VI(b) places on all early-warning radars. By requiring the radars to be on the periphery and looking out, the treaty severely limits their utility as elements of a territorial defense, as they would be extremely vulnerable to direct attack or suppression by other means. They would also be useless for guiding ABM interceptors. Although the ABM Treaty incorporates various qualitative and geographical restrictions on LPARs, it does not place any limits on the number of LPARs that can be deployed for early warning.

Thule and Fylingdales

Soviet Charges

The United States is currently upgrading the BMEWS by replacing mechanically steered radars with much more capable, large phased-array radars. Construction of an LPAR with 240-degree coverage has been completed at the Thule, Greenland, BMEWS site, and an LPAR with 360-degree coverage is planned for the Fylingdales Moor, England, site. Modernization is also being considered for the BMEWS facility at Clear, Alaska. All three installations will receive new computers for data processing and missile-attack assessment.

In October 1985 the Soviet negotiator at the Geneva arms talks, Yuli A. Kvitsinsky, suggested that the U.S. LPARs at Thule and Fylingdales would violate the ABM Treaty, implying that these two new LPARs are not on the periphery of the United States and oriented outward as Article VI(b) requires. The Soviets argued that the ABM Treaty allows only the original BMEWS radars to be located other than on the periphery and oriented outward and that their modernization is not permitted.[57]

The Soviet Union also charges that the modifications under way at the two facilities give the radars ABM potential. The Soviet Union contends that the U.S. improvements violate Article IX of the ABM Treaty, which prohibits the transfer of ABM systems or components to other countries or their deployment outside a party's national territory.

The United States contends that the modified radars constitute legal modernization of facilities that existed when the ABM Treaty was signed in 1972. According to this view, regardless of their configuration the U.S. early-warning installations at Thule and Fylingdales are grandfathered by the treaty and thus exempt from all treaty restrictions. The United States argues that the ABM Treaty generally permits modernization. Proponents of this view note, for example, that Article VII explicitly approves modernization of components or systems that are identified as primarily associated with ABM systems. The United States argues that the BMEWS radars were originally designed as and continue to be early-warning facilities. The ABM Treaty is silent with respect to modernization of early-warning systems. Therefore, the Reagan administration argues, since the treaty generally permits modernization of permitted systems and does not specifically prohibit the modernization of BMEWS, the LPARs at Thule and Fylingdales are entirely legitimate.

Analysis

The central problem at issue in the dispute about Thule and Fylingdales is arriving at a definition of the point at which a radar installation is sufficiently changed that it becomes a *replacement* of the previous facility rather than a *modernization* of the one existing when the ABM Treaty was signed. If the radar is a modernization of a facility grandfathered by the ABM Treaty, it may be exempt from the treaty restrictions. If the modified radar is a replacement, it may no longer be considered the same radar that is grandfathered by the treaty. If it is a replacement, the radar may be subject to all relevant treaty restrictions, including the stipulation that new radars must be deployed on the periphery of a country's national territory and oriented outward.

The Reagan administration has been sensitive to the importance of the distinction between modification and replacement of LPARs. Secretary of Defense Caspar Weinberger stated in his annual report to Congress for fiscal year 1986, "To improve BMEWS' coverage and performance, we are *replacing* obsolete radars at [Thule and Fylingdales] with new phased-array systems similar to PAVE PAWS" (emphasis added). In the Defense Department's annual report for fiscal year 1987, the language changed, stating that the new LPARs at Thule and Fylingdales are "modifications" of existing BMEWS radars.[58]

There are several different ways to inquire into the meaning of the ABM Treaty when there is debate surrounding the compliance of new military systems with the treaty's terms. The treaty language itself may be examined. The negotiating record may be consulted to determine the intent of the negotiators in writing the provisions of the treaty that are at issue. And the treaty may be reviewed as an integrated whole to assess the original intent of the parties.

An analysis of these three sources raises questions about whether the U.S. radars at Thule and Fylingdales are completely in compliance with the ABM Treaty. Yet the evidence is not sufficient to conclude that the radars are clearly in violation. This points up the inadequacy of the ABM Treaty in distinguishing between permitted modernization and the deployment of prohibited new early-warning radars.

The ABM Treaty prohibits the deployment in the future of early warning radars having a power-aperture product of greater than 3 million Wm^2, except on a country's periphery and oriented outward. But the treaty does not mention any method for determining whether an existing facility has been modernized to the point that it constitutes a prohibited new radar. In any event modern LPARs useful for early warning can be expected to have power-aperture products much greater than 3 million Wm^2; for modern U.S. early-warning LPARs they are in the range of 40 million Wm^2.

Since the specific treaty provisions covering LPARs do not provide clear guidance, how, then, is the difference between permitted modernization and prohibited new deployment to be measured? The magnitude of physical improvement of a radar facility is one possible measure of the degree of change. The new LPARs at Thule and Fylingdales clearly share very little with their mechanically steered predecessors in terms of operating principles and hardware. Because the modified Thule LPAR is constructed on the foundation of the previous radar, it could be considered a modernization of the existing radar rather than a replacement. Fylingdales, however, is a physically different radar, not a modification of the existing structure. In fact, although it is at the same base, the new LPAR to be constructed at Fylingdales Moor will reportedly be located at a site some distance from the original BMEWS radar.[59] This raises the question of whether it can legitimately be considered the same facility acknowledged under the ABM Treaty.

But since the treaty does not bar modernization per se, the quantity of change alone is not sufficient to determine that modernization has gone beyond a permissible level. The ambiguities surrounding the distinction between modernizing existing radars and replacing them reinforces the view that it is not possible to rely exclusively on the ABM Treaty text in assessing compliance. Consulting the negotiating record is necessary before conclusions can be drawn about whether or not specific programs or activities are in compliance. It is necessary to consider what the treaty negotiators' intent was in constructing particular provisions.

But what is publicly known from the negotiating record is also ambiguous. There is some indication that classified portions of the ABM Treaty negotiating record confirm the interpretation that the ABM Treaty framers condoned replacement of facilities such as Thule and Fylingdales. Experts involved in the negotiations have written that the U.S. description of the changes at Thule and Fylingdales as permitted modernizations "appears to be consistent with the basic approach of the Treaty."[60] On the other hand, a classified National Security Council report of October 20, 1971, reportedly stated that LPARs could not be constructed at Thule and Fylingdales under the ABM Treaty.[61] John Rhinelander, legal adviser to the SALT I delegation, has cast additional doubt on the view that the modifications at Thule and Fylingdales are permitted: "The revelation, however, that the USG [U.S. government] looked at this issue specifically in the fall of 1971 gives me real pause, because we did *not* clearly preserve our rights to 'modernize.' Overall, I believe the U.S. has the worse of the argument, but the issue is not clear cut."[62]

Like a review of the treaty articles governing radars, what is known publicly of the negotiating record does not provide clear guidance about Thule and Fylingdales. A comprehensive examination of the negotiating record on this point would be helpful. So far, the Reagan administration has not provided the evidence to back up its claim that the negotiating history bears out the legality of the LPARs at Thule and Fylingdales.

In evaluating these radars, we are thus left with the need to determine the intent of the treaty based upon a reading of the agreement as a whole. The fact that the ABM Treaty restricted the deployment of new early-warning radars as a means for constraining the deployment of ABM systems indicates that permitted modernization of existing facilities was not regarded as completely open-ended. If modernization were unrestricted, substantial changes in the nature of existing radars, such as increasing their frequencies by a factor of ten, could greatly enhance their potential. Such changes could enhance the ability of either side to mount an ABM defense and would thus be contrary to the central purpose of the treaty.

In analyzing whether or not the two U.S. radars comply with the ABM

Treaty, it is necessary to determine whether the changes and improvements made to the radars significantly enhance U.S. ABM capabilities and thus defeat the purpose of the ABM Treaty in restricting LPARs as the long–lead-time elements of an ABM system. As discussed, only under certain conditions would LPARs be capable of effective ABM battle management. To perform battle-management functions adequately, an LPAR must be optimized for battle management, defended, and combined with an infrastructure including a system to launch and guide interceptors during the engagement.

In the cases of Thule and Fylingdales, the upgrade of the installations to include LPARs has not been accompanied by any program to decrease the inherent vulnerability of LPARs. The LPAR at Thule is, and the LPAR at Fylingdales will be, optimized for early warning. Both LPARs will operate in the 450-megahertz range associated with early warning rather than at a frequency of about ten times higher associated with ABM battle management. The lower the frequency of such radars, the greater their vulnerability to jamming of nuclear blackout effects.

Thus far, the new LPARs have not been accompanied by the deployment of the necessary infrastructure for battle management. But if they were integrated into an ABM system such as that envisioned by the U.S. SDI program, the long warning time provided by these LPARs could be useful within such a system for detecting incoming attack.

Taking into account the substantial upgrading of the radar facilities, the uncertainty posed by the ambiguity of the treaty provisions, the lack of clear guidance from the negotiating record, and the small increase in ABM potential presented by the radars, the U.S. radars at Thule and Fylingdales represent cases of questionable U.S. compliance with the ABM Treaty. The modernization of the radars is neither unambiguously in violation of the treaty nor clearly in compliance with the terms and intent of the treaty.

As to whether the modernization programs represent questionable compliance even though the radars are not yet operating, the ABM Treaty does not specify when a radar is considered to be deployed. It is widely recognized, based on the negotiating record, that LPARs do not have to actually be operating to be questionable or in violation of the treaty. According to the February 1, 1986, ACDA noncompliance report, to "deploy," in the context of Article VI, means to "site or locate at a particular location. Initiation of the construction of a prohibited radar would constitute a violation of the treaty."[63] Concern about compliance is thus particularly appropriate in the case of the new radar at Thule, which is already completed although it is not yet operating.

Strategic Significance

An evaluation of the military significance of the Thule and Fylingdales radars for the Soviet Union must be based upon the same criterion that has been discussed: Have the new LPARs increased the U.S. potential to mount an ABM defense beyond that which would exist if the United States had such radars deployed only as clearly permitted by the ABM Treaty, on the periphery of U.S. national territory and oriented outward?

The LPAR at Thule is positioned to warn the United States of a possible Soviet attack launched from ICBM fields in the Soviet Union or from submarines in the Arctic Ocean. In its present configuration the radar is capable of detecting objects the size of delivery vehicles at greater distances than would an LPAR with a smaller aperture or lower emitted power, or one located on U.S. territory. Longer U.S. warning time of strategic attack does not increase the military threat to the Soviet Union, but it could be useful if the Thule LPAR were integrated into a fully deployed ABM defense.

The radar planned for Fylingdales reportedly will provide robust early-warning coverage for Great Britain.[64] It will provide early warning of possible intermediate-range–ballistic-missile or submarine-launched–ballistic-missile attack against England. It may also provide minimal early-warning coverage of an SLBM attack along special trajectories against the United States. The radar at Fylingdales could conceivably be useful in assisting other elements of an ABM defense of the United Kingdom or the United States.

However, a single radar facility that is highly vulnerable to direct attack and to nuclear-blackout effects has little utility in an ABM system beyond early warning. As in the case of the Thule radar, Fylingdales by itself adds little to the rapid ABM-breakout capability of the United States.

PAVE PAWS

Soviet Charges

The United States is completing a network of new PAVE PAWS LPARs designed to warn of SLBM attack and to track objects in space. Two PAVE PAWS radars, in Massachusetts and California, have been operational since the late 1970s. Two more, in Georgia and Texas, are scheduled to become operational soon.[65] PAVE PAWS radar facilities are constructed in equilateral triangles incorporating two active faces, which both send and receive radar signals, providing a 120-degree field of coverage for each face. Thus, each PAVE PAWS installation has a 240-degree field of coverage. Even though PAVE PAWS radars are located on the periphery of the United States, their surveillance coverage encompasses large and strategically important areas of the eastern and western United States, including major industrial and population centers as well as areas along the Gulf Coast and the border with Mexico (see map 1).

In the late 1970s the Soviet Union questioned in the SCC whether the PAVE PAWS radars conformed to Article I of the ABM Treaty, which

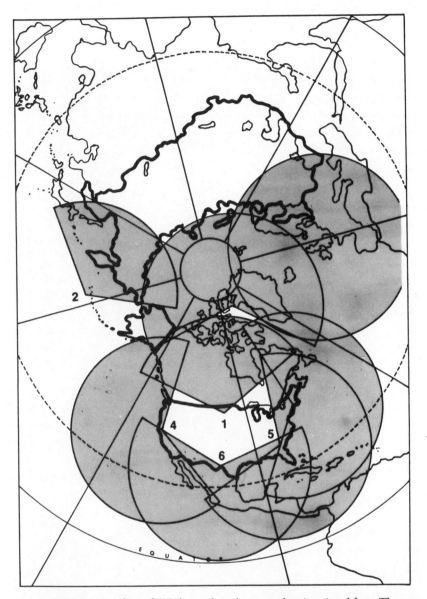

Map 1. **1990 coverage fans of U.S. large phased-array radars** (reprinted from Thomas K. Longstreth, John E. Pike, and John B. Rhinelander, *The Impact of U.S. and Soviet Ballistic Missile Defense Programs on the ABM Treaty* [Washington: National Campaign to Save the ABM Treaty, March 1985], 73)

The perimeter acquisition radar in North Dakota (1) was originally part of the Safeguard ABM system. The Cobra Dane radar on Shemya Island, Alaska (2), is primarily intended to monitor Soviet missile tests. The PAVE PAWS radars at Otis Air Force Base, Massachusetts (3), Beale Air Force Base, California (4), Robins Air Force Base, Georgia (5), and Goodfellow Air Force Base, Texas (6), are located to provide warning of SLBM attack. The mechanically steered radars at Thule, Greenland (7), and Fylingdales Moor, England (8), will be replaced by phased-array radars. All of these radars are also used to track satellites. The area of the fans corresponds to the maximum distance at which an object at an altitude of 500 miles can be detected.

Fig. 8. U.S. PAVE PAWS radar, Otis Air Force Base, Massachusetts (courtesy U.S. Air Force)

prohibits each party from providing a base for an ABM defense of its territory. The aide-mémoire issued in January 1984 by the Soviet embassy in Washington, D.C., stated that the PAVE PAWS radars were "contrary to the commitment" embodied in Article I of the ABM Treaty and that "no measures have been taken by the American side to remove the concern caused by its actions."[66] The United States contends that the ABM Treaty permits PAVE PAWS radars because they are early-warning radars located on the country's periphery and oriented outward, as required by Article VI(b).[67]

Analysis

The surveillance coverage of the U.S. PAVE PAWS program raises significant gray-area questions of ABM Treaty compliance. PAVE PAWS also raises concerns of potentially greater strategic significance than do Thule and Fylingdales, and arguably comes closer to challenging the central purpose of the ABM Treaty—to restrict the construction of long–lead-time elements required for an ABM defense. PAVE PAWS also raises definitional questions regarding key terms in the ABM Treaty.

There are two general viewpoints about the legality of PAVE PAWS coverage. The first contends that, although the radars may not violate the letter of the ABM Treaty, their very wide coverage raises questions about their possible utility as elements of a future U.S. ABM defense. According to this view, the two PAVE PAWS installations in Georgia and Texas are militarily significant, regardless of whether or not they are technically in compliance with more-specific treaty provisions. The second view contends that the radars technically conform to the provisions of the ABM Treaty and offer little ABM potential by themselves.

Analysts who subscribe to the first view consider PAVE PAWS to be a threat to the objective of Article I and Article VI(b). According to this view, the very wide coverage of each PAVE PAWS radar exploits an ambiguity in the ABM Treaty: the lack of a definition of what constitutes "oriented outward." Similarly, those parts of the Soviet LPAR system that are in violation of the ABM Treaty or raise compliance questions could be seen as rubbing against the spirit and intent of Article I.

Based on a literal reading of the ABM Treaty, analysts supporting the second view consider PAVE PAWS radars to be largely consistent with the treaty's terms. In this view, the PAVE PAWS radars can legitimately be construed as early-warning radars located on the periphery of the United States, as required by Article VI(b). It could be argued that the facilities are not deployed precisely on the U.S. coast; but each side seems to have accepted deployment of other LPARs (at Robins Air Force Base, Georgia, and at Pechora, in the Soviet Union) 100–200 kilometers from the other's actual periphery. The ABM Treaty does not define what constitutes the periphery of a country's national territory.

The treaty also neglects to clarify the meaning of the Article I prohibition on providing a base for an ABM defense of national territory. The absence of concise definitions for important treaty language in Article I and Article VI(b) makes it difficult, on the basis of textual analysis, to judge definitively that PAVE PAWS violates any of the treaty's provisions. Moreover, the existence of the PAVE PAWS network is legal; it serves legitimate early-warning functions recognized by the ABM Treaty. Its coverage of U.S. territory and a technical review of PAVE PAWS capabilities suggest there is little basis for accepting Soviet claims that the U.S. could be laying the base for a territorial defense in violation of Article I. However, it is also clear that the location and coverage of the PAVE PAWS radars can be legitimately criticized as a U.S. action that stretches interpretations of Article VI(b) provisions beyond that which the U.S. would be likely to accept for Soviet LPARs.

Strategic Significance

The strategic significance of PAVE PAWS may be evaluated by weighing the difference in capability between the actual system and an alternative configuration that would be clearly compliant with the ABM Treaty. One possible alternative would have been to increase the angle between the active faces of the PAVE PAWS radars, that is, make the faces more nearly parallel, thus causing greater overlap of the coverage area of the individual faces. The result would have been a reduction of the 240-degree total coverage area of each LPAR. To the extent that such a configuration would reduce coverage of U.S. territory, the system would have been more clearly compliant with the treaty. Reportedly, the United States has recently modified the scanning pattern to reduce the coverage of the PAVE PAWS radars in Texas and Georgia, in an attempt to allay Soviet compliance concerns and to provide enhanced warning of close-in Soviet SLBM launches from southern positions in the Atlantic and Pacific oceans. The apparent electronic reduction in coverage provides little assurance that the radars' ability to scan over U.S. territory has been diminished, since their coverage could easily be increased at a later date.

The military utility of the marginal coverage of U.S. territory afforded by the existing PAVE PAWS network is questionable to the extent that any LPAR system could contribute to an ABM defense. PAVE PAWS could assist smaller battle-management radars in identifying and tracking some incoming RVs over the densely populated coastal regions of the United States. Because U.S. LPARs operate at significantly higher frequencies (450 megahertz) than their Soviet counterparts, they may have some limited capability to operate in a nuclear environment.[68] But for the full ABM potential of the PAVE PAWS radars to be realized, the United States would need to defend them and join to them an extensive network of interceptors and battle-management radars. There is no evidence at this time that the United

States has plans to surround the PAVE PAWS radars with such interceptors, to internet them with battle-management radars, or to defend them.

Concluding Remarks

The United States is pushing close to the limits of reasonable interpretation of the ABM Treaty by deploying the new LPARs at Thule and Fylingdales and by completing the PAVE PAWS system in its present configuration.
Thule and Fylingdales represent instances of questionable U.S. compliance
with the ABM Treaty. The United States has failed to support with concrete evidence its grandfathering argument—that modernization of the magnitude occurring at Thule and Fylingdales falls short of creating new radars
prohibited by the treaty. Although Thule and Fylingdales represent programs whose compliance is questionable, by themselves they add little to
the ability of the U.S. to mount a nationwide ABM defense.

The PAVE PAWS radars in Georgia and Texas are also cases of questionable U.S. compliance with the ABM Treaty. They are not clearly within
the provisions of the ABM Treaty as the United States argues. But the PAVE
PAWS radars have very little utility for a future U.S. ABM defense as long
as they are not joined by other ABM components prohibited by the treaty.

Chapter Five

Violation: The Soviet Abalakovo Radar

In July 1983 U.S. intelligence satellites discovered construction of a large phased-array radar at Abalakovo near the town of Krasnoyarsk in Siberia.[1] Partly because of the consternation caused by Abalakovo, the Senate passed an amendment in September 1983 that required an executive-branch report on Soviet arms control noncompliance. Since the first noncompliance report was released in January 1984, the Abalakovo radar has become the centerpiece of the Reagan administration's expressed concerns that the Soviets have systematically violated arms control agreements and that they are laying a base for a territorial ABM defense.

As a compliance issue Abalakovo is in a class of its own. Although the relevant provisions of the ABM Treaty contain some ambiguity, Abalakovo is the only clear-cut treaty violation discussed in this report. This chapter evaluates the legality of the Siberian radar under the ABM Treaty, assesses its military significance, and weighs its impact on the arms control process.

Because the Abalakovo radar did not exist at the time the ABM Treaty was signed and is of a type generally used for early warning, it falls under the Article VI(b) restriction limiting radars for early warning to locations on the peripheries of the two sides' national territories and to outward orientation. Although it is not yet operating, the radar at Abalakovo, like the other Pechora-type radars, will almost certainly have a power-aperture product greater than 3 million Wm^2, subjecting it to the specific restrictions on LPARs contained in Agreed Statement F.

During the late 1970s the Soviet Union began constructing a new class of LPARs to replace its older Hen House radar system. The first of the new radars was at Pechora, near the Barents Sea. Four other LPARs of the Pechora type have been built at sites on the periphery of the Soviet Union, as permitted by the ABM Treaty. The sixth is located at Abalakovo, near Krasnoyarsk (see map 2). Press reports have indicated that the Soviet Union is constructing its seventh and eighth Pechora-type LPARs on the western periphery of the Soviet Union, oriented, respectively, toward the Atlantic and the Mediterranean.[2] The locations of these radars appear to comply with the requirements of Article VI(b) of the ABM Treaty. The two new LPARs will apparently cover the sector between the areas covered by the

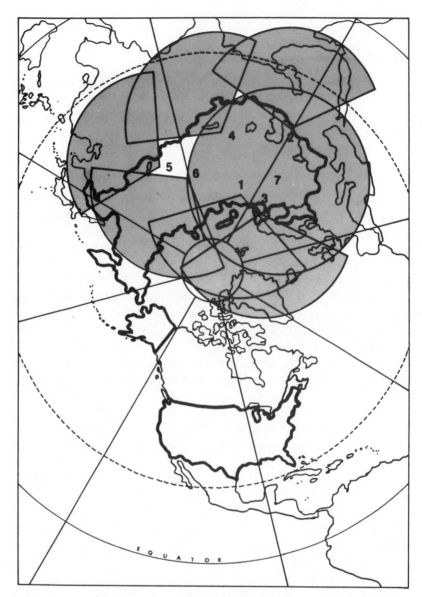

Map 2. **Estimated 1990 coverage fans of Soviet large phased-array radars** (reprinted from Thomas K. Longstreth, John E. Pike, and John B. Rhinelander, *The Impact of U.S. and Soviet Ballistic Missile Defense Programs on the ABM Treaty* [Washington: National Campaign to Save the ABM Treaty, March 1985], 73)

A number of radars of the so-called Pechora type are currently operational or under construction at or near Pechora (1), Lyaki (2), Olenogorsk (3), Sary Shagan (4), Mishelevka (5), and Abalakovo (6). These radars each have a single transmitter face that provides 120 degrees of coverage. The single ABM radar at Pushkino (7), near Moscow, has four transmitters that together provide a full 360-degree coverage. The area of the fans corresponds to the maximum distance at which an object at an altitude of 500 miles can be detected.

Soviet LPARs at Olenogorsk, to the north, and Lyaki, to the south. Hen House radars and the permitted Pushkino ABM radar near Moscow presently scan this sector.[3] It is possible that the two new LPARs are partially designed to detect an attack by NATO long-range theater nuclear forces such as the Pershing II. The Soviets have indicated that the Pechora-type radars are designed for early warning of missile attacks.[4] This argument is supported by the fact that the radars have been observed to operate at the relatively low frequencies (150 megahertz) generally used for early-warning functions.[5]

During the late 1970s the United States expressed concern in the SCC about the new Soviet LPAR network. Because Pechora is located more than 100 miles south of the Soviet coast, the radar could be construed as violating Article VI(b) of the treaty. The Soviets argued in 1981 that, even though they had designed all their Pechora-type LPARs to conform to the terms of the ABM Treaty, it had been necessary to take into account "technical and practical considerations" in their deployment.[6] This statement seemed to indicate that the first LPAR, for example, was located inland at Pechora rather than at a site precisely on the nation's periphery because of logistical and geographical impediments.[7] The United States apparently accepted the location of the Pechora radar as being consistent with the requirements of the ABM Treaty, and the Reagan administration has not questioned the legality of the Pechora radar in its series of noncompliance reports.

U.S. Charge

The United States has judged, on the basis of Article VI(b), that the Abalakovo radar "constitutes a violation of legal obligations under the Anti-Ballistic Missile Treaty" because of its "associated siting, orientation, and capability."[8] The radar is located approximately 400 miles from the nearest Soviet border—the border with Mongolia. More important, rather than looking outward toward the Mongolian border, Abalakovo is oriented to the northeast across some 3,000 miles of Siberia. The United States has also alleged that the Abalakovo radar and "other ABM-related activities suggest that the Soviet Union may be preparing an ABM defense of its national territory" (see chapter 3).

The Soviets assert in public that the Abalakovo radar is designed for tracking satellites and other objects in space, as well as for verification of U.S. compliance with the Outer Space Treaty. The Soviets contend that these functions are permitted under Agreed Statement F of the ABM Treaty. According to the Soviet embassy in Washington: "This radar, the construction of which was started but is not completed, has nothing to do with the obligations assumed by the sides under the ABM Treaty. Its purpose is to follow space objects. On this basis the place for the construction and orientation of the radar was chosen. They [the radar, presumably] make it possible to fill a gap in the zone of monitoring by Soviet radars of space objects and outer space in the eastern part of the country."[9] General Viktor Starodubov reportedly told U.S. representatives at the Strategic Arms Reduction Talks that the radar will monitor flights and landings of manned Soviet spacecraft launched from Tyuratam and Plesetsk, when these flights extend to the east of Krasnoyarsk.[10]

Soviet officials have also stated repeatedly on the public record that the United States will be able to verify Abalakovo's space-tracking capability once the radar is turned on. According to the Soviet embassy: "The purpose of the radar—to follow space objects—can be quite clearly confirmed by experts and by the nature of emissions when the radar starts emitting signals. The regimen of its operation, the power of the emissions and the parameters of the electromagnetic signals were chosen on the basis of the requirements of performing corresponding missions. All that can be verified by national technical means."[11]

Analysis

The siting, orientation, and presumed power-aperture product of the Abalakovo radar are inconsistent with the requirements of Article VI(b) of the ABM Treaty. Despite some ambiguity about how the function of an LPAR is defined, the Abalakovo radar does not qualify for exclusion as a space-tracking or verification radar under Agreed Statement F of the treaty. This judgment supports the Reagan administration's charge that the Abalakovo radar violates the ABM Treaty.

All available evidence contradicts the Soviet assertion that Abalakovo is designed primarily for space tracking or verification, although it might be able to track some future Soviet space-shuttle operations.[12] Abalakovo does not appear to be principally designed for space tracking, nor does it add a significant new capability to existing Soviet space-tracking facilities. The Abalakovo radar faces northeast, a direction that would not allow it to be used for tracking satellite launches from Tyuratam or Plesetsk. (Soviet satellites orbit primarily at inclinations ranging from 47 to 83 degrees [see table 1].) Furthermore, if the Soviets had designed the radar for space tracking, they would have made the angle of the face more obtuse and the radar faces smaller.

The Soviet argument that Abalakovo's purpose will be readily observable when it is operational is not credible. Even if the radar initially emits radiations that suggest it is being used for space tracking, the power and wavelength of the radar are such that the radar could provide early-warning coverage without any external changes observable by U.S. NTM. Furthermore, the SALT I negotiating record makes it clear that LPARs can violate the terms of the ABM Treaty whether or not they are operational. The

Table 1

Orbits of Some Soviet Military Satellites

Perigee–Apogee (km)	Inclination	Apparent mission
35,785–35,785	0°	Communications
19,000–19,200	65°	Navigation
965–1,020	47°	Communications
940–960	83°	Meteorological
855–895	81°	Meteorological
790–810	74°	Communications
620–660	81°	Electronic intelligence (ELINT)
425–445	65°	ELINT ocean reconnaissance (RORSAT)
760–40,000	63°	Launch detection
400–40,000	63°	Communications
365–415	73°	Photo-reconnaissance[a]
250–265	65°	Radar ocean reconnaissance (RORSAT)
172–351	67°	Photo-reconnaissance[b]

Source: U.S. Congress, Office of Technology Assessment, *Anti-Satellite Weapons, Countermeasures, and Arms Control* (Washington, 1985), 37.

[a]Maneuverable; initial parameters for Kosmos 1499 given.

[b]Maneuverable; initial parameters for Kosmos 1454 given.

purpose of the restrictions on LPARs is to prevent the parties from putting into place the long–lead-time elements for a territorial defense.

Strategic Significance

Although there is general agreement among U.S. analysts that the Soviet radar at Abalakovo violates the ABM Treaty, there is a wide range of opinions as to the radar's strategic significance. At the extremes, there are two general assessments of the Abalakovo radar: (1) it is highly significant and could contribute to a Soviet territorial or site defense; and (2) it is not strategically significant because it is vulnerable and therefore could not be relied upon in an ABM defense.

Underlying these different assessments of Abalakovo are different assumptions concerning Soviet strategic-defense programs. For one who believes the Soviets are moving to defend their homeland against ballistic-missile attack, Abalakovo's capabilities, location, and orientation take on considerable significance. For one who dismisses the notion of a concerted Soviet effort to build a nationwide ABM system, Abalakovo's capabilities, location, and orientation may seem to be less of a military concern.

Many administration officials, subscribing to the first view, seem to be convinced that Abalakovo will be fully utilized as an ABM-related radar. They argue that the capabilities of all LPARs must be taken seriously, even if they might be rendered inoperative during a nuclear attack. Those who accept this argument, which underlies the official U.S. view of Soviet programs potentially related to ABM defense, also hold that Abalakovo is well situated to assist in the defense of Soviet SS-11 and SS-18 ICBM fields located nearby. That Abalakovo's coverage area encompasses large portions of Soviet territory is also regarded as providing a substantial ABM capability.

Other analysts doubt that the Soviets are actually moving to deploy a nationwide ABM defense. They also question the utility of any single LPAR for an ABM system, because LPARs are vulnerable and need to be combined with a complex infrastructure to have effective ABM potential. As McGeorge Bundy, George Kennan, Robert McNamara, and Gerard Smith wrote in 1984, "A single highly vulnerable radar installation [Abalakovo] is of only marginal importance in relation to any large-scale breakout from the ABM Treaty."[13] Harold Brown, former secretary of defense, has put forward a similar assessment: "I do not think that [Abalakovo] is a great threat to U.S. security because I do not think that it has that much capability."[14]

Specifically, observers point to the fact that the angle of the radar's two faces, its location, and the 150-megahertz frequency at which Abalakovo will probably operate indicate that it is not optimized to manage a nuclear engagement. Robert M. Gates, deputy director of the Central Intelligence Agency, confirmed before the Senate Armed Services and Appropriations Committees that the Abalakovo radar will probably operate at a low frequency and be susceptible to "degradation from nuclear blast effects."[15] For an ideal hard-site defense of missile silos, the Soviets would have chosen to build the radar closer to existing ICBM fields and would have designed it to operate at a much higher frequency than the Pechora-type radars so that it would not be as vulnerable to blackout effects.

The fact that the Abalakovo radar is essentially identical in exterior appearance to other radars that the Soviets have acknowledged are for early warning—having, in particular, a similar angle of elevation and orientation—is an indication that the radar is designed primarily for early warning of ballistic-missile attack. The siting and orientation of Abalakovo indicate that it is designed to warn of U.S. SLBM launches from the northern Pacific and Arctic oceans and to complement the coverage of U.S. ICBM trajectories over the North Pole provided by the Pechora and

Olenogorsk LPARs (see map 2). According to Harold Brown, "[Abalakovo] is an early warning radar located in the wrong place."[16] The probable coverage area of Abalakovo fills the last remaining gap in the area covered by the Soviet early-warning network, an area not presently covered by either a new Pechora-type LPAR or an older Hen House phased-array radar.[17]

In the debate concerning the military significance of Abalakovo, one distinction is often overlooked. The location of Abalakovo within the interior of the Soviet Union and its orientation over Soviet territory are the only observable features that distinguish it from other Soviet LPARs that comply with the ABM Treaty. A correct analysis of the military significance of Abalakovo must therefore focus on the marginal capability derived from the difference in ABM potential between Abalakovo and an identical radar located on the nation's periphery and oriented outward.

By placing Abalakovo in its present location, the Soviets have intentionally or unintentionally made a trade-off. As now sited, Abalakovo would be able to detect the approach of U.S. SLBMs later in their flight—perhaps after the postboost vehicles would have dispensed the reentry vehicles—than would an identical radar on the periphery. In its 1983 noncompliance report, the administration correctly noted the marginally greater capability the Soviets have gained, asserting that Abalakovo will be able to provide better impact-point prediction for close-in SLBM launches than would a comparable radar or radars on the periphery. Abalakovo's proximity to Soviet ICBM fields enhances this marginal strategic significance. Three SS-18 bases are located behind Abalakovo to the southwest, at Uzhur, Aleysk, and Zhangiz Tobe. One SS-11 base located to the southwest, at Gladkaya, and another base to the southeast, at Svobodny, are conceivably within the coverage area of Abalakovo.[18]

But, as a result of the radar's placement, the Soviets have lost several minutes of early-warning time. This loss stems from the fact that LPARs are able to detect only objects that cross their line of sight, since the waves they emit cannot follow the curvature of the earth to detect objects over the horizon. By placing the radar in the interior of Siberia, the Soviets have decreased the radar's possible coverage of the earlier stages of flight of U.S. SLBMs launched from the northern Pacific.

Finally, no major strategic targets are presently located forward of the radar within its probable coverage area.

The immediate concern raised by Abalakovo is its impact on the vitality of the ABM Treaty. By setting a dangerous precedent for exploiting treaty language, the radar raises the troubling possibility that each side will chip away at the constraints of the ABM Treaty. The U.S. PAVE PAWS program, though not a clear violation, could be seen in a similar light. If such questionable interpretations are not fenced in as they occur, the treaty could become riddled with holes that would undermine its spirit if not its letter. Without frontally breaking out of the ABM Treaty, both sides could bend and stretch the document until it becomes a worthless piece of paper.

In the larger context, Abalakovo has had a more detrimental effect than any other compliance issue on the environment in which U.S.-Soviet arms control efforts take place. Soviet adherence to the implausible space-tracking argument has raised doubts about Soviet explanations of other questionable activities. The Soviets' credibility has been eroded by their poor handling of the Abalakovo issue; this, in turn, has reduced the plausibility of Soviet responses on some of the issues on which the Soviet position may be more legitimate. Moreover, the Soviets' apparent disregard for their treaty commitment in the instance of Abalakovo has caused some past supporters of arms control to doubt Soviet adherence to agreements in general and therefore to question the desirability of negotiating new treaties with the Soviet Union.

Concluding Remarks

The Soviet large phased-array radar at Abalakovo represents a clear-cut violation of the ABM Treaty. When it becomes operational, the radar will have slightly greater potential to contribute to an ABM defense than would such a radar located on the country's periphery and oriented outward. But the evidence suggests that, given the limitations and vulnerability of LPARs, this marginal capability does not by itself lend the Soviets any significant new ABM capability. As Arnold Horelick, former CIA national-intelligence officer for the Soviet Union, stated, Abalakovo represents "no strategic threat in and of itself and is probably at best only a marginal add-on to a breakout capability."[19] As long as LPARs remain highly vulnerable to direct attack and blackout effects, and as long as Abalakovo is not coupled with other ABM components explicitly banned by the ABM Treaty, the radar will remain only a potential threat to U.S. security. Abalakovo has not degraded the ability of U.S. retaliatory nuclear forces to strike Soviet military and civilian assets. At present there is no evidence to suggest that either of these conditions will change in the near future.

Detached from both the implausible Soviet space-tracking argument and the unsubstantiated U.S. charges of pending Soviet territorial defense, Abalakovo clearly has more serious implications for the future of U.S.-Soviet diplomatic relations, including arms control, than it has for U.S. military security.

Chapter Six

Threat of Breach of a Treaty: The U.S. Strategic Defense Initiative

The Reagan administration's dedicated pursuit of the Strategic Defense Initiative raises a number of important questions about U.S. compliance with the 1972 ABM Treaty. The fact that the concern is not centered solely on current U.S. activities complicates an evaluation of these compliance issues. Rather, much of the controversy about the legality of SDI-related endeavors revolves around what the United States intends to do in the near future regarding development and testing of ABM systems. The administration has made assessment of its intentions problematic by arguing for a very controversial, extremely broad interpretation of the ABM Treaty. At the same time that the administration has incorporated that interpretation into U.S. proposals at the Geneva arms control talks, it has pledged to abide for the time being by the traditional, less permissive reading.

This chapter examines three separate aspects of the complex debate over SDI and compliance with the ABM Treaty: (1) the administration's own evaluation of its compliance record with respect to the SDI and its defense of the new, broad interpretation of the ABM Treaty, (2) Soviet charges of U.S. violations of the ABM Treaty, and (3) a review of the concerns raised by various U.S. arms control and defense analysts about the SDI and the future of the ABM accord. The discussion concludes with an overall assessment of the various compliance issues raised with respect to the Strategic Defense Initiative.

Background

In March 1983 President Reagan proposed that the United States begin to develop a shield against nuclear weapons to make deterrence by the threat of retaliation no longer necessary. The human spirit, he said, "must be capable of rising above dealing with other nations and human beings by threatening their existence." He called on the American scientific community to "turn their great talents . . . to the cause of mankind and world peace, to give us the means of rendering these nuclear weapons impotent and obsolete."[1]

By January 1984 the president's call for a world free from the threat of nuclear weapons was transformed under the direction of the Department of Defense (DOD) into the program we now know as the Strategic Defense Initiative. The SDI, according to the DOD, is a "research program . . . established to explore and demonstrate key technologies associated with concepts for defense against ballistic missiles," a program structured to permit "a decision in the early 1990s on whether to proceed to system-level development."[2]

With the introduction of the ambitious SDI program, both the Soviet government and arms control analysts in the United States began to question U.S. intentions with respect to the 1972 ABM accord. The president's interest in moving toward an increasing reliance on strategic defenses seemed to put the administration on a collision course with a treaty that places strict limitations on the testing, development, and deployment of ABM systems. The Reagan administration responded to these concerns by stating that the SDI was formulated to fit within the constraints imposed by the ABM Treaty and by pledging to abide by the terms of previous arms control agreements. According to the 1985 *Report to the Congress on the Strategic Defense Initiative*: "It should be stressed that the SDI is a *research program* that seeks to provide the technical knowledge required to support a decision on whether to develop and later deploy advanced defensive systems. . . . All research efforts will be fully compliant with U.S. treaty obligations."[3]

How long the administration intends to honor this commitment is not entirely clear. The Department of Defense has maintained that none of the tests planned for SDI technologies will exceed treaty limitations until 1991 and that it will be up to some future president to decide the fate of the ABM accord. Recent statements by Secretary of Defense Weinberger and the head of the Strategic Defense Initiative Organization (SDIO), Lieutenant General James Abrahamson, however, have been more equivocal. In his report to Congress for fiscal year 1985, Weinberger wrote that the SDI could be pursued "for the next several years" in a manner consistent with treaty obligations.[4] According to a 1986 *Time* magazine article, General Abrahamson indicated that the SDI might confront a "problem in terms of the narrow interpretation of the Treaty somewhere in 1989."[5]

At present, the administration maintains that all efforts pertaining to the SDI will be fully consistent with U.S. treaty obligations. The administration has detailed its perspective on treaty compliance in its yearly reports to the Congress on the SDI. The administration's analysis divides the work on the SDI into three categories, which it contends are fully justified on the basis of a strict interpretation of the ABM Treaty: (1) conceptual design and laboratory testing, (2) field testing of devices that are not ABM components or prototypes of ABM components, and (3) field testing of fixed, land-based ABM components.

Category 1—Conceptual Design and Laboratory Testing

The Reagan administration holds that conceptual design and laboratory testing are not constrained by any treaty obligations. In fact, there is little question within the United States that laboratory research is freely allowed. The ABM Treaty makes no explicit mention of such activities. The constraints imposed on defensive systems and components, at their most stringent, restrict only development, testing, and deployment.

The administration has also made clear its view of the operational distinction between research, which is clearly allowed, and development, which is severely constrained by the treaty. The official U.S. interpretation is that activities that precede field testing, including so-called early development, fall into the administration's first category and conform to treaty limitations.

Although the Soviet Union and the United States have never formally agreed upon a precise definition of "development," the practices of previous administrations provide substantial precedent for the concept that the dividing line between allowed and prohibited activities lies between laboratory and field testing. This reading of the treaty is based largely on the July 1972 congressional testimony of Ambassador Gerard Smith, chief U.S. negotiator of the accord. According to Ambassador Smith: "The obligation not to develop such systems, devices, or warheads would be applicable only to that stage of development which follows laboratory development and testing. The prohibitions on development contained in the ABM Treaty would start at that part of the development process where field testing is initiated on either a prototype or breadboard model. It was understood by both sides that the prohibition on 'development' applies to activities involved after a component moves from the laboratory development and testing stage to the field testing stage, wherever performed."[6]

The administration has used the Category 1 rationale to justify a number of major SDI-related activities. For example, the ground-based hypervelocity rail gun (GBHRG) experiment is designed to "demonstrate the capability to launch unguided and guided projectiles at hypervelocities from ground-based rail guns." In the initial stages of the SDI program, tests will be carried out "within a laboratory environment."[7] Accordingly, the administration considers the GBHRG experiment, which at present involves only conceptual design and laboratory testing, to be fully compliant with the treaty. In the future the administration intends to test the GBHRG in a fixed, land-based mode at an agreed-upon test site, a type of testing justifiable under its criteria for field testing (Category 3).

Category 2—Field Testing of Devices That Are Not ABM Components or Prototypes of ABM Components

The Reagan administration contends that, in addition to basic research, the ABM Treaty allows field testing of defense-related technologies, as long as the devices that are being tested are not ABM components or proto-types of components. This rationale has in practice implied two fundamental distinctions. The first is between an ABM component, which is proscribed by the treaty, and a subcomponent, or adjunct, which is not; the second is between technologies, proscribed by the treaty, that are field-tested in an ABM mode and those that are not.

Components versus adjuncts. The Reagan administration argues that a variety of defense-related technologies can be tested, or, in the administration's parlance, demonstrated, as long as the devices cannot stand alone as substitutes for ABM radars, interceptors, or launchers. This argument is based on the administration's reading of Article II.1 and Agreed Statement D of the treaty, and on its interpretation of discussions that took place between the U.S. and Soviet sides during the SALT I negotiations. Article II.1 defines ABM systems and components: "For the purpose of this Treaty an ABM system is a system to counter strategic ballistic mis-siles or their elements in flight trajectory, currently consisting of (a) ABM interceptor missiles, which are interceptor missiles constructed and deployed for an ABM role, or of a type tested in an ABM mode; (b) ABM launch-ers, which are launchers constructed and deployed for launching ABM interceptor missiles; and (c) ABM radars, which are radars constructed and deployed for an ABM role, or of a type tested in an ABM mode."

Agreed Statement D extends the definition of ABM systems and com-ponents to include devices that are capable of substituting for ABM launch-ers, interceptors, or radars: "In order to insure fulfillment of the obligation not to deploy ABM systems and their components except as provided in Article III of the Treaty, the Parties agree that in the event ABM systems based on other physical principles and including components capable of substituting for ABM interceptor missiles, ABM launchers, or ABM radars are created in the future, specific limitations on such systems and their com-ponents would be subject to discussion in accordance with Article XIII."

In short, according to the traditional interpretation of the treaty, the re-strictions imposed on development, testing, and deployment of ABM sys-tems and components apply to ABM launchers, ABM interceptors, and ABM radars, or devices capable of substituting for those components.

During the SALT I negotiations U.S. and Soviet representatives discussed the definition of the term "component" and the distinction between a com-ponent and a subcomponent, or adjunct, which would not be subject to treaty restrictions. The negotiators offered the example of an optical tele-scope used in conjunction with an ABM radar as a device that would be exempt. Even if the telescope served as a part of an ABM radar, it would not be able to substitute functionally for the radar.

Although the United States and Soviet Union never formally agreed on a precise definition for "component" either in the SALT I negotiations or subsequently in the SCC, the Reagan administration has made consider-

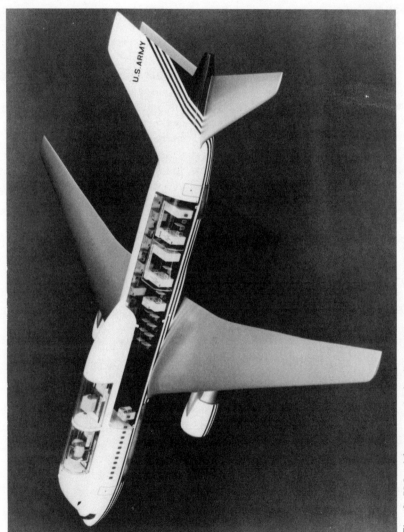

Fig. 9. U.S. airborne optical adjunct (courtesy U.S. Defense Department)

able use of its distinction between components and adjuncts to justify SDI-related work. For example, the administration considers the High Brightness Relay Project, which involves the testing of mirrors in space that are designed to relay the beams from ground-based lasers to their targets, to involve devices that are only subcomponents or adjuncts. The administration describes the test as a manipulation of "technologies which are only part of the set of technologies ultimately required for ABM capability."[8] Therefore, officials contend, "technology demonstrations" of these devices are not limited by the treaty.

Similarly, the administration designates the airborne optical adjunct (AOA) experiment as a Category 2 test because, as the name implies, the technology being tested involves an adjunct and not a component. The AOA experiment is intended to demonstrate the technical feasibility of using optical sensors placed on an airplane to observe ballistic-missile flight tests. The DOD plans to test technologies that perform tasks similar to those previously performed by some radars, namely tasks providing target-tracking data. However, the administration contends that "due to its sensor and platform limitations" the AOA as tested is not capable of substituting for a radar and is therefore not subject to Article V limitations on development and testing of air-based ABM components.[9]

Testing in an ABM mode. The Reagan administration also argues that the ABM Treaty allows testing of defense technologies as long as the tests are not conducted in an ABM mode. Article VI(a) (as well as Article II, already quoted) refers to testing in an ABM mode: "To enhance assurance of the effectiveness of the limitations on ABM systems and their components provided by the Treaty, each Party undertakes (a) not to give missiles, launchers, or radars, other than ABM interceptor missiles, ABM launchers, or ABM radars, capabilities to counter strategic ballistic missiles or their elements in flight trajectory, and not to test them in an ABM mode."

The Standing Consultative Commission has given considerable attention to clarifying what it means to test in an ABM mode (see chapter 8). The SCC has negotiated two agreed interpretations, but both remain confidential. The Reagan administration outlines its understanding of the U.S. commitment in the 1986 SDIO report to Congress: "An interceptor missile is considered to be 'tested in an ABM mode' if it has attempted to intercept (successfully or not) a strategic ballistic missile or its elements in flight trajectory. Likewise, a radar is considered to be 'tested in an ABM mode' if it performs certain functions such as tracking and guiding an ABM interceptor missile or tracking strategic ballistic missiles or their elements in flight trajectory in conjunction with an ABM radar which is tracking and guiding an ABM interceptor. 'Strategic ballistic missiles or their elements in flight trajectory' include ballistic target missiles with the flight trajectory characteristics of strategic ballistic missiles or their elements over the portions of the flight trajectory involved in testing."[10]

The administration places numerous experiments in Category 2, basing its argument on the distinction between testing in an ABM mode and not doing so. For example, the purpose of the space-based kinetic-kill vehicle project is to establish the technology for chemically propelled, space-based interceptors. The nature of the experiment has not yet been fully defined by the SDIO. However, the administration states that no space-based experiment will be tested in an ABM mode and that "intercepts of certain orbital targets simulating anti-satellite weapons can clearly be compatible with [Category 2] criteria."[11]

Similarly, the Significant Technical Milestones experiment, which took place in September 1986, involved two stages of a rocket, which were in closely related orbits. The stages were maneuvered relative to each other in order to "obtain sensor guidance and navigation data." The experiment was concluded when a third stage was made to collide with the second stage in what the administration termed a test of "new guidance equations." According to the administration, the systems tested "[did] not have any ABM capability and the experiment [did] not involve a test in the ABM mode."[12]

Category 3 — Field Testing of Fixed, Land-Based ABM Components

The administration justifies its final category for SDI-related tests by citing Article III of the ABM Treaty. This provision, as modified by Article 1 of the 1974 ABM Protocol, specifically allows for the development, testing, and deployment of a single-site, fixed, land-based ABM system consisting of no more than 100 ABM launchers, no more than 100 ABM interceptor missiles, and a small number of ABM radars in a specified area around the ABM site.[13] Article IV of the treaty allows for 15 additional ABM launchers at test ranges to be used for development and testing of ABM systems.

Article V of the treaty imposes important constraints on the types of systems that may be tested and developed under Article III: "1. Each party undertakes not to develop, test, or deploy ABM systems or components which are sea-based, air-based, space-based, or mobile land-based. 2. Each party undertakes not to develop, test, or deploy ABM launchers for launching more than one ABM interceptor missile at a time from each launcher, not to modify deployed launchers to provide them with such a capability, not to develop, test, or deploy automatic or semi-automatic or other similar systems for rapid reload of ABM launchers."

Article VI and Agreed Statements D and E impose further restrictions. In summary, these provisions allow the development, testing, and deployment of fixed, ground-based ABM systems as long as the testing and deployment take place at agreed-upon locations. According to the traditional interpretation of the treaty, fixed, ground-based ABM systems based on new physical principles may be developed and tested at these locations but not deployed without prior negotiation. Multiple-warhead ABM systems may not be developed, tested, or deployed regardless of their basing mode.

The administration includes three programs under Category 3 in its 1986 report on the SDI: the high-endoatmospheric defense interceptor, a non-nuclear, ballistic-missile interceptor that will "negate" ballistic-missile warheads within the atmosphere; the exoatmospheric reentry-vehicle interceptor, which will negate warheads prior to their reentry into the atmosphere; and the terminal imaging radar, a fixed, land-based ABM radar. For each program the administration pledges to carry out development and testing in full compliance with the terms of the treaty.

A New Interpretation of the ABM Treaty

The administration's three categories of activities provide it with justification, in terms of compliance with the ABM Treaty, for a variety of defense-related endeavors. Recently, the administration has added, on the basis of a reinterpretation of Article II and Agreed Statement D, one more category of activities that it considers to be allowed. According to this broad reading, the accord allows for the development and testing of ABM systems and components based on new technologies, not just at agreed test sites but also in space, in the atmosphere, and at sea.

The administration claims that the language in Article II.1—which defines an ABM system as "currently consisting of (a) ABM interceptor missiles . . . (b) ABM launchers . . . and (c) ABM radars"—means that the restrictions on development and testing of ABM systems and components refer only to technology available in 1972. Abraham Sofaer, legal adviser to the State Department, who performed the official reexamination of the treaty, testified: "The provision can . . . be read to mean that systems contemplated by the treaty are those that serve the functions described and that currently consist of the listed components. . . . The definition in Article II was not merely illustrative but was intended to describe the actual components covered by the treaty."[14]

Administration officials have concluded that Agreed Statement D, which holds that deployment of ABM systems and components based on new physical principles is subject to further negotiation, was added to deal specifically with the question of new technologies. They contend that the restrictions on development and testing of space-based and other ABM systems listed in Article V are not applicable to ABMs based on physical principles other than those referred to in the treaty.

The new reading of the treaty allows the administration an extremely broad latitude for SDI development and testing. However, almost immediately after elaborating the new reading, the administration gave assurances that it intended to follow the old reading, according to which prohibitions on development and testing of ABM systems are binding regardless of the technology upon which they are based. In the past year the administration has maintained not only that the new reading is correct but also that it intends to constrain the SDI within the restrictive interpretation of the treaty for the time being. The SDIO has reported: "The SDI program was originally structured in a manner that was designed to permit it to achieve critical research objectives while remaining consistent with a more narrow interpretation of the ABM Treaty. This being the case, in October 1985, while reserving the right to conduct the SDI program under the broad interpretation at some future time, the President deemed it unnecessary to restructure the SDI program towards the boundaries of the ABM Treaty which the U.S. could observe."[15]

Soviet Charges

In January 1984 the Soviet Union transmitted an aide-mémoire to the United States containing a set of rather vaguely stated charges of U.S. ABM Treaty violations. The charges were made in response to the Reagan administration's first public allegations of widespread Soviet cheating. Several seemed to relate to the Strategic Defense Initiative: (1) testing a Minuteman I as an ABM interceptor, in violation of Article VI, which bans testing of non-ABM systems in an ABM mode; (2) creation of space-based and mobile ABM systems, in violation of Article V; (3) developing MIRVed ABM interceptors, in contravention of Agreed Statement E of the ABM Protocol; and (4) installation of shelters over ABM launchers, violating the prohibition in Article XII on deliberate concealment of ABM-related activities.

This report has already discussed two of these charges, those pertaining to the development of MIRVed ABM systems and the placing of shelters over ABM launchers. The two remaining charges are described here.

Testing a Non-ABM Missile in an ABM Mode

In 1983 and 1984, in a test known as the Homing Overlay Experiment, the United States used a modified ICBM to intercept an incoming missile over the Pacific Ocean. The U.S. experiment involved a fixed, land-based system at Kwajelein Island, a designated U.S. test range, and was therefore considered by the administration to be a Category 3 test, fully permitted by the ABM Treaty. However, the Soviet Union claimed that the United States used a Minuteman I missile as an interceptor and therefore violated Article VI(a) of the ABM Treaty, which prohibits non-ABM missiles from being tested in an ABM mode. The Reagan administration responded that the missile used in the test was modified in such a way that it was distinguishable to Soviet NTM as a Minuteman I, that only the first two stages of the missile were used, and that no Minuteman I missiles were deployed

Fig. 10. Element of U.S. Homing Overlay Experiment (courtesy U.S. Defense Department)

at the time. Therefore, it claims that the United States did not test a non-ABM missile in an ABM mode.

Creation of Space-Based and Mobile ABM Systems

The second Soviet charge is more difficult to pin down. The Soviet aide-mémoire devotes little more than a sentence to the charge that the United States is engaged in the creation of space-based and mobile ABM systems. This allegation may be based on the Soviet reading of Article V. In the U.S. version of the treaty, the provision prohibits the development of a variety of ABM systems. However, the Soviet version uses the Russian equivalent of the term "create" instead of "develop."

As noted, there has never been an agreed-upon, precise definition of the dividing line between research and development. Similarly, there is no agreed-upon definition of the term "creation." The Soviet Union has neither formally accepted nor rejected the U.S. unilateral interpretation of the distinction that allows for early development but prevents field testing. Reportedly, at SALT I the negotiators held discussions to clarify the point and came to an understanding that development is that part of the process that begins with field testing (as noted in the 1972 testimony by Ambassador Smith). Recently, some Soviets have argued that the prohibition on creation of ABM systems includes even the earliest stages of research.[16]

U.S. Concerns About SDI and Compliance

A number of arms control and defense analysts, including former officials involved in the negotiation of the ABM treaty, have raised three distinct sets of concerns about the SDI and compliance with the treaty. Specifically, the analysts have identified as either current or imminent issues the Reagan administration's reinterpretation of the ABM Treaty, its application of the Category 2 justification for SDI-related tests, and its intentions regarding a broad range of future tests of SDI technology.

The Reinterpretation of the ABM Treaty

The Reagan administration's broad interpretation of the ABM Treaty would allow for development and testing of space-based, air-based, sea-based, and mobile, land-based ABM systems and components as long as the technologies used are new—that is not yet in existence in 1972. Although the administration has made a commitment to abide by the old interpretation of the treaty for the time being, the new reading has not escaped scrutiny. One of the most serious critics of the administration on this issue, Gerard Smith, the chief U.S. negotiator of the SALT I accords, has responded to the administration's arguments: "It was not our intention that any type of technology for space-based ABM systems could be developed or tested under the treaty. This has been the official view of the United States Government for more than thirteen years. . . . The differences between the ban on deployment and testing of space-based systems, and the more limited constraints on fixed land-based systems is reflected in . . . Agreed Statement D. This agreed statement does not modify in any way the total ban on the development and testing of space-based systems."[17]

According to proponents of the traditional interpretation, the intent of Agreed Statement D was to strengthen Article III by insuring that ABM systems based on new physical principles would not be deployed in fixed, land-based modes without further negotiation (the deployment of traditional, fixed, land-based systems is not so constrained). Agreed Statement D, it is argued, was never intended to relax the constraints imposed on ABM systems in other parts of the treaty nor to provide exemptions for new technologies based on physical principles other than those specifically restricted in the treaty. According to this view, the intent of Article V from the outset was to preclude the development, testing, and deployment of space-based, mobile land-based, sea-based, and air-based ABM systems and components regardless of the technologies on which they were based. Advocates of the old reading cite Article I, in which each side pledges not to deploy a nationwide ABM system and not to provide a base for such a system, and point to the unlimited duration of the treaty as evidence that the limitations were intended to apply to technology beyond that available in 1972.

Senator Sam Nunn (Democrat, Georgia), chairman of the Senate Armed Services Committee, came to a similar conclusion in March 1987. Nunn conducted a three-part review covering the 1972 Senate proceedings leading up to ratification of the ABM Treaty, subsequent U.S. practice under the ABM Treaty, and the treaty negotiating record. Nunn concluded that the Senate clearly understood at the time the treaty was ratified that it would prohibit the development and testing of mobile or space-based ABM systems using technologies based on "other physical principles," and that the evidence of the Senate understanding was compelling beyond a reasonable doubt.[18]

Nunn also concluded that the statements and activities of the United States and the Soviet Union since the treaty was signed indicated that both sides clearly understood this to be the meaning of the treaty. Finally, Nunn found that the negotiating record supports the Senate's original understanding of the treaty. Nunn called the Reagan administration "in serious error on its position on this crucial issue—wrong in its analysis of the Senate ratification debate; wrong in its analysis of the record of subsequent practice . . . and wrong in its analysis of the negotiating record itself."[19]

Category 2 Justification

There has been considerable controversy surrounding the administration's use of Category 2 justifications for SDI-related technology demonstrations. It is not the administration's reading of the treaty that is in contention but its application of the distinction between components and adjuncts and its definition of testing in an ABM mode.

In the view of many outside the administration, the SDIO has made specious distinctions between ABM adjuncts and components in order to justify technology demonstrations that are not consistent with treaty limitations. As noted, the administration has held that a particular system must precisely perform the function of the components listed in the treaty in order to be considered a component and thus be constrained under Article V.

Administration critics have cited the justification for the airborne optical adjunct test as an example of just such a questionable distinction. The administration considers the AOA an adjunct to the terminal imaging radar, which would use the target-tracking data provided by the AOA and provide direct guidance information to ground-based interceptors.[20]

According to some analysts, the AOA is comparable in every significant way to a component of an air-based ABM radar system, except for the absence of certain data-transfer capabilities. Therefore, in their view, the administration's distinction between adjunct and component is meaningless in this case.[21] A report for the National Campaign to Save the ABM Treaty notes: "The Airborne Optical System performs a role similar to that of the Perimeter Acquisition Radar (PAR) in the Sentinel/Safeguard system [the U.S. ABM system developed in the 1960s]. Radars such as the PAR were clearly considered to be ABM components, and subjected to strict limitations in the Treaty."[22]

Some U.S. analysts have also expressed concern about the administration's application of the definition of "testing in an ABM mode." The so-called endgame of the recent Significant Technical Milestones experiment raised this issue. In the final phase of the experiment one stage of a rocket purposefully intercepted a second stage. Both were accelerating at many times the force of gravity. According to SDIO director General Abrahamson, the collision was meant to test new guidance equations: "We're not trying to pull a stunt here and blow up something in space. . . . What we're really after is a valid technical experiment."[23] However, the test did involve the interception of a vehicle accelerating rapidly in space. Some analysts have noted that during the final phase of the test the rocket stage that was being intercepted had characteristics similar to those of a postboost vehicle of a ballistic missile. Therefore, they conclude, the experiment may have constituted testing in an ABM mode. In the fall 1986 meeting of the SCC, the Soviets were reported to have raised the issue of the Significant Technical Milestones experiment. However, because the meetings were private and the results confidential, it is not clear whether Soviet concerns about the experiment precisely mirrored those raised in the United States.

Potential Violations

Finally, there is considerable anxiety within the U.S. arms control community about a variety of future tests of SDI components planned for the late 1980s and early 1990s. In general, the concern is that the continued active pursuit of the SDI will inevitably lead the United States into a position from which it will be forced either to amend, violate, or withdraw from the ABM Treaty. Table 2 lists planned SDI projects that raise potential problems.

Analysis

The charge leveled by the Soviet Union with respect to the Homing Overlay Experiment, that the United States has tested a non-ABM missile in an ABM mode, does not represent a persuasive case of U.S. noncompliance. According to a number of analysts, the United States has justification for claiming that the use of the significantly modified missile did not constitute a violation of the treaty. According to Sidney Graybeal, former SCC commissioner, the missile was not a Minuteman I but a typical U.S. test vehicle made up of a combination of spare missile components. However, Graybeal adds, "Since the U.S. has called this interceptor a Minuteman I, any future deployment at other than permitted sites would then violate the Treaty's Article VI."[24] John Rhinelander concurred that the U.S. explanation does have merit, but that "it is anything but an open and shut legal case."[25] The issue represents the type of concern that presumably could be laid to rest in the Standing Consultative Commission.

The Soviet allegation that the United States is creating a space-based defense in violation of the treaty is even less substantial than the charge pertaining to the Homing Overlay Experiment. If the Soviet Union does mean to imply that research and early development constitute creation of an ABM system and thus represent a violation, their accusations are not well supported either by the text of the treaty or what is known of the negotiating record.

The administration's statements on the SDI and its own assessment of the related compliance issues prompt two central observations. First, the administration's own rationale does not support the characterization of the SDI as a research program. Although it is true that some of the program remains in the research phase, the administration makes the case that testing of defense-related technologies is allowable in many instances. The administration has given every indication that it will continue to take full advantage of what it interprets as avenues of opportunity in the ABM Treaty to conduct SDI field tests and to move along as far as possible in the exploration of ballistic-missile defenses. Second, though the administration is making some effort to reconcile its current practices with the requirements of the ABM Treaty, its long-term intentions, with respect to how

Table 2

Compliance with the ABM Treaty: Concerns Raised by the SDI

SDI Project	Testing Mode	Testing Period	Concern
Sensors			
Space surveillance and tracking system Detects and tracks warheads during mid-course of flight; could provide tracking and identification information to be relayed for use by midcourse interceptors	Space-based	Early 1990s	If tested in an ABM mode, system would violate Article V.1, which bans testing of space-based ABM components
Airborne optical system Aircraft-based optical sensor system, intended solely for ABM-related applications; original flight test, scheduled for 1987, has been delayed for at least one year	Air-based	Late 1980s	Advanced development and flight testing would violate Article V.1, which bans the development and testing of air-based ABM components
Terminal imaging radar Part of ground-based terminal defense; could be made mobile to enhance survivability	Ground-based (mobile)	Late 1980s	Advanced development in other than fixed, ground-based mode would violate Article V.1, which bans development of mobile, ground-based ABM components
Directed-energy weapons			
Space-based laser triad Consists of Talon Gold pointing and tracking component, Large Optics Demonstration Experiment mirror system, and the the Alpha hydrogen-fluoride chemical infrared laser; Talon Gold telescope attached to space-based laser insures proper aiming at	Space-based	Late 1980s (flight test), early 1990s (integrated demonstration)	Advanced development or testing of Talon Gold or follow-on would violate Article V.1, which bans development and testing of space-based ABM components

Table 2 continued

SDI Project	Testing Mode	Testing Period	Concern
target; in-space demonstration postponed until 1988–89; may be replaced by follow-on system of different name			
Ground-based laser Large, ground-based laser would direct beam to target by a series of space-based mirrors	Space-based (some aspects)	Early 1990s	Although testing of fixed ground-based lasers is not constrained by the treaty, the inclusion of space-based mirrors raises questions concerning Article V.1, which prohibits testing of space-based ABM components
Kinetic-energy weapon Hypervelocity launcher Uses electromagnetic accelerator to propel projectiles at very high velocities; offers prospects of very high rates of fire; space-based demonstrations planned against satellite targets simulating strategic-missile components	Ground-based (initial demonstrations), space-based (later demonstrations)	Late 1980s, early 1990s	Rate of fire—on the order of one shot per second—may violate Article V.2, which requires each party "not to develop, test, or deploy automatic or semiautomatic or other similar systems for rapid reload of ABM launchers." Because of ABM applicability, testing in mode other than fixed, land-based mode would violate Article V.1 even if performed against satellite targets

Source: Thomas K. Longstreth, John E. Pike, and John B. Rhinelander, *The Impact of U.S. and Soviet Ballistic Missile Defense Programs on the ABM Treaty* (Washington: National Campaign to Save the ABM Treaty, March 1985), 51.

it will ultimately interpret the treaty and how long it will strive to abide by a strict interpretation of the accord, are not at all clear. The administration's two-track approach to the new interpretation has made the issue of SDI and compliance a moving target. Administration officials in one instance contend that they are abiding by a narrow interpretation and in the next argue that the treaty allows development and testing of space-based systems. The tenacity with which the administration asserts that the new reading is wholly justified undermines its assurances that it will abide by a strict interpretation.

The administration's new interpretation argues that ballistic-missile defenses based on new technologies do not fall under the definition of ABM systems or components contained in the ABM Treaty and that Agreed Statement D is the only provision pertaining to new technologies. The logical extension of the argument is that deployment of systems based on the new technologies and physical principles other than those discussed in the treaty—should they be developed—could proceed without requiring the United States to withdraw from the treaty. Should the Reagan administration choose to implement the new interpretation, the range of allowed defense-related activities will be enormous, giving both the United States and Soviet Union the latitude to develop and test without restriction ABM systems based on new physical principles. In such an environment the likelihood of rapid breakout from the treaty would be extremely high, and constraints on deployment would be rendered essentially meaningless.

The administration's contradictory signals regarding the old and new readings of the treaty have hampered an open and focused debate on the issue. It is not clear why the administration first publicized its reinterpretation of the treaty and now repeatedly justifies it in the abstract. When critics confront the administration on the issue of noncompliance and the SDI, the administration reverts to the argument that it will conduct the program in accordance with the strict interpretation of the treaty. Regardless of the administration's stated intentions, the new interpretation contradicts what three previous administrations considered to be the clear purpose of the treaty: to prevent the development, testing, and deployment of extensive ABM systems.

Senator Levin's conclusion, that an independent review of the ABM Treaty is an absolute necessity, is well founded. The controversy surrounding the broad interpretation will not finally be resolved until the negotiating record is made available, either publicly or through the analysis of an independent, bipartisan review commission. An open debate based on the record should rightfully precede any attempt to implement a new interpretation of the accord.

The administration's application of Category 2 criteria has brought the United States perilously close to violating the ABM Treaty—if a violation has not yet occurred. Regardless of how one finally balances the administration's arguments against those of its critics, the claim that the airborne optical adjunct and the Significant Technical Milestones experiments are allowed activities clearly underscores an important general trend in the administration's approach to the SDI and compliance, namely, that the administration is willing to test the limits of the ABM Treaty in the interests of aggressively pursuing the SDI. Although the AOA may, for instance, fall short in some detailed respects of what the administration considers a legitimate component, it is clearly intended to be an integral and functionally important part of the SDI.

The United States cannot rely on unilateral interpretations of key provisions, interpretations based on what it sees as expedient for the SDI program, without seriously threatening the ABM Treaty. As Abraham Chayes, the State Department's former legal adviser, has noted: "We are going to keep making up ad hoc and increasingly skimpy legal defenses of particular projects and activities. In the end the treaty will be destroyed, whether we withdraw from it or not."[26] Certainly such practices weaken the credibility of U.S. complaints about Soviet unilateral treaty interpretations and exploitation of loopholes. More important, continued U.S. exploitation of treaty provisions will likely reduce Soviet incentives to continue to comply with the ABM Treaty and other arms control agreements—much as the one instance of Soviet noncompliance (see chapter 5) and the cases of Soviet questionable compliance have decreased U.S. confidence in the arms control process.

In addition, the reinterpretation of the ABM Treaty, prospective pursuit of aspects of the SDI program that would be impermissible under the traditional interpretation, and statements by Secretary of Defense Weinberger calling for early deployment of a strategic defense of U.S. territory all threaten to undercut the basis for the ABM Treaty itself. By pursuing early deployment, the United States would court the possibility of Soviet breakout from the ABM Treaty and other agreements.

If at some future time the United States announces plans to deploy a ballistic-missile defense system, the Soviet Union could, with some legal justification, undertake countermeasures that would cause it to break out of the ABM Treaty. A fundamental concept in both domestic and international law is a country's right to take reasonable measures to offset threats to its national security. When the threat involves violation of a treaty, reasonable measures taken in response can involve treaty breakout.

If the United States were to announce plans for early deployment of a strategic defense and adopt a more permissive interpretation of the ABM Treaty, the Soviet Union could consider the United States to have abandoned the ABM Treaty and to have increased the threat to the Soviet Union in a way that demanded countermeasures not consistent with Soviet adherence to treaty provisions. The Soviet Union could potentially decide to abandon the ABM Treaty.

These compliance concerns are not the only possible effects of such a U.S. policy. If pursued by the United States, the reinterpretation of the treaty and early deployment might increase Soviet incentives to develop offensive forces to overcome a U.S. strategic defense and could decrease sharply the possibility for future progress in strategic arms control.

Chapter Seven

The Sources of Soviet Compliance Behavior

U.S. and Soviet military behavior affects arms control compliance through a complex and interactive process. The two countries subtly signal and test one another about the limits of permissible behavior. Because pinpointing the workings of Soviet internal decision making on national security is difficult, the temptation is great to oversimplify Soviet motivations and behavior and to gloss over the way in which the Soviet approach to compliance interacts with U.S. behavior.

Two concerns officially expressed by the United States in recent years are that the Soviets have a "policy" of violating arms control agreements, and that there is a consistent "pattern" of Soviet violations. Often these two explanations have been linked. A Defense Department report of December 1985 on Soviet noncompliance, entitled *Responding to Soviet Violations Policy,* asserted in both its title and its content that the Soviets have a coherent policy of violating agreements. The report concluded that this Soviet policy has led to a long sequence of arms control violations. According to the report, "The Soviet Union has been violating with impunity its principal arms control agreements with the United States."[1] The White House noncompliance reports have highlighted a "most disturbing pattern of Soviet behavior,"[2] and in congressional testimony and public speeches ACDA director Kenneth Adelman has frequently referred to an "expanding pattern" of Soviet noncompliance.

This chapter describes Soviet compliance behavior as a whole and attempts to identify its sources, paying special attention to the 1979–83 period, when the Soviets made decisions on programs now the subject of compliance concerns, when the Soviet political leadership apparently took no action to ensure strict Soviet compliance, and when Soviet willingness to cooperate with the United States in resolving compliance disputes declined precipitously. All analysis of contemporary Soviet defense policy is to some extent speculative. Within that limitation, we examine both the pattern of Soviet behavior bearing on compliance and the question of whether a coherent Soviet violations policy exists.

Violations Policy

The answer to the question about a violations policy is clear. Neither the record of Soviet compliance with arms control agreements nor what we know about Soviet decision making on national security supports the view that the Soviets have a policy of noncompliance.

The conception that the Kremlin coherently embarks upon policies to violate agreements—treaties that are intimately bound up with the Soviet Union's strategic relationship with the United States and are subject to intensive verification by U.S. intelligence means—reflects a simplistic and mistaken conception of how the Soviet political system operates. In fact, there is considerable debate within the Soviet political leadership about national-security issues, and, as a result, Soviet policies shift over time.[3] A constellation of specific Soviet policies on various issues can, if they coincide, bring the Soviet Union perilously close to violating the terms of agreements. In one current case, the Abalakovo radar, such a set of factors took the Soviet Union clearly over the line between treaty adherence and violation. But such sets of policies are sensitive to both internal and external pressures, and they shift in response to these influences.

The view that the Soviets are systematically cheating on arms control agreements does not follow from the record of Soviet compliance. If the Soviets have a violations policy, they have been singularly inept at realizing significant national-security gains as a result. Let us imagine that the SS-25, encryption, and the Abalakovo radar were part of a coherent Soviet violations policy. Through Abalakovo, the Soviet Union has gained a radar that is suboptimal for early warning, space tracking, or support for ABM battle management. Through the SS-25, the Soviet Union has gained a ballistic missile that is marginally more capable than a clearly permissible version of the same system, but one that may not have sufficient throw-weight to deploy more than the single RV carried by its ostensible predecessor, the SS-13. Through encryption, the Soviet Union may have denied the United States data, but not sufficiently well to prevent U.S. complaints about the SS-25, which are asserted with seeming high confidence by the Reagan administration, based upon evidence from U.S. national technical means of verification.

The only point to a coherent Soviet violations policy would be to realize military gains. It would make little sense for the Soviets to cheat for the sake of cheating, especially considering the damage that allegations about Soviet violations have done to the arms control process and U.S.-Soviet relations. If there is a coherent policy of arms control violations, it is difficult to see how Soviet security has benefited from these three activities or from any of the behavior at issue in the U.S. charges of secondary importance. The minor benefits—perhaps even the harm to Soviet national-security interests—that have accrued from these activities argue against the violations-policy hypothesis.

Soviet Pattern

The issue of whether a pattern exists and, if so, what it is, bears more detailed scrutiny. Officially, the Reagan administration has put a good deal of emphasis on the assertion that there is a pattern of Soviet violations. When questioned about the significance of an ambiguous or dubious charge of Soviet violation, in recent years U.S. officials have asserted that, because of the Soviet pattern, each supposed Soviet arms control violation is significant beyond its specific content. According to ACDA director Adelman: "So we dare not ignore even small Soviet violations much less large ones. Regardless of their particular military significance, violations jeopardize the process and framework, particularly where there is a pattern of behavior. Failure to respond appropriately might lead the Soviets to think that they can violate their commitments with impunity."[4]

The question of whether or not a pattern of violations exists is important for two reasons. First, if a pattern does exist, it may indicate the extent to which there are mechanisms within the Soviet power structure for ensuring compliance with agreements, and the relative importance of arms control considerations and Soviet military priorities when the two conflict. Second, assuming that a pattern of Soviet violations exists, if the Soviets are suspect on a minor issue, this means they could reasonably be suspected of cheating on more major provisions of agreements. Lacking a clear pattern of violations, any attempt to heighten the importance of individual elements of Soviet compliance behavior by reference to the whole is not legitimate.

The case studies in this report do not indicate that there is a consistent pattern of violations of arms control agreements by the Soviet Union. They do, however, point to other patterns in Soviet behavior. The most important of these is that Soviet compliance is highly sensitive to the context of U.S.-Soviet relations, to the perceived threat from the United States, and to prospects for progress in U.S.-Soviet arms control. These factors affect the way in which the Soviet Union interprets arms control agreements and the way in which it responds to U.S. complaints about Soviet compliance. The Soviet Union may also view U.S. behavior and U.S. reaction to Soviet behavior as indicating what interpretations of arms control agreements the United States considers to be permissible and how the United States regards the status of the treaties.

Over the years Soviet behavior has varied with shifts in the U.S.-Soviet relationship in at least six specific ways that are relevant to compliance. First, the Soviets have tended to negotiate agreements to preserve leeway for Soviet systems under development, a practice that has been endemic to the arms control process and has been practiced by the United States as well as by the Soviet Union. Although it may lead to less significant arms control agreements, in a narrower sense this practice tends to favor compliance, ensuring that agreements are constructed in a way that will permit U.S. and Soviet programs to proceed without violating the terms of such agreements.

Second, although the Soviet tendency is to respect the overall limits of arms control agreements, the Soviets do treat some provisions like "Philadelphia lawyers"; that is, they tread as close to the limits as legally possible. During periods of poor prospects for arms control and a high Soviet perception of the military threat from the United States, permissive Soviet readings of treaty provisions have been more numerous and more pronounced.

Third, the Soviet tendency to stretch the meaning of certain provisions to the maximum has been most consistent in the case of subjective qualitative arms control restrictions. Soviet compliance with quantitative limits has been more conservative. The practice of stretching provisions to the limit has historically been more characteristic of Soviet behavior than of U.S. actions, although recent U.S. statements arguing for a permissive view of some ABM Treaty restrictions increasingly exhibit this attitude.

Fourth, the Soviets have, overall, been willing to take steps to bring their military programs into more strict compliance with agreements when the United States has challenged Soviet behavior. But this willingness has varied according to Soviet perceptions of the status of treaties, the prospects for arms control, and the manner in which the United States has advanced its concerns.

Fifth, the Soviet Union has been willing to offer security-related information in the SCC or through other diplomatic channels to clarify or support the Soviet position on compliance when it is challenged. But this Soviet willingness is coupled with the belief that secrecy about military programs should only be compromised in the arms control process when the process is yielding results sufficient to justify the compromise. When the arms control process has seemed to be stalemated, Soviet concerns about U.S. intelligence gathering have heightened, and the Soviet willingness to provide information has declined.

Sixth, when under public pressure about compliance, as in the case of Abalakovo, the Soviets have resorted to convenient explanations that represent only partial truths about Soviet behavior.

Soviet Compliance Decision Making

To explain why Soviet compliance behavior is sensitive to the state of U.S.-Soviet relations, it is necessary to understand how trade-offs between defense priorities and arms control considerations are made within the Soviet system. This is a challenging task. In the absence of information from the Soviet Union about how defense decisions are made, analysts are required to construct explanations that infer the process of defense decision making from observed outcomes.

In the case of weapons procurement more generally, researchers are mainly interested in how the process works to produce the final configuration of weapons. In the case of compliance, muddier and more difficult questions must be confronted: Why are certain programs allowed to proceed in a manner that brings them precariously close to the limits of agreements and, in the case of Abalakovo, that led to a technical violation of an agreement? Did anyone in the Soviet system know that the program in question was close to or over arms control limits? Why does a particular treaty interpretation prevail within the Soviet policy-making structure? These "why" questions are difficult to answer, since one can only hypothesize about the timing of decisions, who was involved in making them, and how the process worked.

Arthur Alexander has pointed to the shortcomings of existing scholarship on Soviet weapons acquisition and has stressed the possibilities for knowing more than we think we can know in this area by integrating data from technical analyses, interviews, Soviet writings, historical background, examination of the hardware itself, knowledge of institutional structures in the Soviet Union, and other sources.[5] However, even using a variety of data, the why of Soviet behavior on Abalakovo, the SS-25, and encryption is not easy to penetrate, and may not be possible to know with certainty.

Declining Internal Policing of Arms Control Compliance

The Soviet Union came closer to clear noncompliance in the late 1970s and early 1980s than previously, including engaging in the only current unambiguous instance of an arms control violation, the Abalakovo radar. One reason for this was that treaty limits tended to affect Soviet military programs more sharply during this period than they inhibited U.S. programs. The efforts to modernize and upgrade Soviet military capabilities brought the Kremlin closer, in other words, to the limits set by agreements than U.S. modernization programs brought the United States. But a more significant cause of the poorer Soviet compliance performance in 1979–83 probably lay in the way the Soviet domestic structure for compliance review interacted with the perceived state of U.S.-Soviet relations and with Soviet expectations of the arms control process.

Initially, the working group considered a hypothesis about Soviet compliance behavior that assumed a loosening of compliance standards in the Soviet procurement process in 1979–83, the period during which all three systems or practices of compliance concern were manifested. This model stressed the differences in magnitude between the more minor questions about Soviet compliance in the past—the "III-X silos" (see chapter 8), the SALT I SLBM launcher dismantlement rate during the 1970s, testing of the SA-5 radar—and the more recent cases. Abalakovo, for instance, is a clearer violation than all of the previous instances except Soviet noncompliance with the Interim Agreement launcher-dismantlement rate in 1976, which was acknowledged by the Soviets and quickly remedied.

This hypothesis did not fit the evidence, however, mainly because decisions on Soviet strategic programs are made quite far in advance. Though the questionable activities may have emerged in 1979–83, the procurement and design decisions relative to the SS-25, encryption, and Abalakovo would have been made much earlier.

One might therefore draw the conclusion that the Soviets simply planned all along to breach the terms of arms control agreements. But this explanation is also unsatisfactory. First, the Soviets have generally provided themselves sufficient leeway in the terms of agreements to ensure that they would not have to violate in order to make planned force modernizations. Second, as mentioned, there has been no previous pattern of clear Soviet violations.

As a result, the working group arrived at a considerably more complex conception of the Soviet internal process that may have produced the decisions on the three cases dealt with at length in this report. The working group concluded that the design of Soviet military programs did not actively change for the worse in terms of compliance in the 1979–83 period. Rather, the Soviet military as a general rule may design programs that tread close to the limits set by agreements. Or the Soviet Union may, as mentioned, negotiate agreements close to the design parameters of systems already under development. In the past the Soviet political leadership may have intervened to constrain programs to fit within the terms of agreements or to take actions to bring programs into compliance when challenged by the United States.

During the 1979–83 period, however, Soviet expectations about the future of the arms control process were low, whereas their estimate of the future military threat from the United States was high. As a result, between 1979 and 1983 the Soviet political leadership may have had very little interest in policing Soviet military programs to ensure a conservative approach toward compliance, and essentially no interest in accommodating U.S. concerns about compliance by altering Soviet behavior. The military procurement system was working as usual during the 1970s; the main difference during the years 1979 to 1983 was that the political leadership probably did not seek to constrain Soviet programs in favor of compliance and did not respond cooperatively to U.S. concerns about Soviet compliance.

Anticipatory Decision Making

Soviet decision making on compliance may be thought to comprise two phases: anticipatory and reactive. The first is the stage at which military programs are under design or development, when compliance concerns might be considered in an anticipatory fashion.

Once the political leadership in the Soviet Union sets the general requirements for weapons in line with strategic necessities, the Soviet military is then responsible for optimizing the design of a system within those parameters. Weapon-design and -development decisions are managed by the Soviet military, which may be subject to less consistent intervention from the political sector than occurs in the U.S. system.[6]

The primary interest of the Soviet military and military industry is in ensuring that Soviet security needs are met, which entails designing programs that are optimal for military effectiveness and economic efficiency. Although aware of treaty limitations, the Soviet military plans programs that exploit the permissible activities to the fullest. In the case of Abalakovo, the military crossed the compliance line in pursuit of efficiency and strategic priorities.

Any routine assessments of compliance with existing treaties made during the development of a military program would probably be performed by the military itself. The Legal and Treaties Directorate of the Soviet General Staff, headed by Colonel General Nikolai Chervov, is most likely the body responsible for assessing the legality of a planned Soviet military program in light of Soviet treaty obligations, if such a judgment were requested. The tendency of such an agency, because it is part of the military system whose goal is to optimize military benefits of weapon systems, would likely be to rationalize a desirable Soviet military program as compliant with the terms of treaties.

Awareness of Treaty Limits

Top Soviet military officials are not unaware of the obligations the Soviet Union has undertaken through arms control treaties. The military has, in fact, had considerable influence in shaping those obligations.

During the 1970s the Soviet military was more influential in the formulation of arms control policy than even the Soviet Ministry of Foreign Affairs, which had titular responsibility for the SALT negotiations. The head of the Soviet SALT I delegation, Vladimir Semenov, a deputy foreign minister, observed in the early 1970s that the Foreign Ministry took a back seat to the military in the formulation of Soviet arms control policy. His ministry's function, he stated, was limited to selecting those formulas for possible agreement that would not interfere with "the realization of Soviet military programs."[7]

Writing in 1979 about the SALT experience up to that point, Thomas Wolfe observed that, in designing arms control agreements, the Soviet leadership was "able to turn for substantive advice only to the bureaucracy whose institutional interests were most at stake in defense policy issues — the military establishment itself. . . . The military . . . can be said to have acquired a substantial amount of leverage both upon national security policy as a whole and upon SALT as an important aspect of it."[8] It was during the early–to–mid-1970s era, the period about which Wolfe and Semenov made their observations, that Soviet decisions about the programs discussed in this report were made.

The elements of the Soviet military leadership involved in arms control in the 1970s included the Ministry of Defense, the Soviet General Staff, and high-level political-civilian-military bodies such as the Defense Council and the Military-Industrial Commission. Representatives of the military-industrial sector, directly responsible for procuring weapon systems, also participated in the SALT negotiations. In 1969 and 1970 Aleksandr Shchukin, a member of the Military-Industrial Commission, and Petr Pleshakov, the Minister of Radio Industry (which has responsibility for radar), both took part in the SALT negotiations. Leonid Smirnov, chairman of the Military-Industrial Commission, was also involved.[9]

The Soviet military's heavy involvement in the negotiating process guarantees that those who oversee military programs are cognizant of the obligations the agreements contain.[10] Pleshakov's ministry, for instance, would have had responsibility for the procurement and construction of the Abalakovo radar. As a participant in the ABM Treaty negotiations, the implications of the planned Soviet LPAR system for ABM Treaty compliance could hardly have escaped his attention. However, there is a natural tension in the Soviet Union, as there is in the United States, between treaty compliance and other considerations related to national-security policies and weapons development.

Given the fact that treaties do contain ambiguities, left to itself the military likely chooses a permissive interpretation of Soviet obligations under the terms of the agreements. The net effect of the Soviet domestic policy-making structure has been that, in the weapon-procurement process, arms control compliance has been weighed against more narrow military priorities in a somewhat fragile balance.

U.S.-Soviet Differences

The main difference between the U.S. and Soviet systems for compliance review does not lie in the formal structure of the internal government processes. In formal structure, the processes are not all that different. The responsibility for executive-branch compliance review in the United States rests mainly with the office of the Director of Defense Research and Engineering, the Defense Department office responsible for the development and design of new weapon systems. Left to itself, DOD may tend to pursue weapon systems that would not comply with arms agreements. For example, many arms control analysts charged that the Dense Pack basing for the MX missile, which was developed by the U.S. Air Force in 1982, would have violated the Interim Agreement ban on new fixed ICBM launchers, in force at the time. Nonetheless, Dense Pack was endorsed by the Pentagon and even by President Reagan in a public address in November 1982.

In the United States the State Department legal adviser and the general counsels of the Defense Department and ACDA have a role in making judgments about the compliance aspects of prospective weapon systems. Their approach fluctuates, however, with the political interests of particular administrations. Where these individuals have become involved, they do not necessarily play a watchdog role with regard to treaty compliance. In a case in 1985, in which the State Department legal adviser was asked to review U.S. obligations under the ABM Treaty in light of the SDI program, the result was an extremely permissive interpretation of U.S. obligations.[11]

The real difference between the U.S. and Soviet systems for compliance review is societal rather than structural. The Soviet Union lacks the legislative and public constituencies that lobby for compliance with arms control agreements in the United States. In the United States these constituencies exert an oversight function, consistently balancing the more permissive interpretations of the military and often the executive branch as a whole to produce policies that generally uphold treaty compliance. In the Soviet Union there is no open press to question government interpretations of treaty provisions, no independent legislative body to examine the compliance aspects of weapon systems in their design phase through Arms Control Impact Statements (or to threaten funding cutoffs for programs that exceed treaty limits as the U.S. Congress did in 1986), and certainly no independent arms control community to establish a Campaign to Save the ABM Treaty, as was the case in the United States. Finally there is no agency in the Soviet Union equivalent to the U.S. Arms Control and Disarmament Agency to coordinate arms control policy and to serve as an advocate within the government for a more restrictive reading of treaty provisions, as ACDA has done at times in the United States.

There is thus no effective anticipatory oversight of compliance with agreements built into the system in the Soviet Union. To the extent that such anticipatory oversight would occur, it would probably only be through the strong commitment of a general secretary or other Politburo members to ensure Soviet compliance, which might lead them, for example, to examine Soviet military programs for their compliance with agreements or to alter programs to conform to treaty obligations. Because there is no broadly based constituency for compliance in the Soviet Union, the balance between military priorities and compliance has been particularly sensitive to changes in the Soviet perception of the prospects for arms control and of the U.S. military threat.

The Soviet political leadership's intervention in military procurement for various reasons has been noted in a number of cases.[12] According to Michael MccGwire: "The record shows that during [the] design and development period, a high proportion of major Soviet weapon systems have undergone significant changes in their role, their method of employment, and their production schedules. This has been the result of changes in requirements that themselves stemmed from changes in the external environment, in internal priorities, or in operational concepts."[13]

A case has been made that in 1970–71 the political leadership decided to bring Soviet ICBM silo and launcher construction programs into congruence with the expected limits of the SALT I Interim Agreement. MccGwire has examined the apparent Soviet plans for a force of ICBMs based on 336 deployments per year from 1966 onward. In the first half of 1969, MccGwire argues, the Soviets cut back the deployment of ICBMs targeted on North America to a level matching U.S. ICBMs targeted on the Soviet Union, more than halving the production rate to 144 ICBMs per year.[14]

Then, according to Raymond Garthoff, in anticipation of the limits on offensive forces, agreement on which was reached in the SALT negotiations in May 1971, the Soviet leadership stopped ICBM launcher construction altogether, freezing their land-based missile force at the number then deployed or under construction.[15] These two actions may have been a signal to the United States that the Soviet Union was strongly interested in the completion of the SALT I agreement and intended to support it.

Perhaps because of its own heightened sense of threat, top Soviet political leaders might have been disinclined to raise compliance concerns about Soviet military programs in the late 1970s and early 1980s. Soviet military procurement operated as usual, treading perhaps harder on the terms of agreements because of the deeper qualitative limits imposed by SALT II. This situation probably produced the period of Soviet compliance that was poorer than previous practice. Soviet compliance deteriorated until the end of 1983 then gradually improved. The improvement may have indicated that the top Soviet leaders saw better prospects for arms control and thus once again took an interest in Soviet compliance.

Reactive Decision Making

Once the United States has raised a compliance concern in the SCC, the Soviet Union must contemplate a position to defend its behavior, negotiate an understanding to tighten the treaty provision at issue, accuse the United States of violations, or follow some other policy approach. The influence of the military in this second stage of decision making is still strong. All three Soviet SCC commissioners have been prominent military general officers: General G. I. Ustinov, General Viktor Starodubov, and, presently, General Vladimir Medvedev. The Soviet SCC delegation, like other arms control negotiating teams, is staffed and supported by the Legal and Treaties Directorate of the General Staff.

When the United States complains about Soviet compliance, the Soviet political leadership and other security and foreign-policy institutions of the government necessarily become involved in examining Soviet military programs from the standpoint of treaty compliance. The involvement of institutions interested in wider Soviet foreign-policy goals than the military causes the Soviet political leadership to take other factors into account—including the state of U.S.-Soviet relations, the prospects for arms control, and its view of the U.S. military threat—in determining its response to a U.S. compliance concern.

Two special press conferences, held in Moscow in May and June of 1985 to discuss the U.S. decision to abandon SALT II, illustrate the broader involvement once a U.S. compliance challenge has been made. The press conferences took place at the Soviet Foreign Ministry, and the spokesmen were Chief of the Soviet General Staff Akhromeyev, and Soviet Deputy Foreign Minister Bessmertnykh, giving joint status to the defense sector and the Foreign Ministry in dealing with compliance questions.

Participation in the reactive stage extends beyond the Foreign Ministry, sometimes involving specialized institutions with expertise or jurisdiction related to the agreement in question. The State Committee on the Utilization of Atomic Energy has shared influence with the Foreign Ministry in governing Soviet nuclear exporting practices that have implications for compliance with the Non-Proliferation Treaty.[16]

Decisions on the Soviet position in the SCC may be made in a special interagency group, including representatives of the Central Committee, the Defense Ministry, the General Staff, the Foreign Ministry, institutions with special expertise, and the KGB. This broad involvement may explain why the Soviet Union was relatively open during the 1970s to understandings negotiated through the SCC that sought to tighten treaty provisions and hence placed further restraints on Soviet military programs.

The involvement of a broad constituency does not insure that the Soviet Union will compromise in order to resolve compliance disputes. Once a U.S. challenge has been made, the Soviet political and military leadership must make a policy calculation based on its perception of the status of U.S.-Soviet relations and the prospects for future arms control agreements, and therefore its interest in compromise versus pursuit of unilateral military priorities. During periods when the Soviet perception of the U.S. threat is high, the political leadership may be more susceptible to the military leadership's permissive interpretations about compliance with agreements. In periods of productive arms control negotiations, the Soviets have exhibited both more restraint in the procurement process as it affects compliance and a greater willingness to take ameliorative action at the request of the United States, making trade-offs in favor of maintaining good relations with the United States and furthering the arms control process.

Patterns of Behavior

The characteristics of the Soviet internal process just described produce the patterns of Soviet compliance behavior mentioned at the beginning of this chapter.

Negotiating to Preserve Existing Programs

Because of the influence of military priorities in arms negotiations, the Soviet Union has historically negotiated agreements to provide leeway to proceed with programs already in the design or development pipeline. An example of this Soviet practice was the SS-19 ICBM, developed in the early 1970s and deployed subsequent to the signing of the SALT I agreements. The Soviets protected their ability to deploy the SS-19, necessary in their view as part of their MIRVing program, by avoiding a precise definition in the Interim Agreement of what constituted a "heavy missile." The Soviets refused to accede to U.S. Unilateral Statement D, which identified a heavy ICBM as any missile greater than the largest "light" ICBM then operational on either side—the Soviet SS-11.

The misconception has persisted in the United States that the SS-19 constitutes a violation of the SALT I agreement. Secretary of State Henry Kissinger created the impression in the United States, through congressional briefings at the time of SALT I, that the agreement would preclude Soviet deployment of new, heavier ICBMs. In fact, according to Garthoff, the Congress misconstrued Kissinger's testimony. The Interim Agreement contained a restriction on the expansion of the "dimensions" of existing ICBM silos (no more than 10–15 percent). Kissinger conveyed the impression that this limit would prevent deployment of ICBMs significantly larger than the SS-11. In fact, a 15 percent increase in each of the dimensions—depth and diameter—was equal to a 52 percent increase in volume, a change quite ample to accommodate the SS-19.[17]

The Soviet delegation reportedly informed U.S. representatives during the SALT I negotiations of the general size and character of two new Soviet ICBMs, and said that the existence of these ICBMs was the reason the Soviet Union could not accept the U.S. proposed definition of a light ICBM as one equal to or smaller than the SS-11. U.S. intelligence also confirmed this Soviet interpretation of SALT I during the 1972 Moscow summit.[18]

According to Rand Corporation analyst Arnold Horelick: "It was clear from the way their programs were going that there would be something lighter than a heavy missile and heavier than a light missile, and the unwillingness of the Soviets to nail down that distinction obviously meant that they had something in-between, which was closer to heavy. We signed anyway." In Horelick's view, "If we are willing to sign such a provision, we, as well as the Soviets, should bear some of the blame."[19]

Although this approach has raised questions about Soviet arms control compliance, the Soviet Union has hardly made a secret of its intention not to be bound by military restraints on its programs other than those precisely embodied in the terms of agreements. President Nixon reported that the following statement was made to him by Soviet General Secretary Brezhnev at the SALT I summit in June 1972: "Mr. Brezhnev made it absolutely clear to me that in those areas that were not controlled by our offensive agreement that they were going ahead with their programs."[20]

What Nixon did not add, according to Garthoff, is that he told Brezhnev that the United States would uphold the provisions of the agreements but would also proceed with military programs consistent with the limits.[21] The United States has engaged in quite similar behavior to that of the Soviet Union, holding out, for example, for an exemption for one "new type" of ICBM in SALT II to protect the MX program. The United States also refused to negotiate a MIRV ban in the Interim Agreement, in order to permit completion of the U.S. ICBM and SLBM MIRVing program then in progress.

The United States also held out for including a ban on long-range–cruise-missile deployment only in the two-year SALT II Protocol, to permit U.S. deployment of cruise missiles in the European theater. Likewise, the United States would agree to a ban on flight testing or deployment of mobile missiles only if it would expire in two years, in order to protect the U.S. MX program.

This pattern has been characteristic of superpower behavior in the arms control process, each side seeking to preserve key modernization options. Needless to say, it has substantially weakened the ability of arms control agreements to regulate and/or limit many of the most important military activities of the two superpowers.

Exploiting Ambiguities

In its military programs, as well as in its international behavior more generally, the Soviet Union charts a course as close as possible to the limits embodied in the agreements it has signed, usually stopping just short of violating the letter of the law. Where ambiguity about the meaning of provisions exists, the Soviets have exploited it to advance their high-priority national-security goals.

This same pattern of behavior has been visible in the Soviet approach to the explicit and tacit rules of conduct governing Soviet activities in Cuba. The Soviet pattern since 1962 has been one of testing the limits of the Kennedy-Khrushchev understanding that the Soviet Union would refrain from introducing offensive forces into Cuba, which the Soviet Union agreed to observe in return for a U.S. guarantee not to attempt another invasion of Cuba. This understanding left ambiguous the question of what constituted offensive forces in Cuba. The Soviet Union tested the limits of this agreement by commencing in 1970 to build servicing facilities for nuclear missile–carrying submarines at the Cuban port of Cienfuegos. It was only when the United States made clear that it considered "offensive forces in Cuba" to include support for strategic offensive submarines that the Soviet Union halted construction of the servicing facilities.[22]

This pattern has been clearly evident in the Soviet attitude to arms control compliance. Consider the Soviet approach to the "concurrent testing" provision of the ABM Treaty. In this case, the Soviet Union has come so close to exceeding the limits of an agreement that, with U.S. worst-case assumptions or verification uncertainties, it is debatable whether Soviet behavior is in compliance.

This Soviet approach to the terms of agreements continues to be seen today in the Soviet position on encryption. In the absence of a definition of "impede," the Soviet Union construes the meaning of the SALT II provision to permit almost complete encryption of telemetry. This raises the issue of whether Soviet behavior is interfering with U.S. verification.

The same type of behavior is practiced by the United States, but with less consistency. Different U.S. administrations are committed in varying degrees to the expansion of U.S. military capabilities and thus tread close upon the limits of agreements more irregularly than do the Soviets, who throughout the arms control era have maintained a high commitment to new weapon programs.

It is common practice by the Soviets to provide strong signals in the negotiating process about their interpretations of agreements, and especially about provisions that they find less than satisfactory. When a provision that the United States wants badly will interfere with an ongoing or projected military program of importance to the Soviet Union, and the United States is unwilling on principle to yield its position, the Soviets have made it clear by the way they negotiate that they will stretch the interpretation of that particular provision to the breaking point.

The areas that have sparked the greatest U.S. concern about Soviet compliance are those about which the Soviets have expressed the greatest reservations during negotiations, and which they have refused to agree to except in the last phase of negotiations, when compromises are sometimes made for the sake of concluding the agreement. The Soviets have signaled to the United States their interpretations of these treaty provisions throughout the arms control negotiating process, but the United States has not been attuned to these signals and has failed to adjust its expectations about Soviet compliance accordingly.

Thus, it should not be altogether surprising that compliance controversies have arisen over the new-type and encryption provisions of the SALT II agreement. Agreement on these provisions was achieved only in the final weeks of the seven-year SALT II negotiations. The Soviet Union had strongly resisted qualitative limits that would restrict improvements to ICBM guidance as well as an absolute ban on ICBM modernization.[23] They agreed to the 5 percent modernization limit on the physical parameters of ICBMs only in the spring of 1979, shortly before the treaty was signed.

A similar sequence characterized the negotiations on encryption. Although there was some sentiment in the U.S. intelligence community for a complete ban on encryption in SALT II, neither the United States nor the Soviet Union would agree to such a provision. But the Soviet position throughout much of the negotiations was more extreme: that flight-test telemetry was not relevant to verifying SALT II compliance and should not be restricted by the treaty. The result of the Soviet dislike for encryption restraints was the lawyerly formulation on "impeding" verification through encryption, which sought both to protect Soviet secrecy in the testing of such missile parameters as accuracy and to safeguard U.S. access to telemetry related to SALT II limits.[24]

The Soviet Union's dislike of restrictions on encryption and on new missile types, and its determination to exploit to the full the ambiguities it had succeeded in preserving in the agreement, led to questions about Soviet compliance. In pushing to the limit the provisions allowing encryption short of impeding and 5 percent changes in the parameters of ICBMs, Soviet behavior differed only in degree from past practice. It is remarkable that the United States did not interpret the Soviet hesitations about the new-type provision of SALT II as a signal, in light of the existence in the pipeline of several new Soviet ICBM types.

The tendency of the Soviets to exploit ambiguities has varied somewhat over time with the phasing of their major military modernization programs. The tendency also varies over time according to the interests of the political leadership in restraining Soviet programs as designed by the military.

The Soviets' "Philadelphia lawyer" approach does not in itself constitute bad faith toward treaty provisions. During periods when the political leadership has manifested greater interest in accommodation with the United States, the Soviet Union has been willing in a number of cases to accept more restrictive language regarding treaty provisions, when such a tightening or clarification is applied jointly to U.S. and Soviet activities through the SCC. Such was the case in 1985, when an agreement was reached in the SCC to prohibit concurrent operation of SAMs and ABM radars (see chapter 8).

The Secrecy–Arms Control Trade-off

The leaders of the Soviet Union, and of Russia before the revolution, have treated control over the outside world's access to information about their country—and especially its military forces—as an important component of national power. Only with great reluctance and foot dragging have Soviet leaders conceded that sharing some information about their military programs may be necessary in the arms control process, to increase the other side's confidence, to enhance verifiability, and to aid in the resolution of compliance disputes by clarifying Soviet practices under question.

Soviet leaders view the sharing of any militarily sensitive information as potentially useful to an adversary for intelligence purposes, and thus as a compromise on the part of the Soviet Union. The extent to which this is true is poorly understood in the United States. The Soviet view is that any sharing of information, through enhanced verification procedures like on-site inspection, should only take place when such concessions are absolutely necessary to secure some significant advantage.

A key Soviet work on verification, published in 1983 by Roland Timerbayev, the deputy Soviet ambassador to the United Nations, makes this point abundantly clear. Unless they occur in the context of significant progress in arms control, the Soviet position has been that verification measures are simply an attempt to legitimize U.S. intelligence gathering on Soviet programs. Timerbayev refers frequently to the "principle of proportionality in verification and disarmament."[25]

The importance of this principle is quite evident in recent Soviet practice. One trend that emerges clearly from the compliance picture of the late 1970s to the mid-1980s is that, as the prospects for arms control declined, the Soviet tendency to be wary of divulging security-related information increased. The Soviets were willing to provide less voluntary data on military exercises in performance of their Helsinki Final Act obligations. They were less willing to provide information in the SCC to aid in the resolution of compliance disputes. The increasing level of Soviet encryption of missile–flight-test telemetry after 1979 can also be seen in this light.

The Soviet Union had been willing until 1979 to move toward an unprecedented (albeit still limited) level of openness about its military programs, in deference to the requirements of the arms control process. The Soviets have always seen this greater openness as a trade-off for arms control benefits. With the deterioration of the arms control process, the Soviets were quick to see this trade-off as a one-way street.

Partial Explanations Under Pressure

It is characteristic of Soviet behavior, especially when publicly challenged by the United States about activities related to key Soviet national-security interests, to resort to partial truths to rationalize their activities. This has been the hallmark of the Soviet response to the controversy surrounding the Abalakovo radar, the one case in which the Soviet Union has clearly contravened the terms of an agreement.

The Soviet position on Abalakovo has been that the radar is to be used for space tracking. This explanation has been offered by a number of Soviet officials, including former Ambassador Anatoly Dobrynin and Chief of the General Staff Sergei Akhromeyev, and it has been the Soviet position in the SCC.[26] Various data, including the location, orientation, and angle of the radar's antennae have been cited to support this explanation.

It is true that the radar may have space-tracking capabilities. But this begs the question of whether space tracking is its only or primary function. The Soviet position in the case of Abalakovo is highly reminiscent of a small number of other cases in which the Soviet Union has expressed a partial truth to explain Soviet behavior.[27] A recent, parallel case was the affair of the Soviet "combat" brigade in Cuba in 1979, when the Soviet Union claimed that the unit in question was involved in training Cuban soldiers in the use of Soviet weapons. Taken literally, this was correct, but it was not the full story. The brigade probably also had a number of other functions.

Decision-Making Patterns and Abalakovo

These Soviet tendencies—preserving existing programs, stretching the meaning of treaty provisions, increasing secrecy when arms negotiations are unproductive, resorting to partial truth under pressure, and especially the unwillingness of the political leadership to constrain military programs or accommodate U.S. concerns when arms control is stalemated—all came to bear on the current cases of concern about Soviet compliance. They were at work most notably in the case of the Abalakovo radar.

To understand the likely sequence of decisions affecting these programs, it is necessary to estimate the timing of Soviet decisions. Table 3 depicts the working group's best estimate about the timing of Soviet decision making on the SS-25, encryption, and the Abalakovo radar. Initial procurement decisions on the three Soviet activities of greatest compliance concern were probably made between 1971 and 1975. Decisions to flight-test the SS-25, to approve deployment of the radar, and to increase encryption were all probably made at later dates.

In the case of Abalakovo, the decision to upgrade the Soviet early-warning network through the Pechora-type LPARs was likely to have been made at the time the Eighth Five-Year Plan was approved in 1971, prior to the conclusion of the ABM Treaty. The general area of Abalakovo's siting may also have been set at this time; in addition, there was some urgency to begin its construction in order to address the emerging threat of the Trident SLBM program. Given this timing, the Soviets may not have recognized that the location of this particular radar would be likely to conflict with ABM Treaty obligations.

In all likelihood, the Soviet Defense Council, and possibly the Politburo, would have approved the decision to build the radar system as a whole. Final approval for the construction of individual LPARs to be built during particular five-year plans would probably have been given at the time each plan was approved. Thus, construction of a second group of radars, including Abalakovo, the preceding radar at Michelevka, and perhaps others,

Table 3
Chronology: Abalakovo, SS-25, Encryption

	1971	1974	1975	1976	1978	1981	1982	1983	1985	1986	1988–89
Abalakovo	Pechora system probably approved			LPARs at Abalakovo and Michelevka probably approved	Construction probably begins			United States detects in July		External construction complete	Operation expected
SS-25			Requirement for SS-25 likely determined			First flight test expected but delayed	Go-ahead for flight test probably given in October	First flight test conducted in February	Deployment begins		
Encryption		United States notes first Soviet encryption			United States notes increased encryption in SS-18 test	United States notes second major increase, to current level					

was probably approved in 1976. Site preparation for Abalakovo likely began in 1981, with U.S. detection occurring two years later, in July 1983.

Reasons for Siting of Abalakovo

A combination of economic and strategic rationales may well have led the Soviet military to the Abalakovo site for the sixth in the Soviet network of early-warning LPARs. If one charts the placement of the Pechora-class LPARs, it is clear that they have been constructed in priority order, first to close the gaps in Soviet early-warning coverage, and then, when that task was accomplished, to respond to the deployment of new U.S. offensive nuclear forces.

The Soviet need to place an early-warning radar in this particular area was relatively urgent. New U.S. long-range Trident C-4 SLBM deployments in the northern Pacific in the mid-to-late 1970s, and the prospective deployment of the D-5, had made it imperative that the Soviet Union close a gap in early-warning coverage on the country's northeastern perimeter. Prior to Abalakovo, this area had probably not been effectively covered by Hen House radars, the older generation of Soviet early-warning radars that the Pechora-class radars were designed to augment or replace. This area constituted the last remaining complete gap in the Soviet early-warning network.

The Soviets continued to add LPARs to their network after Abalakovo, but only to replace or add to the capabilities of existing Hen House radars. The later deployments followed the secondary pattern of Soviet response to increased U.S. threats. Two LPARs under construction beginning in 1985 or 1986 along the western periphery of the European Soviet Union will provide early warning for the short–warning-time Pershing II, deployment of which began in late 1983.[28] They will also augment Hen House coverage for the European part of the Soviet Union.

For coverage of the northeastern area, the Soviet Union may have faced a choice. They could build two LPARs on the periphery of the Soviet Union—one to the north on the Arctic Ocean, and one to the east on the Sea of Okhotsk. Or they could build a single LPAR set back from the border. Such a radar would cover a much wider area, a short distance out from the Soviet coastline, than one located on the periphery (see map 3). A third possibility might have been to accept poorer coverage by building a more expensive single radar facility on the northeastern coast, designed especially for its location and climatic conditions.

A number of factors likely affected this Soviet choice. If the Soviets had chosen to build radars on the periphery, they would have been forced to build on permafrost, which would not only present construction difficulties, thereby increasing costs, but could also degrade the functioning of the radar. The heat from the facility could melt the permafrost layer underneath, creating instability in the radar structure. The Soviets have skirted

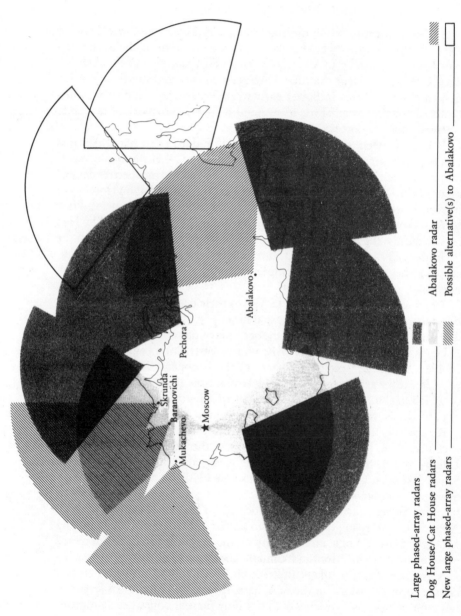

Large phased-array radars ▬▬▬▬▬
Dog House/Cat House radars ▬▬▬▬▬
New large phased-array radars ▨▨▨▨▨

Abalakowo radar ▨▨▨ ☐
Possible alternative(s) to Abalakovo ▬▬▬▬▬

Map 3. **Possible alternative coverage fans of Soviet large phased-array radars** (adapted from U.S. Defense Department. *Soviet Military Power*, 5th ed. [Washington, March 1986], 44)

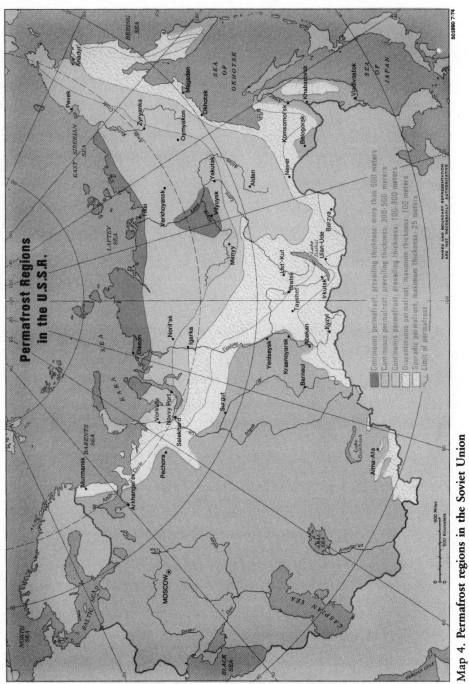

Map 4. **Permafrost regions in the Soviet Union**

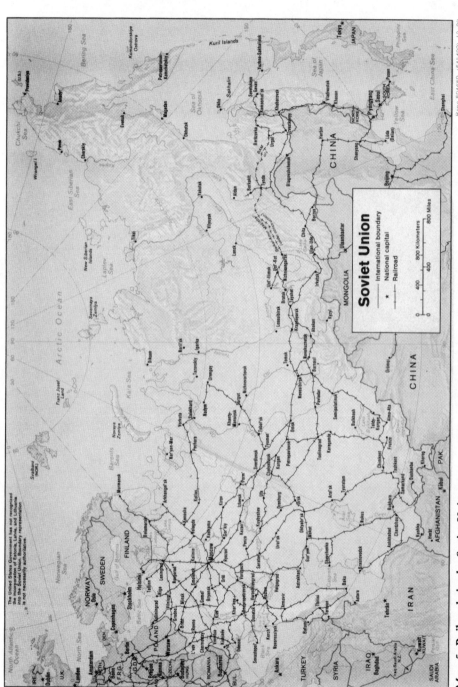

Map 5. Railroads in the Soviet Union

the permafrost border in deploying their LPAR network (see map 4). The only site without permafrost in northeastern Siberia is apparently the tip of the Kamchatka Peninsula, which might have provided only partial coverage of the early-warning gap, and might have had to be complemented by a second radar on the Arctic Ocean.

Second, two radars, or one specially designed radar, would have been substantially more costly to the Soviet Union than the facility built at Abalakovo. The U.S. Defense Intelligence Agency conservatively estimates the cost of each face of the two-faced Pechora-class radars at between $300 million and $400 million. Other sources estimate that the cost is higher.[29]

Third, a site more northerly than Abalakovo would have been remote from ground transportation lines, and this would have presented further logistical problems in constructing the radar (see map 5). The trans-Siberian railroad extends to Krasnoyarsk, which is a short distance from the Abalakovo site overland or via the Yenisey River. The previous five Soviet LPARs are all located near major railways.

Fourth, the interior location of the radar potentially provides better impact-point prediction for incoming warheads than would sites on the periphery. But, because of its setback, the Abalakovo radar represents a degraded early-warning capability in comparison to the functioning of two such radars built on the periphery. Because of the location of Abalakovo, the Soviets are likely to lose six minutes of early warning of U.S. SLBM attack.[30] Also, because of the angle of its faces in relation to the curvature of the earth, the field of the Abalakovo radar may be less capable than radars on the periphery of detecting certain depressed-trajectory SLBM attacks, should the United States develop such a capability in the future. Even these drawbacks were probably accepted as a trade-off in favor of economy and the ability of the radar sited at Abalakovo to contribute to the tracking of space vehicles, including flights of the Soviet space shuttle.

Fifth, the Soviet Union may have also had a strategic reason for siting the radar so far west. MccGwire argues that in 1966 a major reformulation of Soviet strategic thinking occurred. Revised Soviet military doctrine held that if a war occurred with the United States it might not result in a cataclysmic nuclear war. After 1966 Soviet doctrine envisioned the possibility of a conventional attack on the Soviet Union from the east, as part of a protracted East-West conflict. MccGwire contends that after 1966 Soviet military strategy envisioned a fallback defense perimeter at the Yenisey River, to protect European Russia from such an attack. According to MccGwire, beginning in the early 1970s, when this doctrinal shift began to affect military programs, all new major Soviet fixed military assets not related to the Asian-Pacific theater, whenever possible within the limits of operational requirements, were located west of the Yenisey River fallback defense perimeter.[31] The Abalakovo radar lies just west of the river.

From the standpoint of economics, ease of construction, reliable functioning, strategy, and effective coverage, the decision to site the radar at Abalakovo made considerable sense. It also may be that insufficient funding was provided to the military industry to place a radar or radars on the periphery, given the greater expense of constructing such a facility nearer the coast. These concerns obviously prevailed over any arms control considerations in the Soviet military in selecting its preference for siting the radar.

We have noted that adjustments in Soviet programs to ensure compliance with agreements probably only occur through intervention of the top political leadership. How much did the Soviet leadership know about the compliance questions raised by the radar? According to Garthoff, Georgiy Arbatov, director of the Soviet Union's Institute of the USA and Canada, has claimed that the decisions on the siting of the radar were made at a relatively low level in the Soviet system, without Politburo or Defense Council review, in 1978–79.[32]

This may be an attempt by the Soviet Union to attribute the radar siting decision to a low-level bureaucratic error. One factor that argues against low-level decision making is the cost of such a radar system. Any military decision involving the expenditure of from $600 million to $800 million, depending on which estimate is correct (and potentially twice that amount, if the debate was between building two radars on the periphery and one inland), almost certainly involves high-level Soviet decision makers. Decisions on strategic systems and nonroutine matters, the former of which did and the latter of which could have characterized Abalakovo, are thought to be forced upward to high levels in the Soviet system.[33]

Even assuming that the Abalakovo issue reached the Politburo, it is unlikely that the military industry would have presented the question of the radar site as a compliance issue. When the Pechora system as a whole was considered in 1971, documents, including a list of locations for the radar and other data, would probably have been presented to the Politburo. But in 1971 the ABM Treaty was not yet finalized. The Soviet Union was still holding to the position that LPARs other than those specifically for ABM uses should not be limited by provisions such as that later embodied in Article VI(b), which restricted LPARs, other than those for verification or space tracking, to the periphery. There would have been no immediate compliance issue related to Abalakovo in 1971.

An expenditure limit for the radar could have been set by higher authority, causing the military-procurement organs to design the facility in a non-compliant site to stay within the financial constraints imposed. Even if the radar was put before the Politburo or Defense Council around 1976 for a final construction decision, representatives of the Soviet military-industrial sector would not have tended, on their own, to raise a compliance issue posed by the proposed siting of the radar. Brezhnev or other Politburo members would have been highly unlikely to scrutinize defense plans in sufficient detail to ask about the compliance of any one component with agreements. Had they done so, Politburo members would likely have been assured that the radar was in compliance.

The top Soviet leadership tends to work on the basis of specialization. The Politburo has its recognized experts on agriculture, energy, and defense matters. The ruling body as a whole tends to defer to the individual or group of members with greatest expertise on the subject at issue. If the Politburo members prominent in defense policy, which during this period were the general secretary and Defense Minister Ustinov, either did not take issue with a position presented by the military industry or actively supported it in order to stay within budgetary limits, then the remainder of the political leadership would probably have deferred to their colleagues.

Somewhere in the Soviet defense establishment, at some point, someone must have been aware that the radar could be considered a violation. But the first time senior Soviet leaders were likely to have learned that the Abalakovo radar presented a compliance problem may have been when the United States raised the issue in the SCC. Even had they questioned the site of the radar, Politburo members might well have been assured that, if the United States were to protest the location of Abalakovo, the Soviet Union could always stress its space-tracking functions. If Soviet political leaders recognized the compliance problem, they decided to pursue it no further.

Role of the Political Leadership

Construction of the Abalakovo radar likely proceeded despite the clear compliance problem it would present because of two additional factors that decreased the probability that the Soviet political leadership would raise compliance concerns regarding its site.

The first of these factors might have been the relatively mild U.S. response to the siting of an earlier Soviet radar. In 1981 the United States raised questions in the SCC about the location of the first Soviet 1970s-vintage LPAR, located at Pechora. This site was about 200 kilometers inland from the periphery of the Soviet Union, near the Barents Sea. Following the SCC discussion, the United States accepted this radar, despite its distance from the border of the Soviet Union. This may have signaled to some elements of the Soviet national-security bureaucracy that the United States would accept installations this far from the periphery as being within ABM Treaty limits. The Soviets may have perceived U.S. interests in preserving the ABM Treaty regime to be strong enough in the late 1970s to allow for the Soviet interpretation on Abalakovo.

As discussed elsewhere, the Soviets may have tried to float a trial balloon in 1981 to test out this more permissive interpretation of the meaning of "periphery." At the October 23 session of the SCC, the Soviets responded to U.S. concerns about the Pechora radar by stating that the location of the radars had to take account of "technical and practical considerations involved in their placement." This statement was reportedly repeated at the SCC in 1982.[34] This does not, of course, explain how the Soviet Union could have believed that the United States would accept a radar located 700 kilometers from the Soviet border with Mongolia and oriented across much of northeastern Siberia.

A second factor that might have induced the Soviet leadership to approve the deployment decision, despite its implications for compliance, was the probable lower saliency of arms control compliance concerns due to increased perceptions of the U.S. military threat. Such perceptions were likely to have decreased the leadership's interest in constraining military programs in favor of compliance. Soviet political leaders may have been unwilling to intervene in the Abalakovo project in a manner that would sacrifice efficiency in order to uphold strict compliance. When the issue was later raised by the United States, neither political nor military leaders had much incentive to work through the SCC to resolve compliance disputes as had occurred in the 1970s, because of their view that the United States was in the process of abandoning its own arms control commitments.

Soviet Perceptions in the Early 1980s

During 1981 and 1982 the West was afforded an unusual public glimpse of the Soviet military's heightened sense of threat from the United States and its view of its implications for the status of arms control treaties. In the July 1981 issue of *Kommunist*, the Communist Party theoretical journal, Chief of the General Staff Marshal Nikolai Ogarkov wrote a striking article. In it he stressed the increased threat to Soviet security from the West since the advent of the Reagan administration. He argued that the United States was pursuing a course for achieving military superiority over the Soviet Union. As a major trend in U.S. policy, Ogarkov insisted that the U.S. administration was "working to wreck the treaties that have been concluded with the Soviet Union, and also the talks on limiting and reducing armaments." Ogarkov charged that the United States was undermining the SALT I agreement, the ABM Treaty, and SALT II. He noted, "Many high ranking administration officials, the President included, are openly stating that the SALT II treaty allegedly places the United States at a disadvantage and must therefore be radically revised."[35]

Ogarkov proceeded to state that the Soviet Union would not permit the United States and its allies to gain military superiority over the USSR. He argued for a greater capacity to mobilize Soviet armed forces and for placing Soviet society on a "war footing" in response to this perceived threat. He concluded, "Taking into account the increased complexity of the international situation, it is essential to convey to the Soviet people, in a more profound and better reasoned form, the truth about the existing threat of the danger of war."

Ogarkov's rather alarmist position on the U.S. threat was balanced by a less extreme article that appeared shortly thereafter, written by Defense Minister Dmitri Ustinov. Ustinov echoed Ogarkov's concern about what he also perceived to be the U.S. quest for superiority. In marked contrast to Ogarkov's exhortations to put the Soviet Union on a "war footing," however, Ustinov stressed the peaceful intentions of the Soviet Union and the benefits of the détente of the 1970s.

Ustinov did concur with one important judgment found in Ogarkov's article: that the United States was in the process of abandoning its commitment to existing arms control agreements. Ustinov said of the United States: "Another aspect of the activities of the present administration also stands out. It is gradually undermining many treaties and agreements. For example, the head of the Pentagon has cast doubt on the treaty between the Soviet Union and the United States on limiting the anti-ballistic missile systems. He said that the United States might demand a review of this treaty if the circumstances suited it." Ustinov proceeded to point out Washington's undermining of other agreements:

> The Washington Administration believes that SALT II is not advantageous to the United States. It should be carefully studied, so they say. This is a strange way of operating: First they say that the treaty is not unacceptable and then they say it should be studied. In what way is it not advantageous to the United States? . . .
>
> Judging by the statement of the present leaders of the United States they find a shortcoming in the treaty in the fact that it was founded on the principle of equality and uniform security. It is precisely this alone that constitutes an obstacle to the treaty becoming valid. "SALT II should be revised in favor of the United States" is the demand of the White House. One would like to recall in this connection the words of L. I. Brezhnev at the 26th CPSU Congress: "We shall not consent to an agreement which would give unilateral superiority to the United States. There must be no illusion on this score."[36]

The Ogarkov and Ustinov articles are usually cited as evidence that a policy debate took place among senior members of the Soviet political and military leaderships during this period over the nature of the threat posed by the new Reagan administration's defense policy, and the means by which the Soviet Union should respond. But Ogarkov and Ustinov were in absolute agreement on one point—that the United States did not intend to uphold existing arms control agreements, particularly the ABM Treaty and SALT II.

This apparent perception among top Soviet defense officials appeared two years before any indication that the Reagan administration intended formally to accuse the Soviet Union of arms control violations, and indeed before the United States made significant movement toward abandoning SALT II or embarking on the strategic defense program that would raise the question of U.S. compliance with the ABM Treaty. The perception also preceded by more than two years the detailed Soviet accusations that the United States was violating agreements, citing specific U.S. programs and specific provisions of treaties. Precise Soviet charges were made public only after U.S. charges of Soviet violations began in early 1984, and only in response to specific U.S. complaints.

In light of the later questions about Soviet compliance, it seems significant that Ogarkov and Ustinov both chose to stress this particular point at this particular time. There is no way to know whether a debate about treaty compliance was occurring within the Soviet government during these years. But by emphasizing U.S. noncompliance with arms control agreements, certainly Ustinov and Ogarkov were providing justification to any elements of the Soviet political leadership that may have been arguing for a Soviet approach to defense procurement that gave preference to military preparedness over concerns with arms control compliance.

Already low within the Soviet system because of the lack of built-in mechanisms for oversight, the saliency of arms control compliance concerns for the top political leadership probably dropped substantially in the last two years of Brezhnev's tenure and during the brief regimes of Yuri Andropov and Konstantin Chernenko. During this period the military leadership of the Soviet Union projected a high level of concern about the increased military threat from the United States and about the apparent lack of U.S. regard for its arms control commitments.

Ogarkov, and perhaps Ustinov as well, may have advocated a position within the Soviet defense policy–making structure that downplayed arms control concerns as the Soviet Union moved to counteract the effects of the Reagan administration's strategic modernization program. The argument that the United States was preparing to abandon its arms control commitments could have proven persuasive against any concern within the Soviet political leadership that Soviet initiatives could provoke the United States to break out of existing arms control limits; by mid-1981 Ogarkov and Ustinov were portraying the United States as having already taken that step. This was precisely the period during which any final intervention in the radar program would need to have been made to bring it into compliance with the ABM Treaty.

Given Ustinov and Ogarkov's view that the United States had already moved to abandon its arms control commitments, their view that the Soviet Union needed to take major steps to balance the high level of threat from the United States probably increased in saliency within the Soviet leadership, and any view that argued for the high saliency of arms treaties or their interpretation in a "strict constructionist" fashion likely fell into disfavor. No one within the Soviet political leadership could be expected to impose a restrictive interpretation of arms agreements on the Soviet Union when it was perceived that the United States was following a permissive interpretation of its obligations.

It was in this climate that the Soviet General Staff and Ministry of Defense were in all likelihood stressing the urgent need to complete the Soviet early-warning network, to protect their land-based forces against preemption through production of a single-warhead, mobile ICBM, and to deny the United States all possible data about Soviet weapon systems. Given also the economic pressures on the Soviet system, it is easy to see how their recommendations to the political leadership about how to close the gap in the Soviet early-warning network in the most economical and efficient manner might have gained the necessary support.

Changes in Soviet Behavior Since 1983

After 1983 a quiet but noticeable improvement was visible in Soviet compliance practices and attitudes toward resolving disputes. Since that time no new instances in which the Soviets violated an agreement, as in the case of Abalakovo, or trod on the margin of violation, as in the cases of the SS-25 and encryption, have been reported. Since 1983 the Reagan administration has said that no further evidence of what it believed to be Soviet chemical- or biological-weapons violations was noted after that date. The production rate for Soviet Backfire bombers has reportedly declined from slightly above thirty aircraft per year to slightly below that number. In 1985 the alleged SS-16 components were removed from the Plesetsk test site.[37] The Soviet Union has reportedly begun dismantling Bison bombers. In addition, in the SCC the Soviet Union acceded to a further restriction on ABM testing to inhibit concurrent operation of ABM and SAM components. In 1986 the Soviet Union also provided more information to Western scientists concerning the 1979 anthrax outbreak near Sverdlovsk (see chapter 3).

It is likely that the resumption of strategic arms negotiations in 1982 and their reinvigoration in 1985, the U.S. policy of interim restraint with regard to SALT II compliance after 1983, and the U.S. suggestions from mid-1985 that its inclination to abrogate SALT II could be held in check if the Soviet Union took "constructive action," encouraged a stricter Soviet approach to compliance.[38]

Up to a certain point the U.S. use of the SCC in 1981–83 to raise compliance concerns to the Soviet Union may have served a useful function in engaging the compliance issues among a wider spectrum of actors within the Soviet government. The result may have been an effort to improve Soviet behavior in areas where military activities were leading to U.S. concern, and where changes in Soviet practice would not decrease Soviet military preparedness. This effort demonstrates Soviet willingness to deal with compliance issues, once the issues have been joined in such a way to engage a broader segment of the Soviet decision-making elite.

Yet the Soviet Union will not take steps to change its behavior in areas where it fears that unilateral corrective action would be prejudicial to Soviet security. It is instances such as these that remain at the heart of the compliance dispute today.

Changes Under Gorbachev

The most important cause of the more conservative Soviet compliance behavior since 1983 may be the advent of the post-Brezhnev leadership, and particularly the coming to power of Mikhail Gorbachev. Since March 1985 Gorbachev may have taken steps to arrest the Soviet slide toward noncompliance as part of a new effort to promote progress in arms control agreements, a process that began under Andropov in 1983. Gorbachev is clearly interested in concluding a new series of arms control agreements with the United States, and he may possess the political clout to raise objections to military programs on compliance grounds when he feels that Soviet treaty performance might impede the negotiations. One can speculate that Gorbachev may have taken steps in 1985, 1986, and 1987 to bring certain Soviet military programs more clearly into compliance with the terms of arms control treaties.

By 1986 there were signs that Gorbachev was changing the Soviet approach to arms control, and to verification and compliance as part of that process. The timing of several Soviet initiatives related to verification and compliance suggests that they were partly a Soviet effort to meet President Reagan's criteria, set out at the time U.S. withdrawal from SALT II was announced in May 1986, that if the Soviet Union took some unspecified positive steps on arms control or compliance, the United States would reconsider its withdrawal from the treaty. These signs took three distinct forms.

First, the Gorbachev leadership made proposals for resolving the key remaining compliance disputes. In particular, in early October 1985 at the Geneva arms control negotiations and a year later in the SCC, the Soviet Union offered to stop work on the Abalakovo radar if the United States halted its plans to upgrade the Thule and Fylingdales Moors radars, followed by a discussion of the permissibility of these three LPARs.[39] This represented a tacit Soviet admission that the Abalakovo radar is a compliance problem. If the Abalakovo radar is a violation of the ABM Treaty, the Soviet Union has argued, then the two upgraded U.S. radars would violate the treaty provisions that restrict new early-warning LPARs to the periphery of the national territory. Also, in response to U.S. charges on encryption, the Soviets have asked the United States in the SCC to specify the parameters for which it needs to receive unencrypted data to verify SALT II provisions, whereupon the Soviet Union would provide that data. Although neither of these positions may be acceptable to the United States, they signal a recognition by Gorbachev that resolving these two compliance issues will require some Soviet accommodation.

Second, Gorbachev has made institutional changes in the domestic Soviet structure for formulating arms control policy. These changes include the establishment of a new arms control section of the Foreign Ministry, under the direction of Viktor Karpov, the former Soviet chief representative at the Geneva arms control talks.[40] A new arms control section has also been formed within the International Department of the Central Committee, headed by General Viktor Starodubov, a former Soviet SCC commissioner and former deputy to General Chervov at the Legal and Treaties Directorate of the General Staff.

It is unclear what responsibilities Gorbachev will delegate to these new arms control bureaus. Their sole purpose may be to improve Gorbachev's control over defense- and foreign-policy decision making, an objective that he has pursued more generally through his reshuffling of top defense- and foreign-policy figures. Or these bureaus may be used primarily to coordinate the content of Soviet arms control diplomacy.

These new departments, particularly that in the Foreign Ministry, could play an internal advocacy role in the Soviet Union for a more conservative approach to arms control compliance. If interests in compliance were to become more institutionalized within the Soviet system, rather than simply depending upon the interests and perceptions of a particular political leadership, the compliance performance of the Soviet Union could be significantly improved. Better Soviet compliance, in turn, could enhance the effectiveness of U.S.-Soviet arms control agreements.

Finally, there is some evidence that the Soviet Union is becoming more open to cooperative verification measures. In 1985 and 1986 the Gorbachev leadership produced a number of proposals for verification measures that have progressively departed from the traditional Soviet hesitancy to discuss or implement significant cooperative verification procedures. The placement of seismometers near the Soviet test site at Semipalatinsk in a cooperative arrangement between the Soviet Academy of Sciences and the U.S. Natural Resources Defense Council, official talks with the United States about measures to enhance the verifiability of the TTBT in August 1986, and acceptance of overflight inspections of troop maneuvers at the Stockholm Conference on Security- and Confidence-Building Measures in Europe are three recent examples of the new Soviet openness about verification.[41] It is too early to tell whether these initiatives will lead to progress on the thornier issues, such as encryption, but the trend is heartening.

Chapter Eight

The Standing Consultative Commission

Background

Early in the SALT process the SALT negotiators conceived the Standing Consultative Commission as a mechanism to address the inevitable disagreements that arise about compliance with arms control agreements. In anticipation of agreements after SALT I that would further limit strategic nuclear weapons, in Article XIII of the ABM Treaty the framers of the treaty charged the SCC with a wide range of tasks. These include negotiation of agreed U.S.-Soviet interpretations of treaty provisions, consideration of "proposals for further measures aimed at limiting strategic arms," and contemplation of "changes in the strategic situation that have a bearing" on the treaties under the SCC's jurisdiction. The SCC was designed as a deliberative body, with no inherent authority to enforce either compliance with treaties or joint interpretations of agreements reached through the SCC.

The intentional flexibility of arms control agreements made the creation of a body such as the SCC necessary. That the United States and Soviet Union provided for the SCC through SALT I indicated their recognition that the strategic situation is dynamic and that there is an ongoing need to adapt agreements so that they may endure despite technological change or other developments unforeseen when they were negotiated. The SCC is based on the presumption that the signing of an arms control treaty marks the beginning rather than the end of the arms control process. Written agreements are meaningful to the extent that they are effectively implemented by the signing parties.

The SCC was formally established by the Memorandum of Understanding Regarding the Establishment of a Consultative Commission, signed by the United States and Soviet Union in December 1972. The memorandum charged the SCC with promoting the objectives and implementation of the ABM Treaty, the Interim Agreement on the Limitation of Strategic Offensive Arms, and the Agreement on Measures to Reduce the Risk of Outbreak of Nuclear War.[1] The SCC has produced several agreements advancing the implementation of these accords and has clarified ambiguous treaty language in fulfillment of its charter.[2] For example, the ABM Treaty prohibited the testing of missiles, launchers, and radars "in an ABM mode," a vague phrase that was clarified in 1978 through an agreed statement and then further clarified through the SCC in 1985.

The SCC's responsibilities were expanded under SALT II to include negotiation of "procedures for replacement, conversion, and dismantling or destruction of strategic offensive arms" covered by the agreement and maintenance of an "agreed data base on the numbers of strategic offensive arms" on each side (Article XVII.2[e] and .3). Because the United States did not ratify SALT II, the procedures have not been completed and the data base has not been maintained.

The memorandum of understanding directed each party to send a commissioner and a deputy commissioner to the SCC, plus staff as deemed necessary. It was left to the discretion of each country to construct bureaucratic support for the SCC according to its respective governmental structure.

To date there have been four U.S. commissioners and one acting commissioner: U. Alexis Johnson (1972, while the SCC was being formally established), Sidney N. Graybeal (1973–76), Robert W. Buchheim (1977–81), Brigadier General John R. Lasater (acting commissioner, 1981), and General Richard Ellis (1981 to present). An interagency working group supports the U.S. SCC delegation. The group is chaired by a representative of ACDA and includes representatives from the State Department, the Office of the Secretary of Defense, the Joint Chiefs of Staff, and the intelligence agencies.

Bureaucratically, the United States treats the SCC as an instrument of the executive branch's authority to conduct foreign policy. Although instructions for the U.S. SCC delegation have typically been formulated through an interagency process, the ultimate decisions about use of the joint body emanate from the White House through the National Security Council. The president sends to the Congress occasional classified reports providing accounts of substantive agreements reached in the SCC. The reports are usually sent to six congressional committees: the Senate Committee on Foreign Relations and the House Committee on Foreign Affairs, and the armed services and intelligence committees of both houses. Until the 1980s these reports provided almost the only links between the SCC and the legislative branch. In recent years, however, increased interest in the SCC among some U.S. legislators has contributed to a confrontational approach that has decreased the effectiveness of the SCC.

The Soviet Union has emphasized the importance of the SCC and has sent highly qualified military representatives to serve on the Soviet delegation. To date there have been three Soviet SCC commissioners: General Major G. I. Ustinov (1973–79), General Viktor P. Starodubov (1979–86), and General Vladimir Medvedev (1986 to present). Although the Ministry of Foreign Affairs has always assigned the Soviet deputy commissioners, the commissioners and their supporting military staff have reportedly played the more dominant role in the SCC deliberations.

The SCC is thus not an autonomous body, but rather a tool in the hands of the Soviet and U.S. governments. Because the U.S. and Soviet delegations to the SCC receive their instructions from their respective governments, the SCC's effectiveness depends greatly on the manner in which the United States and Soviet Union decide to utilize the joint body. The mandate of the SCC is broad, leaving to the U.S. and Soviet governments the choice of whether to use the SCC minimally or maximally as a joint consultative forum to implement the terms of arms control agreements. Historically, the two countries have chosen to invoke only a small portion of the SCC's mandate, employing it almost solely to discuss technical compliance issues and to negotiate practical measures for the implementation of agreements. Nonetheless, from its inception in 1972 until the early 1980s, the two countries effectively used the SCC to increase the viability of the arms control process. It clarified ambiguities surrounding military activity and related treaty language, and it drafted procedures for the implementation of agreements (see appendix D).

Evaluating the effectiveness of the SCC is difficult because the SCC's proceedings and accomplishments are cloaked in secrecy. At the time the SCC was established, the Soviets insisted on the stipulation in the SCC regulations that the commission shall conduct all proceedings in private and may make them public only with the express consent of both commissioners. Each government does announce the conclusion of agreed statements and common understandings. Although the SCC regulations do not require that the texts remain classified, the texts have never been made public by either government. One can sketch a picture of the SCC's internal functions only by assembling scattered pieces of evidence and relying on the recollections of people who have participated in the SCC process. Although not ideal, this combination of sources permits one to reconstruct much of what has led to a breakdown of the SCC's effectiveness during recent years.

Two U.S. Approaches to the SCC

U.S. presidents Nixon, Ford, and Carter encouraged the work of the SCC and generally regarded it as a mechanism that advanced U.S. security interests by promoting Soviet compliance. A 1983 report by the Carnegie Endowment for International Peace, representing a broad spectrum of views on national security, assessed the role of the SCC, noting that it had not yet been confronted with a clear case of noncompliance: "There seems to be general agreement . . . that the SCC has served a very useful role as a mechanism for heading off misunderstandings and providing a forum for clarifying both past conduct and future obligations on points of detail."[3]

The beginning of the 1980s marked a watershed in the way the United States and Soviet Union chose to use the SCC to address compliance concerns. During the Reagan administration, the SCC has become the object of increasing controversy in the United States. Top administration officials have publicly criticized the SCC's performance and questioned its usefulness for resolving compliance concerns. In a November 1985 memorandum to the president, Secretary of Defense Caspar Weinberger called the SCC a "languid, confidential, and ineffective forum," used by previous administrations to excuse Soviet violations. Secretary Weinberger also praised the Reagan administration for its policy of publicizing what it considers to be Soviet cheating, and he urged the president to publicly denounce the SCC.[4]

This section contrasts two distinct U.S. approaches to the SCC: the problem-solving strategy of the Nixon, Ford, and Carter administrations and the public diplomacy of the Reagan administration. Through the problem-solving approach, previous U.S. administrations sought patiently and privately through the SCC to clarify activities or situations causing concern about compliance, occasionally calling on high-level officials of the U.S. and Soviet governments to resolve difficult issues in the context of the SALT negotiations. Through its public-diplomacy approach, the Reagan administration has denigrated the utility of the private SCC channel and sought instead to publicize cases of Soviet "cheating" and to use U.S. and European public opinion as a lever for changing Soviet compliance behavior.

An examination of the two strategies and their results points to the greater empirical success of the problem-solving approach in clarifying ambiguous treaty language and military activity, improving compliance with existing agreements when it has been questionable, and thus supporting the effective implementation of arms control agreements. The public-diplomacy approach may have resulted in some minor improvements in Soviet behavior. However, these small advances have been outweighed by the adverse effects of the public polemics on resolution through the SCC of major disputes and thus on the ability of the arms control process to function through ongoing and necessary settlement of compliance disputes.

The problem-solving approach employed by the United States during the 1970s proved more productive than the public-diplomacy approach of the 1980s for a variety of reasons. First, because of the ongoing arms control process and expectations for future agreements in the 1970s, incentives were high on both sides to resolve disputes through the SCC and thus keep the process on track. The failure of the SALT II Treaty to obtain ratification in 1979 interrupted the efforts of the SCC to reach agreement on implementation procedures for SALT II. Once the United States began to make charges of Soviet violations in 1981, the Soviet approach in the SCC swung sharply, from a response to U.S. concerns that had sometimes been grudging, but had also been forthcoming in the past when the incentive was high to reach a compromise, to a response of tit-for-tat accusations and denial of U.S. charges.

Second, there were positive direct links during the 1970s between the SCC and arms control negotiations and between the SCC and higher levels of the national governments of the two countries. These links aided the work of the SCC by providing supplementary avenues for pursuing agreement on interpretation of the provisions of arms control treaties.

Third, because the problem-solving approach insulated SCC deliberations from the political environment, compromise may have been easier for both sides in reaching agreed interpretations of arms control provisions. Because it was accompanied by polemics about arms control cheating, the public-diplomacy approach created suspicion about the public opinion–shaping motives of one side in raising a compliance concern about the other.

Fourth, during the 1970s U.S. presidents and officials at high levels of the executive branch were supportive of efforts to reach agreement in the SCC. The U.S. SCC commissioners received more encouragement than they have during the 1980s to seek agreements in the SCC, and the commissioners were less subject to the type of competing and contradictory influences, from within the U.S. bureaucracy, that in the 1980s have had the effect of frustrating agreement.

Finally, the problem-solving approach realistically assumed the possibility of divergent interpretations of agreements and lent itself to a patient effort to reach common understandings about the meaning of treaty provisions. The public-diplomacy approach, on the other hand, has been based on a strong presupposition that the Soviet Union is cheating in every case in which the two countries maintain a different interpretation of treaty provisions. Thus, in the 1980s U.S. officials have impatiently moved beyond discussion in the SCC to public accusations of Soviet cheating, or even bypassed the SCC altogether.

This evaluation of the two U.S. approaches to the SCC analyzes cases in which the two approaches were applied, illustrating the effects of the approaches on the compliance concerns and the implications of the outcomes in each case for the status of treaties and for U.S. security.

Problem Solving: The Approach Under Presidents Nixon, Ford, and Carter

In the 1982 edition of *Arms Control and Disarmament Agreements*, the U.S. ACDA recognized the SCC's success in resolving issues of treaty interpretation: "Both the United States and the Soviet Union have raised a number of questions in the Commission relating to each side's compliance with the SALT I agreements. In each case raised by the United States, the Soviet activity in question has either ceased or additional information has allayed U.S. concern."[5]

One reason for the SCC's success was the significant personal political investment of Presidents Nixon, Ford, and Carter in the arms control process, an investment that gave them a particular interest in resolving compliance problems. They recognized that treaties are imperfect and that interpretations of ambiguous provisions can vary; and they believed that private negotiation offers a better chance for resolution of compliance disputes than public diplomacy. Consequently, they relied on the effective and low-profile SCC mechanism to find solutions to what were essentially technical compliance problems and avoided injecting them directly into the milieu of U.S.-Soviet political relations. The two governments' commitment to additional arms restraints encouraged the smooth functioning of the SCC by creating incentives to clear up ambiguities that threatened to obstruct further progress.

Secretary of Defense James Schlesinger's testimony before the Senate Armed Services Committee in 1975 typified the diplomatic restraint exercised by the Nixon, Ford, and Carter administrations. Schlesinger characterized questionable Soviet activities as ambiguities rather than violations: "We believe that the Soviet Union has been, and today is, in compliance with the terms of the SALT agreements. There are, however, some ambiguities in certain activities underway in the Soviet Union which need clarification."

Although they exhibited restraint in public, these administrations acknowledged the need to register their concerns with the Soviets. In his testimony, Secretary Schlesinger outlined the compliance strategy of the Nixon and Ford administrations, an approach later to be adopted by the Carter administration: "One could expect the Soviets to tread at the limits of the SALT agreements. If unchallenged, we then should expect them to overstep and go beyond the limits. If such activities are challenged as they occur, the strategic risk might be regarded as acceptable."[6]

Throughout the 1970s the United States chose to challenge the Soviets privately in the SCC. In order to avoid unnecessary confrontation, the U.S. delegation to the SCC was careful to raise compliance concerns with the Soviets only after the concerns had been substantiated by intelligence data. The U.S. commissioners would present concerns as questions rather than as accusations. The two delegations would then work to find mutually acceptable revisions of treaty language that would serve to reduce ambiguities about the meaning of provisions in relation to new technologies or behavior and to prevent future interpretations of treaty language that might be used to justify activities the treaty intended to proscribe.

Because both sides were actively pursuing new arms control initiatives, there was a generally constructive link between the SCC and the SALT II negotiations. The SCC and the negotiations reinforced one another, as complementary elements of the effort to realize effective and equitable restrictions on nuclear weapons. The SCC delegations occasionally encountered difficulties on particular issues and looked to cabinet-level officials to facilitate the negotiation of agreements or understandings. For example, between 1972 and 1975, through personal contact, Secretary of State Henry Kissinger and Ambassador Anatoly Dobrynin broke impasses in the SCC over technical issues. Neither side wanted such issues to arouse hostilities that could contaminate the SALT negotiations. By facilitating the implementation of SALT I, the SCC strengthened the consensus that arms control enhanced U.S. security and thus added to the momentum toward a SALT II agreement.

The link between the SCC and the SALT talks sometimes operated in the reverse direction. Both sides occasionally used the existence of the SCC as a rationale for deferring difficult issues rather than confronting them in the SALT negotiations, where they might obstruct progress. According to Strobe Talbott's account of the SALT II negotiations, Soviet negotiator Semenov agreed to the ambiguous language restricting telemetry encryption partly because he thought it provided the SCC with an adequate basis for addressing any questions that might arise. According to Talbott, U.S. negotiators believed that the SCC could effectively protect U.S. access to Soviet telemetry needed for verification.[7] This reasoning was a reflection of the consensus that the SCC was operating effectively and the desire of some officials in the Carter administration to realize a SALT II agreement, even if doing so meant accepting wording that was less than ideal.

In the SALT I and II negotiations both sides also sought to position themselves to support their interpretations of treaty provisions in later debates about compliance. As a general rule, the United States strove for greater specificity than the Soviet Union. When the United States could not convince the Soviet Union to agree to a particular provision, such as one specifying stricter limits on telemetry encryption than were ultimately contained in SALT II, it often sought at least to provide a legal peg on which to hang its future arguments. The United States sought treaty language that could be used to support the U.S. position. Both sides issued unilateral statements staking out their positions on points of detail that they believed were not sufficiently explicit in the final treaty language. The two sides also used the negotiating record—the accumulation of all formal and informal exchanges between representatives of the two parties—to establish positions that would help explain how the ultimate treaty provisions were formulated, should issues of interpretation arise later in the SCC. In the case of encryption, U.S. negotiators viewed the treaty provisions and negotiating record as sufficient basis for arguing the general principle that verification of the terms of SALT II should not be made more difficult by either side. But the general language of the treaty provision also provided the Soviet Union with a legal peg for its contrasting argument that Soviet encryption did not impede U.S. verification if the United States was able to obtain the data it needed. This is precisely the type of circumstance that has resulted in the intricate ambiguities taken up by the SCC.

Although the prevailing U.S. evaluation of the SCC during the 1970s was positive, its handling of issues involving Soviet compliance provoked significant criticism. Melvin Laird, former secretary of defense, wrote in late 1977, "The evidence is incontrovertible that the Soviet Union has repeatedly, flagrantly, and indeed contemptuously violated the treaties to which we have adhered." Despite secret diplomatic efforts, Laird argued, "Soviet violations have increased progressively, in both number and seriousness."[8] The manner in which the two sides used the SCC entailed a process that was frustrating to some participants and observers and did not yield results as quickly as some would have liked. Despite such criticism, and even though results were sometimes long in coming and agreements were achieved step-by-step, the SCC was considered a uniquely useful tool for influencing Soviet behavior and clearing up uncertainties. Achievements realized through the SCC process were made possible by the fact that it was a little-known forum, which enjoyed relative obscurity outside the two governments and which was generally insulated from the public controversy surrounding the SALT negotiations.

Issues resolved by the SCC during the 1970s. An examination of the record shows that, by using the problem-solving approach in an environment conducive to arms control, the SCC clarified several types of ambiguities during the 1970s. The SCC dealt successfully with three different types of questions involving treaty interpretation: (1) ambiguous military activity related to clear treaty language, (2) clear military activity related to ambiguous treaty language, and (3) ambiguous military activity pertaining to ambiguous treaty language. Clear military activity pertaining to clear treaty language would not present a compliance concern unless the activity were an outright violation. There was no such case during the 1970s.[9]

1. Ambiguous activity related to clear treaty language: Soviet launch-control facilities. In 1973 the United States suspected that the Soviet Union was constructing new missile silos prohibited by the Interim Agreement, Article I, which stated that each party shall not "start construction of additional fixed, land-based intercontinental ballistic missile (ICBM) launchers after July 1, 1972." The treaty language was clear enough, but the Soviet activity was ambiguous as observed by U.S. national technical intelligence means. The Soviets maintained that what the United States named "III-X silos" were launch-control facilities. The United States accepted the Soviet argument after additional intelligence became available and the Soviets provided clarification in the SCC.

2. Clear military activity related to ambiguous treaty language: Minute-

man shelters. In 1973 the United States began construction of shelters over Minuteman silos during conversion from the Minuteman II, single-warhead ICBM to the Minuteman III, MIRVed ICBM. The Soviets were disturbed, since the shelters could have been used to disguise launcher modifications that were restricted by the agreement. The Soviet Union argued that the shelters were not in conformance with Article V of the Interim Agreement, which requires each side to avoid "deliberate concealment measures which impede verification by national technical means of compliance with the terms of this Interim Agreement." The United States contended that the purpose of the shelters was to protect workers from environmental conditions rather than to conceal the launchers, and that the shelters were consistent with Article V.[10]

The military activity itself was clear, but the precise meaning of "deliberate concealment" was uncertain. At issue was the relationship between the shelters' intent, which was environmental protection, and their effect, which was concealment from verification by national technical means. The effect of the shelters was to obstruct the ability of Soviet satellites to verify parameters, such as the size of ICBM silos, that were regulated by the Interim Agreement. The Soviets argued convincingly that, regardless of U.S. intentions, the impeding effect of the Minuteman shelters raised questions about U.S. compliance with the Interim Agreement.

Some U.S. analysts argued at the time that the Minuteman shelters should be removed because they established a dangerous precedent. By attempting to legitimize measures that obstructed verification by national technical means, the United States was opening the door for the Soviets to construct similar shelters over their ICBM silos. Soviet construction of such shelters would be troubling to the United States, creating uncertainty about the size of Soviet silos or the types of missiles deployed by the Soviet Union. The implications of such Soviet activity for Soviet treaty compliance and the U.S. deterrent could be serious. But, U.S. experts warned, the United States would have little basis for arguing in the SCC against such Soviet shelters, since it was the United States that had set the precedent.

Corrective U.S. action was slow in coming. Not until 1977, after the Minuteman modernization program had been completed, did the Air Force modify its use of shelters over Minuteman silos. The Soviets never elected to build similar shelters, and the two sides reached a common understanding in the SCC in 1977 that neither side would use shelters that impede verification by national technical means.[11]

The handling of the Soviet launch-control facilities and the Minuteman shelters influenced the U.S.-Soviet interaction in subsequent SCC deliberations regarding compliance issues. The Soviets raised the Minuteman shelter issue only after the United States raised the III-X silo issue. Since then, the Soviets have responded to each U.S. concern raised in the SCC with a concern of their own. The case of the silo shelters also helped to establish a practice by each party of being very slow in taking corrective action to alleviate the concerns of the other party.

3. *Ambiguous military activity related to ambiguous treaty language: the Soviet SA-5 radar.* Concurrent testing of ABM components and SAM radars or testing them in an ABM mode has been a long-standing issue in the SCC. The ABM Treaty sought to foreclose the upgrade of non-ABM military hardware by prohibiting each side from giving missiles, launchers, or radars ABM capabilities or testing them in an ABM mode.

But the phrase "in an ABM mode" was left vague, apparently intentionally, in the text of the ABM Treaty.[12] A U.S. unilateral statement issued just before the conclusion of the ABM Treaty negotiations asserted that the United States would consider testing a radar in an ABM mode to consist of making "measurements on a cooperative target vehicle" that has the characteristics of a strategic ballistic missile or making "measurements in conjunction with the test of an ABM interceptor missile or an ABM radar at the same test range." The caveat was added, "Radars used for purposes such as range safety or instrumentation would be exempt from application of these criteria." Apparently the United States considered the terms "range safety" and "instrumentation" to be self-explanatory and in need of no further definition. The Soviet delegation did not concur with the U.S. unilateral statement and did not consider itself legally bound by it.

The Nixon administration had reason to believe in 1973 and 1974 that the Soviets were using a radar associated with the SA-5 system to track ballistic-missile tests.[13] Because the SA-5 system was widely deployed throughout the Soviet Union, it might, if upgraded to track strategic ballistic missiles, eventually have contributed to a Soviet territorial defense. A debate took place within the U.S. intelligence community about whether the Soviets were seeking to upgrade the SA-5 system for an ABM role or were merely using the system for range instrumentation. The fact that the Soviets had other radar systems at their ABM test ranges that could be used for instrumentation raised doubts that the SA-5s were needed for that purpose.

In the SA-5 case the Soviets exploited the ambiguous language of the ABM treaty to justify actions that were also ambiguous, that is, not clearly prohibited by the agreement. The United States sought to use the SCC to clarify the language of the treaty so that the observed Soviet activity could be placed clearly inside or outside of its provisions and dealt with accordingly.

The Soviet activity of concern ceased "a short time" after the United States raised the issue in the SCC, according to a 1978 Carter administration compliance report. Soviet upgrade of the SA-5 radar to an ABM radar would have required continued testing and "extensive and observable modifications" to other parts of the SA-5 air-defense system; and the Carter administration concluded that the Soviets had not made such additional modifications as of early 1978.[14]

The SA-5 case highlights the step-by-step process by which the SCC has been used to bring the sides to agreement. Like the case of the silo shelter, the case of the SA-5 system demonstrates the ability of the SCC to induce slow corrective behavior. The deliberations in the SCC began under President Nixon; they were pursued by President Ford; and an agreed statement was reached under President Carter. Admittedly slow, this procedure yielded a comprehensive agreement in 1978 that clarified (1) what constitutes an ABM test range as discussed in Article IV of the ABM Treaty, (2) what constitutes testing in an ABM mode, and (3) permitted uses of air-defense and other non-ABM radars at ABM test ranges. Each side agreed not to conduct "concurrent testing of air-defense components co-located at the same test range" and not to use air-defense radars "utilized as instrumentation equipment" to make measurements on strategic ballistic missiles.[15]

Continued operation of SAM radars during ABM-component tests at Soviet ABM test ranges, however, continued to concern U.S. analysts. Some ambiguity remained as to what constitutes a test. In 1985 the two sides reached a common understanding in the SCC that amplified the 1978 agreement to prohibit concurrent operations of air-defense components co-located at the same test range.

Some SCC advocates point to the SA-5 case as evidence that the SCC has effectively halted ambiguous but potentially dangerous Soviet activity before it adversely affected U.S. national security. These supporters argue that the United States used the SCC to realize results that protected U.S. interests and reinforced the arms control process. Critics of the SCC argue that U.S. efforts in the SCC did not deter the Soviets from continuing to test the SA-5 in an ABM mode and that the Soviets ceased these tests only when their program had concluded. One could make a similar argument with respect to the United States' continued use of large Minuteman shelters long after the Soviets objected to their use through the SCC. Critics also contend that the 1978 agreed statement failed to curb Soviet activity that was causing concern and did nothing to obstruct Soviet efforts to lay the base for a national defense against ballistic-missile attack. This argument was one of several issues concerning compliance with SALT I raised during the SALT II ratification debate.

The Watershed: Problem Solving to Public Diplomacy

As arms control came under attack in 1979, compliance became an increasingly contentious issue. The SCC came under scrutiny by opponents of SALT II, forcing the Carter administration to defend the effectiveness of the consultative forum. With the advent of the Reagan administration, the predominant view in the U.S. government was that the SCC was an ineffectual forum, which had failed to obtain changes in Soviet behavior. After 1979 the SCC became increasingly ineffective as a mechanism for constructive discussion of compliance concerns. This watershed in the SCC's effectiveness coincided with the general downturn in U.S.-Soviet political relations and a distinct change in the manner in which the two governments used the SCC.

Candidate Ronald Reagan campaigned against the "fatally flawed" SALT II Treaty and brought to the White House an attitude toward nuclear-arms control that was fundamentally different from that of his predecessors. Reagan initially rejected the possibility of future arms agreements and threw into question the status of those already in existence. Intense bureaucratic struggles were waged over the utility of arms control agreements on two interrelated fronts: policies with respect to any future strategic arms reduction talks (START) or intermediate-range nuclear forces (INF) agreements, and policies with respect to agreements already in place.

One aspect of the Reagan reassessment of existing accords was a detailed examination of the Soviet compliance record. Members of the Reagan transition team for ACDA compiled lists of alleged Soviet violations in early 1981, and the president's General Advisory Committee on Arms Control and Disarmament was tasked in 1982 to conduct a yearlong study of Soviet noncompliance with arms control agreements. What Secretary Schlesinger and other officials of prior administrations had deemed ambiguous Soviet activity, the new administration identified as elements of a deliberate pattern of Soviet cheating.

This change in viewpoint altered the U.S. approach to handling compliance concerns and quickly affected the way in which the United States used the SCC. For example, U.S. officials reportedly raised once again the issue of the Soviet SS-19 ICBM, charging that it did not comply with a U.S. unilateral statement, following the Interim Agreement, that asserted that the United States would consider any ICBM larger in certain parameters than the Soviet SS-11 to be a prohibited new heavy missile. The U.S. chargé d'affaires in Moscow, Jack Matlock, reportedly notified the Soviet deputy foreign minister, Georgi Kornienko, that the SS-19 was an example of how the Soviets had distorted the spirit of agreements, behavior that would no longer be acceptable.[16] The executive branch accompanied such diplomatic forays with public statements questioning the reliability of the Soviets as negotiating partners. During previous administrations such public charges of Soviet noncompliance had been voiced primarily by conservative legislators or by private individuals or organizations.

The new administration viewpoint included a conviction held by many officials that going public was the only way to get the Soviets to bring their behavior into line with U.S. interpretations of treaty language. Supporters of public diplomacy for airing compliance issues believed that the Soviets had systematically violated their arms control commitments during the 1970s in an effort to achieve military advantage. The administration felt obliged to inform the public of the extent of Soviet cheating and to take military steps to counterbalance its effects. The new administration judged the private diplomatic efforts of the past to have failed. According to the 1984 GAC report: "Near total reliance on secret diplomacy in seeking to restore Soviet compliance has been largely ineffective. The U.S. record of raising its concerns about Soviet noncompliance in the Standing Consultative Commission and through various high level diplomatic demarches demonstrates the ineffectiveness of this process."[17]

The utility of the SCC, a vestige of the SALT process, was for the first time seriously questioned inside the government. U.S. participation in the SCC encountered direct opposition within the administration immediately after President Reagan took office in January 1981. The SCC session scheduled for that spring was postponed for several months, while an internal debate ensued about whether to utilize the joint consultative body.[18] The nonratification of the SALT II Treaty during the Carter administration had already undercut the SCC process, causing the SCC to cease ongoing efforts to conclude implementation procedures for the treaty.[19] Now the SCC and the agreements it was designed to support were the target of vocal criticism by U.S. government officials.

The Reagan administration decided later in 1981 to continue to send SCC delegations to meet with the Soviets in Geneva but did not resolve what the U.S. approach would be in the SCC. In subsequent years bitter bureaucratic battles over the U.S. stance ensued between representatives of the State Department, on the one hand, and ACDA and civilian officials in the Defense Department, on the other hand. Some friction of this nature was de rigueur, but it became more acute as representatives of the DOD and ACDA attempted to block the problem-solving approach that had endured since the SCC had been established. Under Presidents Nixon, Ford, and Carter, questions to the Soviets had been stated in a diplomatic manner: "We are concerned about this particular activity. Could you explain it to us?" The Reagan administration favored a more confrontational approach: "We view this particular activity as a violation. What are you going to do about it?"

The uncertain status of the unratified SALT II Treaty posed a difficult problem for the United States and tempered the enthusiasm of the new administration for aggressively criticizing Soviet practices through the SCC. Opponents of SALT II recognized that raising SALT II issues in the SCC might be interpreted as legitimizing the "fatally flawed" treaty; they did not want to discuss issues related to an agreement not regarded by the United States as being in force.[20] By the time the SS-25 became an issue in early 1983, the administration had committed itself to refrain from "undercutting" SALT II and therefore felt it could raise concerns about Soviet compliance with SALT II.

Although the United States did refer to the SS-25 as a compliance concern in the SCC, it chose to pursue the issue primarily through other diplomatic channels, which were not bound by secrecy.[21] This U.S. movement away from utilizing the SCC began to erode the SCC's viability and subject the joint body to the politics of public diplomacy.

Not only did the administration bypass the SCC as a conduit for discussing compliance issues and publicly attack its effectiveness, but also some opponents of the SCC within the administration used the instructions to the U.S. SCC delegation, whose role it was to serve the administration, to undermine the delegation's effectiveness. For example, ACDA officials attempted to deny Commissioner Ellis authority to complete the bomber-dismantlement procedures under SALT II because the ambiguous status of SALT II made them irrelevant.[22] Also, in 1985 representatives from the Defense Department reportedly prevented the U.S. SCC commissioner from proposing, as a means of dealing with the dispute over the Abalakovo radar, a ban on new large phased-array radars.[23] These tactics hamstrung the ability of the U.S. SCC delegation to search for mutually acceptable solutions to the unresolved compliance issues and to develop implementation procedures.

For advocates of the SALT agreements within the bureaucracy, on the other hand, the SCC became a point of defense against those officials who sought to loosen the provisions of the treaties or break out of them altogether. In other words, for its supporters the SCC gradually changed from a mechanism for enhancing and strengthening the treaties it covers to a mechanism for struggling to maintain the achievements of the past.

1982 ABM Treaty review. Article XIII of the ABM Treaty delegated to the SCC the responsibility for conducting an ABM Treaty review every five years. In 1977 the two sides apparently agreed without much debate that the treaty was still serving their national-security interests. But preparation for the 1982 ABM review was a hostile and bitter bureaucratic contest inside the U.S. government, as factions within the Reagan administration fought over the desirability of maintaining the treaty. The preparations for the 1982 ABM Treaty review conference typified the sort of confrontation that occurred within the U.S. government between advocates of public diplomacy and proponents of using the SCC for problem solving as this approach had been used during the previous administrations.

The chief U.S. negotiator for the START talks, General Edward Rowny, argued persistently that the ABM Treaty review should be incorporated into the START negotiations. Richard Perle, assistant secretary of defense for international security affairs, apparently tried to prevent the United States from issuing a statement confirming its commitment to the ABM Treaty, because the question of U.S. compliance was still an open issue in the administration.[24] In the end, the administration did not adopt proposals to offer amendments to the ABM Treaty or to announce its withdrawal from the agreement, and the review session itself apparently passed rather smoothly.[25] A joint statement affirming the viability of the ABM

Treaty and the SCC was issued at the end of the SCC special session on December 15, 1982.[26]

Compliance reports. Although more moderate members of the administration successfully sheltered the SCC from arms control opponents in 1982, events in 1983 increased momentum toward public confrontation with the Soviets on compliance issues. Specifically, press reports stated that the administration considered the Soviet SS-25 ICBM and the new Soviet LPAR at Abalakovo to be violations of SALT II and the ABM Treaty, respectively. These two cases were largely responsible for congressional requests for an executive-branch review of Soviet compliance practices. In January 1984 the administration released the first such compliance report.

The release of the first formal, public accusations of Soviet cheating in the history of the nuclear–arms control enterprise fundamentally changed the way in which the United States and Soviet Union deal with compliance questions. Rather than pursue the issues patiently through the SCC, the United States chose to take compliance issues directly to the public, once they had been mentioned to the Soviets in the SCC. As a result, the Soviets engaged in tit-for-tat responses, charging the United States with a host of violations, some of which were new and others of which simply raised issues that the SCC had dealt with previously.

This escalation of charges of cheating, exemplifying the move toward public diplomacy, has had a generally destructive impact on the SCC. The administration contends that its efforts to bring the leverage of public opinion to bear on the Soviets has compelled the Soviets to change some of their practices. But vestiges of the problem-solving approach, not public diplomacy, have largely been responsible for the modest gains realized through the SCC during the Reagan administration.

1985 SCC common understandings. Two new SCC agreed statements and two Soviet corrective actions taken in the 1980s were built upon the base of previous administrations' discussions and understandings illustrating the step-by-step process that yields results in the SCC. The SCC concluded two common understandings in June 1985. The first of these enhances the 1971 "Accident Measures" Agreement through a provision for use of the U.S.-Soviet hot line in case of a terrorist nuclear threat. The understanding represented a continuation of the SCC's responsibility for implementing that agreement and is important given the parties' strong mutual interest in averting nuclear terrorism. The second common understanding further clarifies the ABM Treaty through an agreement that neither side will conduct concurrent operations of SAM radars and ABM components co-located at the same test range. The concurrent-operations agreement represents a further attempt to distinguish between permitted and prohibited military activities as they relate to ABM Treaty language concerning testing in an ABM mode. The two sides had agreed in principle to this understanding as early as 1983, but final agreement was delayed because of internal bureaucratic disputes on the U.S. side.

After these two formal agreements were concluded, the United States used the SCC to encourage the Soviets to bring some activities that were of concern to the United States into clearer compliance with agreements. The United States was concerned that the Soviets were not properly dismantling Bison bombers as they were required to do to stay under SALT II limits. But because the SALT II bomber-dismantlement procedures were never completed, the United States was unable to determine clearly whether or not the Soviet approach to dismantling was in compliance. Sometime after the United States raised the issue in the SCC, the Soviets apparently began dismantling the aircraft in a fashion accepted by the United States. Also, after the United States alleged that the SS-16 ICBM had been secretly deployed in violation of SALT II, the Soviets took action to convince the United States that the SS-16 was not deployed at the Plesetsk test site.[27]

New compliance concerns. Although the modest advances realized through the SCC during the early 1980s indicate that it continued working, if only to a minimal extent, the two sides have not effectively used the SCC to resolve any of the new compliance concerns raised by either country since 1981. Most important among these from the U.S. viewpoint have been questions surrounding the SS-25, encryption, and Abalakovo.

The SS-25 and encryption issues are of the type that the SCC dealt with successfully in the past: They are technical issues pertaining to somewhat unclear treaty language. The Abalakovo radar, on the other hand, represents a completely different type of issue than any brought previously to the SCC: It is the first issue that the SCC has confronted that represents a clear-cut violation. The Abalakovo radar raises a difficult question: Can the SCC consultative process handle an actual violation of an arms control agreement, or does a clear violation require unusual diplomatic measures?

SS-25. The Soviets first flight-tested the SS-25 in February 1983. The United States has charged that the SS-25 violates the new-type provision and the limitation on the RV-weight–to–throw-weight ratio contained in the SALT II Treaty (Article IV.10, Third Agreed Statement). The Soviets insist that the SS-25 is a permitted modernization of the SS-13 ICBM. The two sides have not used the SCC to clarify the actual characteristics of the SS-25 and SS-13, nor do they seem to have explored other, more creative options for resolving the differences between the two sides.

Precisely what is included in measurements of throw-weight for the purpose of treaty compliance is the question at issue in the SS-25 case. Both sides have made repeated public statements asserting their positions regarding the SS-25 but have not seriously pursued an agreement in the SCC on the definition of throw-weight. The United States used the SS-25 "violation" as one rationale for its decision to scrap the SALT II Treaty. Upon withdrawal from SALT II in November 1986, the United States formally abandoned attempts to resolve the SS-25 and other SALT II compliance issues through the SCC.

Telemetry encryption. Soviet encryption of missile–flight-test telemetry is extremely troubling to American intelligence analysts, who rely on such data to verify the characteristics of Soviet weaponry. But SALT II recognizes that some telemetry encryption is permissible, so long as it does not impede verification by national technical means of the provisions of the treaty. The language of the restriction has proven to be extremely problematic, and the two sides have been unable to reach any clarification in the SCC.

In January 1979 the United States notified the Soviet Union that it would consider the levels of encryption observed on a recent series of tests of the SS-18 ICBM to be a violation of the SALT II Treaty, which was still under negotiation.[28] The Soviets continued to encrypt a high percentage of their test data, but the Reagan administration was hesitant to raise the issue in the SCC because of the uncertain status of SALT II. In May 1982 the administration adopted its policy of not undercutting SALT II, and in the fall SCC session it raised the encryption issue.

In subsequent SCC deliberations the Soviets have offered to make telemetry available for those parameters about which the United States specifies information is necessary for verification of SALT II.[29] The United States has refused the offer, contending that, by specifying parameters, the United States would reveal sensitive U.S. verification capabilities to the Soviets. The U.S. intelligence community has argued strongly and successfully against entertaining the Soviet offer.

The SS-25 and encryption issues are similar to the issues that were resolved in the SCC during the 1970s. The two parties could find a technical solution by striking a compromise between the Soviet Union's need to protect its sensitive data and the U.S. need to verify Soviet capabilities. These two objectives are not necessarily irreconcilable. But the atmosphere of the SCC has become so polarized that exploration of creative possibilities to deal with issues such as encryption has been stifled. The deadlock in the SCC and the public accusations from both sides have resulted in a complete lack of progress on the encryption issue.

Like the SS-25 issue, the encryption issue in a sense became a moot question once the United States decided to scrap the SALT II Treaty. But with widespread belief in the United States that any new treaty on strategic nuclear weapons should incorporate more effective provisions restricting encryption, the SCC deliberations on encryption could still be very useful. By defining "encryption" and other key words, the SCC could lay the basis for more effective encryption restrictions in future agreements.[30]

Abalakovo. The Soviets rejected a U.S. request for a special SCC session after the United States discovered the Abalakovo radar in July 1983. The United States then raised the issue in the regular fall 1983 session, which began on September 22. The Soviets contended that the radar was intended for space tracking, and that the United States would be able to verify the radar's purpose once it was operational (see chapter 5). The United States rejected the Soviet argument, contending that the capabilities, location, and orientation of the radar were not optimized for space tracking.[31]

As the one clear case of Soviet noncompliance, the Abalakovo radar has become such a volatile political symbol in the United States that resolution would be difficult at the level of the SCC. Moreover, Abalakovo, unlike other compliance issues, has no available technical solutions. The radar is simply located in the wrong place and has permanent characteristics that cannot be changed.

On one level, the Abalakovo dispute represents a failure by the Soviet Union adequately to use the joint consultative process of the SCC. There may have been compelling technical reasons for the Soviet Union to build the radar where it is located, including economic efficiency and effectiveness of the radar for early warning, its intended use. Ideally, in anticipation of technical problems associated with siting Abalakovo clearly on the Soviet periphery and oriented outward, the Soviet Union would have sought clarification through the SCC of the ABM Treaty provisions dealing with LPARs. The Soviet Union and United States might have jointly pursued a new interpretation of the ABM Treaty that could have allowed the radar, perhaps with special arrangements for U.S. verification of the radar's use only for permitted functions. Or, seeing a common interest with the United States, in light of new U.S. LPAR programs, in constraining the location and capabilities of LPARs, the Soviet Union might have sought a common understanding to reinforce ABM Treaty restrictions.

The fact that Abalakovo represented a treaty violation made it inherently unlikely that the Soviets would engage in a full-fledged effort to consult with the United States about the radar problem, as they did in the case of SLBM dismantlements during the 1970s. The political climate of the early 1980s rendered such an effort impossible. Therefore, the radar issue, alone among the compliance questions of the early 1980s, should have emerged from the SCC, once discussion became deadlocked, to be dealt with constructively through other diplomatic means.

Although the problem-solving approach has proved more productive than public confrontation in the resolution of compliance issues, occasionally an issue arises that is beyond the scope of the SCC. It is important to distinguish such issues from those that can be pursued through the SCC. Such an issue must represent a clear violation rather than ambiguous behavior or treaty provisions. The Abalakovo radar was the only violation in this category during the early 1980s. As such, it should have been addressed by the United States in a manner clearly distinct from more ambiguous questions about treaty interpretation.

If the United States is to be able to convey to the Soviets the seriousness of its concern about a violation, it is crucial for the United States to distinguish that violation from activities that are ambiguous. The Reagan administration did not make such a distinction, but buried the concern about Abalakovo among numerous other issues, of the type amenable to SCC resolution, to the detriment of impressing upon the Soviet Union the seriousness of the radar issue.

Failure to resolve the Abalakovo issue has been primarily the result of Soviet intransigence and use of a flimsy rationale to justify the radar. But the lack of effective avenues of dialogue between the United States and Soviet Union in the 1980s has been a contributing cause of the deadlock. Had there been functioning arms control negotiations in Geneva in 1984, it might have been possible for the United States to deal with the Abalakovo issue by including consideration of the Soviet radar in a more general discussion of restrictions on LPARs and ABM systems. But from the time the INF and START talks were broken off, at the end of 1983, until early 1985, when the new comprehensive negotiations began, the SCC was the only operating U.S.-Soviet conduit for discussing strategic-weapon issues. Had there been the type of effective back channel that existed until 1976 between Kissinger and Dobrynin, the two countries might have been able to find a mutually acceptable solution to Abalakovo before construction reached an advanced stage and before the issue became divisive. But no such informal mechanism existed in the early 1980s. The Abalakovo radar would have posed a difficult problem under any circumstances, but the issue emerged at a particularly inauspicious stage in U.S.-Soviet relations.

Even before direct remedies moved beyond reach, the SCC should have discussed the questions posed by Abalakovo. The siting of LPARs presented a general problem for ABM Treaty compliance, a problem that was clearly emerging by the late 1970s. The creep of LPARs away from clearly permitted siting and configuration began with the Soviet Pechora radar and has continued with the U.S. PAVE PAWS radars in Georgia and Texas, the Soviet Abalakovo radar, and the U.S. Thule and Fylingdales radars. The United States and Soviet Union should have utilized the SCC in an anticipatory fashion, in line with its broad mandate, throughout the late 1970s and early 1980s to discuss measures to implement the ABM Treaty provisions restricting LPARs from having ABM potential. Instead, the SCC became a victim of polemics about alleged violations.

By arguing that Abalakovo's purpose was space tracking, the Soviets exploited a loophole provided by ambiguities in ABM Treaty provisions covering LPARs. With a return to a problem-solving approach by the two sides, the SCC might still function usefully to reduce such ambiguities and might bring about U.S.-Soviet agreement on steps, consistent with the ABM Treaty, for more effective restraint in the future siting of LPARs. Although the Soviets initially were uncooperative in discussing Abalakovo, the importance of the radar issue has gradually been impressed on the Soviets, largely through the contacts between Soviet officials and private U.S. nongovernmental experts. Over time the Soviets have provided more information about the radar facility while still publicly maintaining the space-tracking argument. Since late 1985 the Soviet Union has appeared eager to resolve the Abalakovo issue. In November 1985 the Soviet Union made an offer in the Geneva arms control negotiations, repeated at the fall 1986 SCC session, which implicitly recognized that the Abalakovo radar violates the ABM Treaty. The Soviets offered to stop construction on Abalakovo if the United States stopped construction on the new Thule LPAR and scrapped plans for the new Fylingdales LPAR. The Soviets contend that the Thule and Fylingdales radar programs violate the ABM Treaty because they involve new early-warning LPARs not located on the periphery of the United States. The United States contends that they are permitted modernizations of radars that existed at the time the ABM Treaty was signed. Although it is questionable whether the issue of the Abalakovo radar, as a clear violation, should be linked to any other issue, the Soviet proposal does indicate a willingness to address the Abalakovo problem.

Concluding Remarks

During the 1970s the SCC operated slowly but adequately to address U.S. and Soviet compliance concerns and to design procedures to implement agreements. The transformation of the SCC from a functioning forum that dealt with compliance concerns in the 1970s to a stalemated enterprise in the 1980s prompts several observations. First, U.S. and Soviet use of the SCC mechanism, throughout its existence, has been less than ideal. Both the United States and Soviet Union have practiced behavior in the SCC that has impeded its functioning. Each side has responded in an extremely leisurely manner to compliance concerns raised by the other side. Slow Soviet adjustment of its SA-5 program and even slower U.S. response on Minuteman shelters typified such behavior. Both countries have also tended to raise concerns in a tit-for-tat fashion, preventing the SCC from concentrating on important issues. Behavior of this sort has created frustrations with the SCC, opening the commission up to the sort of attack launched within the United States in the 1980s. If the SCC mechanism is to work in the future, each country must make a greater effort to address compliance concerns in a more responsible manner.

Second, the SCC is not likely to deal effectively with clear violations that are not acknowledged by the offending party. Higher-level diplomatic means must be available to address such violations, but must only be adopted upon clear determination that violations have indeed occurred. The SCC should continue to address issues that surround treaty ambiguities. For the sake of credibility and effectiveness, neither side should mix concerns about clear violations with concerns about ambiguous behavior.

Third, the United States and the Soviet Union have not utilized the SCC to the full extent of its charter. The SCC has the mandate to consider trends on the horizon that could affect the treaties under its jurisdiction. One such trend in the late 1970s and early 1980s was the movement of the two countries away from clear compliance with the ABM Treaty in their siting of LPARs. The two countries clearly should have used the SCC to approach this trend in a joint, problem-solving fashion and should in the future exhibit the foresight to discuss military developments that potentially threaten treaty compliance.

Finally, the SCC cannot be fully insulated from the overall trend in U.S.-Soviet relations. The effectiveness of the SCC is inextricably linked to the momentum of the arms control process and is dependent upon the desire of both sides to use the SCC as a tool to cultivate greater clarity and relevancy of arms control agreements. It is no coincidence that the most productive years of the arms control process were also the most productive years in the SCC. Anticipation of SALT II during the 1970s gave each side incentives to continue to adhere to the Interim Agreement and to resolve disputes in order to maintain its effectiveness. The effective operation of the SCC gave SALT negotiators assurance that the provisions they were drafting could be refined and revised at a later date if they proved to be less than perfect. The interaction between the negotiations and the SCC generally reinforced the arms control process.

In the tense atmosphere of the 1980s, the SCC has attempted to function without the support of productive arms control negotiations. The Soviets have not always been forthcoming with information in response to U.S. concerns, nor have they always proven eager to resolve issues. Opponents of existing and future arms agreements in the United States have attacked the SCC directly. Abalakovo has presented a new type of compliance concern—an actual violation. The Reagan administration's use of public diplomacy has precluded exploration of options that might have led to resolution of compliance issues when they first arose. Rather, the administration has chosen to characterize the configuration of the SS-25 and Soviet encryption, as well as many more minor concerns, as violations by the Soviet Union of its political and arms control commitments, using these as evidence in their public accusations of Soviet cheating. And yet, it was within the proven capabilities of the SCC to resolve those issues by clarifying the ambiguous treaty language pertaining to them.

In recent years the SCC has been asked to deal with tougher issues than it has ever faced before, in a highly confrontational atmosphere. In the 1980s the body has not found the support it needs from the high levels of the U.S. administration. Although the SCC can be protected from critics outside government, as it was during the 1970s, it is more difficult to shelter the delicate SCC mechanism when opposition to its functioning to resolve disputes emanates from within the government itself.

Ambiguities in treaty language will inevitably give rise to uncertainties of interpretation, in ways that could not have been predicted by arms control negotiators. Without a body such as the SCC, functioning as an integral part of the arms control process, treaties become out-of-date and irrelevant. Until the United States and Soviet Union return the SCC to its role of facilitating U.S.-Soviet agreement on procedures for implementing agreements and reaching joint treaty interpretations, and, indeed, until they expand and improve the SCC's role, no existing or future arms control agreement will be capable of operating effectively over time.

Chapter Nine

Conclusion: Compliance and the Future of Arms Control

The United States and the Soviet Union stand at a crossroads. Down one path lie measures to strengthen existing arms control agreements and to use them as the basis for future restraints on weapons and behavior that will improve national and international security. The other path leads toward dismantling the arms control limits that have been achieved over the past thirty years. The patterns of behavior that have been exhibited by the United States and the Soviet Union since the early 1980s are leading both countries down the second path.

Although the fundamental interest of the two sides in arms control has not changed, changes in the political environment since 1979 have led the United States and Soviet Union to become embroiled in a wide-ranging controversy over compliance with agreements. By exaggerating problems and failing to resolve disputes, Washington and Moscow have generated a perceived crisis in compliance with arms control agreements. This perceived crisis has undermined confidence in arms control as a method of improving security. Now, as a result, compliance with arms control agreements faces a real crisis of major proportions. Movement to withdraw from treaties by the United States, and potentially by the Soviet Union in response, not only weakens existing accords, but also sharply decreases the possibility for any new arms control agreements in the future. This concluding chapter provides a summary description of the present compliance situation and explores the reasons for the impending compliance crisis; the final section proposes a new U.S. strategy for strengthening arms control compliance and for reinvigorating the process for resolving compliance disputes.

Overall Pattern of Compliance

As a result of its review, the working group reached conclusions about the current arms control compliance situation in three areas: the overall compliance picture, the process of resolving compliance disputes, and the political context within which arms control agreements operate.

The allegations that either the Soviet Union or United States routinely violates arms control agreements are false. A net assessment points strongly to a U.S. and Soviet record of compliance, not noncompliance, with the terms of arms control agreements. Today, the majority of control agreements remain free of any significant compliance concerns.

Central Provisions Upheld

Even when compliance has been questioned, the most central provisions of arms control agreements have been upheld. In the case of SALT II, for example, until the United States withdrew from the treaty in November 1986 both sides respected the important numerical ceilings and subceilings on offensive nuclear forces, which had helped to preserve the essential stability of the nuclear balance.

Arms control agreements have provided a strong net benefit for U.S. security. Their provisions have rendered the nature of Soviet nuclear forces more predictable, decreased the danger of conflict that could possibly lead to a nuclear war, and decreased the negative environmental consequences of nuclear-weapon testing.

Not only has the U.S.-Soviet pattern until recently been one of compliance with arms control agreements, but when one party to an agreement has challenged the other with regard to compliance, until the early 1980s the pattern was one of accommodation to resolve disagreements. In some cases this adjustment involved changes in the behavior of the United States or Soviet Union. In other instances the parties cooperated to clarify the activities in question in a way that put compliance concerns to rest.

In the early 1980s the process of accommodation broke down. Although programs begun during the 1970s have been the targets of allegations of noncompliance, most of the signs of dissatisfaction about compliance from 1980 on have been an expression of general frustration about the state of U.S.-Soviet relations and the arms control process. Even considering the Abalakovo radar—the one, clear Soviet violation—there has been no major, overall change in the level of compliance by either country.

Lack of Net Assessment

Nonetheless, in annual noncompliance reports produced by the Reagan administration since 1983, there has been an overemphasis on alleged Soviet violations of agreements (and no reference to potential U.S. violations). The U.S. approach has lacked a net assessment, which must be the basis for any reasoned analysis of arms control compliance. The impression created by this U.S. concentration on alleged Soviet violations—that the Soviet Union is in widespread violation of its arms control commitments—is simply not accurate. Soviet compliance performance does not justify the November 1986 U.S. decision to terminate its pledge not to undercut the SALT II Treaty and to withdraw from the 1972 Interim Agreement, nor does it warrant U.S. withdrawal from any other arms control treaties.

Nor do most of the Soviet charges of U.S. noncompliance stand up to scrutiny. The overwhelming majority of U.S. and Soviet charges of noncompliance relate to ambiguous treaty provisions or ambiguous behavior. Such questions will predictably arise, illustrating the ongoing need to interpret treaty provisions in light of developments in technology and behavior. With the exception of the Abalakovo radar, the U.S. and Soviet behavior that has been the subject of charges of noncompliance involves either so-called gray areas, or activities that are questionable but are not clear violations. The working group's findings regarding gray-area issues and questionable compliance can be grouped into six categories:

1. Issues that have been previously resolved through the Standing Consultative Commission. Soviet charges regarding the Shemya radar and Minuteman missile shelters have been adequately resolved in the SCC. U.S. concerns relating to the Soviet Union's concurrent testing of SAMs and ABM radars have been adequately dealt with through a 1985 common understanding achieved in the SCC, unless new concerns about Soviet behavior come to light.

2. Questions that are no longer relevant because of unilateral changes in the behavior of one party. U.S. charges relating to Soviet violation of SALT II SNDV limits, SS-16 ICBM deployment, the Backfire production rate, and the Helsinki Final Act military-exercise notification requirements have been made irrelevant by unilateral Soviet corrective action. Until August 1985, when the Soviet Union began a nineteen-month moratorium on nuclear testing, the Kremlin repeatedly violated the LTBT through emissions of small amounts of radioactivity, released during underground nuclear tests, which crossed Soviet borders into other countries. These were apparently inadvertent violations, similar to U.S. venting or seepage prior to the 1980s. Such emissions have in the past exposed neighboring countries and Soviet citizens to low-level radioactivity. It would be considered a violation if venting that caused detectable radioactivity to cross Soviet borders were to occur in the future.

3. Allegations that are based on questionable evidence or uncertain methodologies for determining violations. U.S. allegations of Soviet noncompliance with the Backfire range limit and the 150-kiloton limit of the TTBT are unsupportable, based on the best technical evidence available. In the TTBT case, the methodological limitations in measuring the yield of underground nuclear tests are well known. A Soviet charge concerning MIRVed ABM interceptors is irrelevant; no such interceptors have been tested by the United States. Allegations that the Soviet Union has violated both the Geneva Protocol and the Biological Weapons Convention have not been substantiated.

4. Questions that relate to the early planning of a questionable system. Soviet complaints about the Midgetman ICBM are not relevant, since the system is only in its early planning stages. U.S. complaints about Soviet movement toward an ABM territorial defense are based on an exaggeration of the capabilities of individual ABM system components and on a disregard for basic limitations in the Soviet infrastructure that would make it difficult for the Soviets to field such a system.

5. **Charges that are vague or do not relate to the actual provisions of an agreement but that have been made for tit-for-tat reasons.** The Soviet Union has charged that the United States has violated the SALT II Protocol, the Non-Proliferation Treaty, and the confidentiality of SCC proceedings and has circumvented SALT II through the deployment of the Pershing II missiles in Europe. Some of these charges are vague, and others fail to relate to precise obligations assumed by the United States in arms control agreements. The Soviets appear to have made these charges largely for purposes of evening the score.

6. **Issues of treaty interpretation or implementation about which common understandings or agreed statements could be reached through the SCC if the process of dispute resolution were functioning effectively.** A smaller subset of the gray-area compliance issues are appropriate for discussion in the SCC, with the objective of seeking common interpretations to resolve existing ambiguities about treaty language or behavior. Among the issues that should be addressed in the SCC are the mobility of ABM components, rapid reload of ABM launchers, ABM capabilities of SAMs, verification of missile-launcher association, and procedures for dealing with remaining facilities at sites for dismantled ICBMs. In addition, improved cooperative verification procedures would increase confidence in compliance in several areas where U.S. or Soviet behavior has unilaterally improved, such as the apparent Soviet removal of SS-16 components from the Plesetsk test site. These are relatively minor, technical issues, which could be resolved in the SCC with the proper will and spirit.

Three Areas of Questionable Compliance

Although overall compliance has been good, in a few areas U.S. and Soviet programs are a cause for concern. Since 1980 both countries have begun to stretch treaty provisions in a manner that, if it were to continue, could prove extremely destructive to arms control agreements. In each of the cases of questionable compliance, there is disagreement between the two sides about how to interpret treaty obligations. These disputes could be resolved and measures could be taken to close treaty loopholes that have allowed questionable interpretations to arise. Again, such an approach would require sufficient will on both sides to resolve the disputes.

In the case of the Soviet SS-25 ICBM, the two countries disagree about which components of an ICBM must be included in measuring the throw-weight of a missile for purposes of determining compliance with the SALT II one-new-type rule. The dispute over Soviet encryption of missile–flight-test telemetry involves interpretation of the SALT II provision that prohibits the impeding of verification through encryption. In both cases the Soviet Union has adopted an excessively permissive interpretation of its treaty obligations.

U.S. modernization of its LPARs at Thule, Greenland, and Fylingdales Moor, England, raises the question of compliance with the ABM Treaty provision that all such new LPARs must be restricted to the "periphery of the national territory and oriented outward." The ABM Treaty prohibits the deployment of such radars for early warning "in the future" unless they are so located and oriented. The treaty thereby implies that early-warning radars that existed at the time the treaty went into effect may remain, but it does not explicitly grant permission to modernize such facilities. The U.S. program raises a question about the distinction between the modernization of existing radars and the creation of a new facility that could have utility for an ABM system.

The U.S. PAVE PAWS program is creating a network of radars that will provide substantial coverage of U.S. national territory and population, raising a question as to whether PAVE PAWS are oriented outward. In the cases of the Thule and Fylingdales radars, and the two PAVE PAWS radars in Georgia and Texas, the United States is adopting a very permissive interpretation of its treaty obligations.

None of these activities, by itself, has major national-security implications for either side. The SS-25 may offer the Soviets somewhat greater throw-weight than permitted, but as long as the fractionation limits of SALT II were in force the missile was still limited to one warhead. Lacking those fractionation limits, the SS-25 constitutes a somewhat more important military issue.

Soviet encryption probably has the most significant consequences for U.S. security of any Soviet practice discussed in this report. It is possible that the United States can verify Soviet SALT II compliance using data from unencrypted telemetry and other sources, but with less precision and confidence and with greater difficulty than if the United States had access to Soviet telemetry. Because of the high level of Soviet encryption, the United States may have less confidence in the future in its ability to verify Soviet compliance with those provisions—such as the SALT II 5 percent limit on modifications to existing ICBM types—that demand precision in verification.

From the standpoint of Soviet security, the Fylingdales and PAVE PAWS radars, in particular, could theoretically play a role in an ABM defense of Europe or the United States, respectively. But each of the radars is a highly vulnerable target, making it unsuited for ABM purposes, and is not part of a network of components that could give it certain ABM potential.

The permissibility or impermissibility of each of these questionable activities could be substantially clarified through the SCC if the United States and Soviet Union were committed to strengthening the terms of the treaties in question. Each dispute involves treaty provisions that were imprecise when they were written and are today in need of new interpretation and application in light of developments in military technology.

SDI: Compliance Concerns

In issuing statements endorsing the early deployment of strategic defenses and in advancing a permissive reinterpretation of the ABM Treaty, the United States today risks undercutting the very basis on which that agreement rests. As submitted to Congress in 1986, the administration's SDI program will be compliant with the traditional interpretation of the ABM Treaty for the next three years. But in pursuit of SDI some Reagan administration officials are adopting a highly permissive approach toward a treaty in force and of unlimited duration.

Of particular concern are statements by Secretary of Defense Caspar Weinberger and Attorney General Edwin Meese, among other officials, stating the U.S. intention to deploy an ABM system in the near future, in a configuration that would almost necessarily violate the treaty; the administration's reinterpretation of the ABM Treaty to permit development and testing of non-fixed and non-land-based strategic-defense technologies, on the basis of highly questionable legal analysis; its use of inappropriate, legalistic distinctions in planning tests of components of such exotic systems; and its pursuit of certain specific experiments that could in the future violate the ABM Treaty.

These statements and prospective activities are of concern primarily because they could serve as a basis for a Soviet decision to abandon the ABM Treaty, based on the Soviet right to take steps to offset increased threats to national security. Such a breakdown in compliance with the ABM Treaty is not in the long-term interest of the United States.

The SCC could productively examine future tests planned for the SDI program in light of ABM Treaty obligations. The SCC could also review the negotiating history and provide a forum for both countries to express their views about ABM Treaty obligations that are at issue in the debate over the restrictive versus permissive interpretations of the treaty.

Abalakovo Is Only Violation

Among the forty charges of noncompliance leveled by both countries, only one—the Soviet large phased-array radar at Abalakovo—is a clear-cut, current violation of an agreement. In rationalizing this violation, the Soviet Union has sought to exploit a loophole in the ABM Treaty permitting LPARs for space tracking and verification to be located other than on the periphery of a country's territory and oriented outward.

The United States is unable to establish by national technical means of verification that Abalakovo is a radar for space tracking or verification. The United States can reasonably conclude that the radar's purpose is early warning, because the radar fills a gap in Soviet early-warning coverage and because it is the same in design as the other Pechora-class radars located around the periphery of the Soviet Union, which perform this function. The radar's early-warning capability must be considered a violation of the ABM Treaty because the installation is neither on the periphery of the Soviet Union nor oriented outward.

The military significance of this radar, without other components of a nationwide ABM system, is small, just as new U.S. LPARs by themselves have little strategic significance. The case against the radar would be stronger if the ABM Treaty contained more-precise criteria for distinguishing radars for space tracking or verification from those for early warning. Yet the United States must regard this Soviet violation of the ABM Treaty seriously; the U.S. government must discourage Soviet noncompliance with arms control agreements even when such noncompliance has little direct military significance.

U.S. and Soviet Behavior Is Interactive

There is no evidence to suggest that the Soviet Union has a policy of violating arms control agreements. However, Soviet compliance behavior does reflect the leadership's sensitivity to a host of external factors, including the state of U.S.-Soviet relations, the character of U.S. foreign and military policies, and the health of the arms control process.

The Soviet Union typically designs weapon systems for maximum military value and economic efficiency, often drawing a fine line between compliance and noncompliance. In some cases, political intervention in the military procurement system may be required to ensure that a Soviet weapon system does not violate the terms of an arms control agreement. This domestic situation has produced a tendency on the part of the Soviet Union to push up against the limits of the obligations that it has assumed in arms control treaties.

Even so, U.S. behavior and the state of U.S.-Soviet relations to some degree affects whether or not the Soviet system produces outcomes that are questionable from the standpoint of treaty compliance. Intervention in the military-procurement process by Soviet political leaders is less likely to occur if U.S.-Soviet relations are tense, if the Soviet perception of the U.S. strategic threat is heightened, and if the arms control process is stalemated. Soviet perceptions in the late 1970s and early 1980s—that U.S. interest in future arms control agreements and commitment to compliance with existing accords had declined—may have contributed to the leadership's lack of interest in imposing a conservative view of treaty obligations on the Soviet procurement system. The lack of such intervention may have shaped Soviet decisions on the Abalakovo radar, the level of Soviet encryption, and the configuration of the SS-25 missile.

From 1981 through 1983 Soviet behavior was characterized by a decreased willingness to work with the United States to resolve compliance disputes, a decreased willingness to alter Soviet behavior in response to U.S. compliance concerns, a decline in the amount of information about Soviet weapon programs the Soviet Union was willing to share to support arms agreements and to resolve compliance disputes, and a tendency to resort under pressure to partial truths about Soviet behavior, particularly in the case of Abalakovo.

Beginning in 1984, the Soviet attitude toward compliance altered somewhat, and since the advent of the Gorbachev leadership in March 1985, some changes in the Soviet position have become evident. The Soviet leadership took steps that could strengthen the internal constituency for compliance in the Soviet Union. Soviet representatives have also made proposals in the SCC to resolve both the encryption and the Abalakovo disputes. Unilateral measures were taken to improve Soviet compliance in several respects, and a new Soviet approach to verification emerged, stressing more cooperative measures. In particular, the Soviet Union may have taken steps, beginning in 1986, to respond to the Reagan administration's proposition that, if Soviet behavior improved in unspecified ways, the United States might reconsider its decision to abandon the SALT II limits.

Compliance as Political Issue in United States

It is hard to escape the conclusion that Soviet compliance with arms control agreements became a more divisive political issue in the United States than might otherwise have been the case because of the highly manipulative manner in which many U.S. critics of arms control chose to characterize and frame the problem. The phenomenon dates back at least to 1979, during the debate over ratification of the SALT II Treaty, when political forces opposed to SALT II adopted the tactic of raising exaggerated concerns about the Soviet compliance record. Lacking any detailed evaluation of Soviet behavior, preparatory to the 1980 election campaign the Republican party adopted the position that the Soviet Union had not complied with its arms control commitments. The 1980 Republican party platform asserted Soviet noncompliance, and charged that the Carter administration had downplayed Soviet cheating.

The politicization of the compliance debate intensified in 1982, when the Reagan administration tasked the General Advisory Committee on Arms Control and Disarmament, historically a source of advice on measures to strengthen the arms control process, to conduct a search for Soviet arms control violations. The resulting 1983 GAC report further politicized the issue by charging the Soviets with widespread cheating but failing to provide a convincing analysis in support of its position. The report simply applied new and inappropriate standards to old issues, many of which did not relate to Soviet commitments undertaken in arms control agreements.

In part through congressional pressure, the process of reporting on alleged Soviet arms control violations was institutionalized in the United States in what can only be characterized as a highly destructive manner. As part of the defense-procurement process, the White House was required, by Public Law 99-145, passed by Congress in the summer of 1985, to report annually to Congress on Soviet noncompliance. But the charge to the White House did not include a net assessment of Soviet compliance versus Soviet noncompliance, nor did it require any examination of U.S. behavior. The focus on alleged Soviet violations, all but one of them identified by this report as inaccurate, ambiguous, or no longer relevant, has served to keep the image of widespread Soviet arms control violations before the public eye.

The three reports that the White House produced to satisfy congressional requirements applied standards to Soviet behavior that were inconsistent from one year to the next. Soviet activities were classified by the 1985 White House report according to the certainty with which the administration believed a violation to have occurred. The February 1986 report classified activities according to the legal status of agreements.

The trend in the three White House reports was to move from a lesser to a greater number of charges each year: seven in 1984, thirteen in 1985, and eighteen in 1986. In fact, a closer reading of the reports suggests something quite different: Only four of the eighteen charges in the February 1986 report were said to be violations of *legal* commitments. Yet the total number of charges highlighted in the reports rose from year to year, creating a perception that the number of Soviet violations had steadily increased.

Charges of Soviet noncompliance and U.S. strategic modernization plans were also linked in U.S. policy in a manner that decreased the credibility of U.S. objections to Soviet behavior. In 1986 U.S. officials cited Soviet noncompliance to justify abandonment of the SALT I Interim Agreement and the SALT II Treaty. Moreover, the emphasis on Soviet violations tended to shift from year to year in relation to priorities in Reagan administration strategic-weapon programs. The 1985 report highlighted Soviet SALT II violations, as the United States contemplated withdrawal from that agreement in order to permit deployment of further MIRVed strategic systems. The 1986 report emphasized alleged Soviet movement toward a territorial ABM defense, as the administration pursued its SDI program. These links created the perception, in the minds of Soviet leaders and among some U.S. constituencies, that the Reagan administration was complaining about Soviet noncompliance in order to rationalize and therefore facilitate U.S. abandonment of its arms control commitments.

The United States took insufficient notice of the Soviet proposals that were made after 1984 to resolve compliance disputes in the SCC, particularly with regard to Abalakovo and encryption. As indicated, there is evidence to suggest that the Soviet Union embarked on an effort to improve its compliance behavior and to resolve compliance disputes in response to the May 1986 announcement by President Reagan that he would take such Soviet actions into account in his decision regarding U.S. SALT II abrogation. For the most part, the Soviet effort went unnoticed by the U.S. government.

In addition, various Defense Department and ACDA officials have sought to undercut the ability of the U.S. SCC commissioner, General Richard Ellis, to pursue resolution of compliance disputes with the Soviet Union. Attacks on the effectiveness of the SCC, particularly from the Defense Department in November 1985, have served to further weaken the commission. In an environment in which the U.S. secretary of defense is quoted by the press as referring to the SCC as an "Orwellian memory hole down which U.S. concerns have been dumped like yesterday's trash," the SCC cannot function successfully.[1]

Through this politicization of the compliance issue in the United States, the Reagan administration has at times behaved as if it desired to withdraw from all existing strategic arms control agreements with the Soviet Union. The United States has acted in a fashion that undercuts the essential process of resolving disagreements that arise with regard to treaty compliance, rather than seeking to make the process work. This, combined with Soviet stretching of the terms of agreements and stubbornness in dealing with many of the compliance issues, has caused the arms control process to lose its give-and-take. If this situation continues, there is little hope for arms control over the long term.

Dispute Resolution Has Broken Down

The reason that so many gray-area issues and areas of questionable compliance have persisted between the United States and Soviet Union is not that compliance has always been poor or that it has degraded substantially in recent years. The situation persists because of the breakdown, beginning in the early 1980s, of the mechanisms for resolving compliance disputes.

Since the early 1980s the SCC has been unable to function successfully in a climate of tense U.S.-Soviet relations, Soviet intransigence, U.S. accusations of Soviet noncompliance, and the virtual stalemate in strategic arms control negotiations. The movement in U.S. policy from problem solving through the SCC to public confrontation has greatly decreased the effectiveness of the SCC.

U.S. public diplomacy may have succeeded in producing some small improvements in Soviet compliance behavior, but its impact has been negligible in resolving the major compliance issues. During the 1970s the SCC dealt reasonably effectively with such compliance problems as the Soviet "III-X" launch-control facilities, the U.S. Minuteman missile shelters, and the Soviet SA-5 radar. But in the 1980s none of the major compliance issues— encryption, PAVE PAWS, Thule/Fylingdales, the SS-25, SDI, or the Abalakovo radar—have been successfully addressed through the SCC. Only two, rather minor, common understandings have been reached, both completing work begun during the Carter administration. In the 1980s the SCC was forced to deal with tougher compliance issues than before, in a tense political climate and lacking unified support from the U.S. administration. As a result, the SCC was rendered ineffective as a U.S.-Soviet mechanism for resolving disputes.

The driving force behind the compliance disputes of the 1980s has not been a crisis in arms control compliance but rather a crisis of confidence in the underlying basis of U.S.-Soviet security relations, and thus in the practical manifestations of this relationship: arms control agreements. The Soviet Union and United States are both in some measure responsible for the crisis. The causes lie partly in the political forces at work in each country and partly in deeper trends in their security relationship.

Political Forces

The Soviet tendency to stretch the terms of arms control agreements to accommodate Soviet military programs contributed to U.S. frustration with the arms control process that became evident at the end of the 1970s. The Soviet Union has had an insufficiently strong internal constituency to argue for restrictive interpretations of Soviet arms control obligations. The lack of such a constituency has made the Soviet Union a difficult partner for the United States, which has a relatively strong compliance constituency.

Since 1981 the Soviet Union has been insufficiently open with the United States, both in the SCC and through other diplomatic channels, about providing information to support its positions regarding compliance. The Soviets have not backed up their statements about the throw-weight of the SS-13, for instance, by providing the necessary supporting data. Initially the Soviets were also reticent to discuss U.S. compliance concerns in the SCC, contributing to the stalemate in the commission. And they exhibited a lack of precision in their tit-for-tat charges of U.S. noncompliance in response to the U.S. allegations.

On the U.S. side, the Reagan administration's temporary but sharp public rejection of negotiated arms control in 1981 caused the Soviets to doubt the U.S. commitment to past agreements and to further progress in arms control. Following an eighteen-month hiatus, during which the president repeatedly referred to the SALT II Treaty as "fatally flawed" and declined to resume strategic arms control negotiations with Moscow, the administration returned to what had been a consistent U.S. policy over the previous two decades: to seek moderation of the U.S.-Soviet nuclear-weapon competition through arms control. Despite this shift in policy, the signals that the U.S. government projected in 1981–82 about the possible abandonment of the arms control process have had a persistent effect on U.S.-Soviet relations and on the arms control process. Through its effect on Soviet perceptions and decisions, and on the process of resolving compliance disputes, this detour in U.S. policy has exerted an extremely negative influence on the compliance situation.

Deeper Causes

It would be a mistake to attribute the compliance crisis solely to the perturbations of politics and of U.S.-Soviet relations in a narrow sense. The compliance disputes between the United States and Soviet Union are symptomatic of deeper dissatisfactions on both sides with the terms of existing arms control agreements.

The underlying cause of the compliance problems that do exist and of the trend toward U.S. treaty abandonment is the shared U.S. and Soviet concern about security—or insecurity—and the consequent pursuit by both sides of strategic defensive technologies and measures to increase the accuracy and lethality of land-based forces. The high level of threat each country perceives creates strong motivations on both sides to move ahead with strategic defense and with new ICBM systems that are mobile and survivable, avenues of military development that have been restricted by past arms control treaties.

Strategic defense has been stringently limited by the ABM Treaty on the assumption that such defenses could never be reliable and that the competition in offensive forces would be intensified if an attempt to deploy defensive systems were undertaken. Treaties have established ceilings to freeze the number of offensive strategic-missile launchers on both sides. Treaties have limited new ICBM types to constrain qualitative improvements and to encourage the deployment of more-survivable sea-based forces. The logic of the limitations contained in the ABM Treaty, SALT I, and SALT II continues to have validity today. Yet it is precisely these provisions of these particular treaties that are now threatened by U.S. and Soviet policies.

Today strategic arms control agreements face the most crucial test of their fourteen-year history. The test is whether the arms control constraints that have been devised can withstand strong pressure from both sides to pursue the very type of programs that have been limited. In 1987 the military programs of both superpowers threaten to contravene important treaty limits.

Soviet practice has been to seek further developments in both offensive and defensive forces by stretching the terms of agreements. U.S. policy in recent years has been to dispense with such limits overtly. Although the methods of pursuing these objectives are distinctive, matching the closed nature of Soviet society, on the one hand, and the more open nature of U.S. society, on the other, the results for arms control are much the same. Arms control limits cannot reasonably be expected to endure when they are hard-pressed by the desire for military developments that contravene both the underlying premises and the specific restrictions of agreements, unless there is a functioning arms control process to balance desires for new programs with arms control restrictions.

Yet no strategic arms control agreement has been successfully concluded and ratified by the United States since 1972, a lapse of fifteen years. No strategic arms control agreement has been successfully *negotiated* since 1979. This means that the provisions of existing agreements have become dangerously out-of-date in relation to new military technologies and that developments in the military sphere have not been integrated into arms limitations.

The ability of current arms agreements to endure is highly dependent upon the perception that arms control is an ongoing process and that current limitations will be followed by other restrictions that will continue to equalize the military balance and forestall unilateral advantage. When this process breaks down, the incentives decline to comply with existing limits, and incentives increase to redress the perceived military threat by unilateral means.

The Impending Crisis

As a result of some Soviet stretching of treaty provisions, U.S. exaggeration of the problems with treaty compliance, and the inability of both sides to move toward a resolution of the outstanding compliance disputes, arms control now faces a crisis that is quite real, even if it is based upon false perceptions. The United States has withdrawn from its commitment not to undercut the SALT II Treaty and from the Interim Agreement. This U.S. step—which is not justified by the actual record of Soviet compliance with the SALT agreements—removes all existing constraints on strategic offensive nuclear forces. No strategic arms control agreement to replace these limits is yet in sight. The future of the ABM Treaty is also uncertain, because of the Soviet violation of the agreement in the case of the Abalakovo radar and the U.S. push for a more permissive interpretation of the treaty to accommodate the SDI program.

The situation with regard to existing arms control agreements raises serious doubts about the prospect for new accords in the future. It is highly questionable whether the United States and Soviet Union will be able to conclude any new strategic arms control agreements along the more radical lines that have been under discussion, such as 50 percent reductions in offensive nuclear forces, as long as both countries continue to emphasize violations and fail to move toward resolution of disputes relating to existing accords.

Lacking a functioning process of dispute resolution, there is little prospect that, even if new agreements are reached, the two countries will be able to sustain them over time. Progress toward an INF agreement notwithstanding, there is a significant disjunction between the public perception that nuclear arms control negotiations are proceeding and the reality that many of the minimal limits of the past rest on increasingly shaky ground.

Need for a Compliance Strategy

Compliance with arms control agreements is arms control in practice, and it is critical for the arms control process. Yet the U.S. government today lacks an effective approach to evaluating and strengthening compliance with arms control agreements. It is clear that whatever elements of a compliance strategy the United States has been pursuing for the past six years have not worked. Although the Soviets have altered some programs to improve compliance since 1984, they have not changed their behavior in the areas of most concern—the SS-25, encryption, and Abalakovo—in response to U.S. pressure. The key mechanism for refining the meaning of treaty provisions and for ensuring compliance, the SCC, has become paralyzed.

The apparent U.S. compliance strategy during the past six years has consisted of arriving at unilateral interpretations of the meaning of treaty provisions, publicly accusing the Soviets of violations, demanding changes in Soviet behavior publicly and privately, and embarking on an arms control breakout policy of its own in pursuit of strategic modernization. All of these steps have been taken in an atmosphere of increased military competition, no progress toward new arms control agreements, and tense political relations. Although this strategy may have served other political purposes and needs, it has abjectly failed in its only legitimate purpose: ensuring that the Soviets comply with arms accords and improve their behavior where they are treading on treaty limits.

Recommendations: A U.S. Strategy for Ensuring Compliance

Arms control is a process that, to function successfully, requires give-and-take between the negotiating partners. In addressing current U.S.-Soviet compliance issues, the main objective should be to restore the process of give-and-take, which will require the cooperation and support of both the U.S. and Soviet governments.

To help restore the process, the United States should take action in five areas. First, the U.S. government should improve the process for evaluating and dealing with compliance issues. Second, the United States should take more constructive steps to resolve existing compliance disputes, which are a political barrier to new arms accords and which represent ongoing issues that will need to be dealt with in any new arms control agreements. Third, the United States should take steps to improve the incentives for the Soviet Union to comply with agreements, and to encourage the Soviet leadership to strengthen its internal constituency for compliance. Fourth, the United States should reaffirm its commitment to existing arms control agreements, thereby helping to restore confidence in the process of dispute resolution. And fifth, the United States should draw on its experience concerning compliance during the past two decades in pursuing the type of provisions in new agreements that will strengthen compliance.

Improving the U.S. Process for Dealing with Compliance

Viewing Soviet compliance behavior in isolation contributes to the exaggeration of compliance problems and impedes the process of resolving disputes. In the future the United States should base evaluations of Soviet compliance on the concept of *net assessment.* Future U.S. annual reports on compliance should include an assessment of Soviet compliance as well as noncompliance *and* an assessment of U.S. compliance and noncompliance.

To give impetus to the process of net assessment, the House Armed Services and Foreign Affairs committees and the Senate Armed Services and Foreign Relations committees should conduct hearings on the manner in which U.S. assessments of Soviet noncompliance have been prepared since 1983, on the substance of the charges of noncompliance that have been made by the United States, and on the state of the SCC and the process of resolving compliance disputes. These hearings should draw on testimony not only from the administration but also from former arms control and intelligence officials, as well as other expert witnesses who can offer additional historical and technical perspectives on the current situation.

Through these hearings the Congress can form an independent judgment about the reasons the arms control dispute-resolution process has broken down and can generate a more comprehensive picture of compliance with existing agreements. This judgment should then be used by the Congress to inform its actions that seek to help resolve existing compliance disputes, that affect future U.S. compliance with agreements, and that influence U.S. approaches in future arms control negotiations. On the basis of the information emerging from such hearings, the Congress can make a net assessment about whether past arms control agreements have served the U.S. national interest.

The controversy over Soviet compliance has distracted attention from measures that the United States could implement to improve the functioning of arms control agreements. In particular, the membership of the General Advisory Committee on Arms Control and Disarmament needs to be reconstituted. Appointees selected to represent a particular ideological viewpoint should be replaced by distinguished senior statesmen and scientists who have worked extensively in the arms control field. The GAC should resume its roles of foreseeing challenges to existing agreements that arise from new developments in technology and policy and of discussing effective new approaches to arms control. Such a group of senior experts on arms control is sorely needed in the latter role today. To ensure continuity, some members of the GAC should continue to serve the government despite changes in administration.

The ability of the SCC to function well in seeking resolution of compliance disputes is key to the successful implementation of arms control agreements. To the extent possible, the U.S. SCC commissioner should be protected from efforts to influence U.S. policies in the SCC arising from different elements in the bureaucracy. The SCC commissioner is currently appointed by the president but operates under instructions emerging from an interagency process that reports to the president. It has been recommended elsewhere that in place of the present system the SCC commissioner report directly to the president, through the assistant for national security affairs.[2]

In theory at least, there is nothing wrong with the existing process. But, to work effectively, it requires substantive presidential involvement to resolve disputes between various agencies. President Reagan has not played this role effectively, either directly or through coordination by the national security adviser. In the future, both the president and his national security adviser must be attentive to the importance of the SCC for resolving compliance disputes, and the White House must provide strong support for the SCC commissioner's work through better oversight and coordination.

U.S. national-security officials should also refrain from making inflammatory public statements about the SCC. The U.S. secretary of defense's reference to the SCC as an "Orwellian memory hole" in an official 1985 document is the type of statement that only undercuts the SCC's effectiveness. Statements of this nature demonstrate to the Soviet leadership the lack of support for the dispute-resolution process in the U.S. government. Consideration should be given to creating a more prominent public role for the U.S. SCC commissioner, and to the SCC's issuing an annual report summarizing progress made in the consultative body.

Finally, it is easy for a U.S. administration to play on public suspicions about Soviet cheating, through exaggerated accounts of Soviet arms control violations and neglect of the positive aspects of the Soviet compliance record. It is a more difficult task for a political leadership to give a genuine reading about the health of arms control agreements, conveying the complexities of interpretation and implementation that such agreements naturally involve. In dealing with compliance issues, the public, the press, and the Congress can and should play a more central role, including pressing the administration to convey the balance of U.S. interests in making the arms control process work rather than simply highlighting alleged instances of Soviet noncompliance.

Resolving the Existing Disputes

It is important for the U.S. public to understand that, because of the lack of enforcement mechanisms in the international arena, arms control treaties are not like criminal statutes. Resolving disputes related to treaties, therefore, requires a continuing negotiation rather than a simple determination of guilt or innocence. What are claimed to be right and wrong interpretations of a treaty will be less persuasive than what continues to be in the interests of both parties. What was intended when a treaty was negotiated is likely to be less important than what the parties can continue to agree on over time. And, when one or both sides refuse to participate in the ongoing negotiation, the process cannot work.

The point of suggesting measures to resolve existing compliance disputes is not to propose the exact set of steps that should be taken by each side. Such a balance of measures is better left to diplomats to achieve. The goal of U.S. policy should be to reinstitute the give-and-take of the arms control process, to get the process of dispute resolution moving once again. The recommendations in this chapter are meant to be illustrative of possible steps the United States and Soviet Union might take in pursuit of that objective.

In dealing with existing disputes, the United States should avoid actions that respond to Soviet activities by mimicking the Soviet behavior in question, thereby loosening the terms of agreements and contributing to the trend toward noncompliance. The objective of U.S. actions should be to convey the message that agreements are to be respected and upheld. The United States should underline this message both through its own behavior and through its response to Soviet activities. The general U.S. approach, if dispute resolution fails, should be to offset any real Soviet military or political advantage gained through noncompliance or questionable compliance. At the same time, the United States should continue to adhere to arms control agreements, working to strengthen them in ways that will prevent noncompliance or questionable compliance in the future.

Rather than abandoning SALT II—an action not warranted by any evidence about Soviet noncompliance with the agreement—the United States should work to strengthen the provisions of the treaty and to reduce ambiguities (while reserving the right to neutralize through measures that do not violate the treaty any Soviet military advantage that may have been gained through questionable compliance with the agreement). The Reagan administration should preempt possible congressional action to compel U.S. compliance with the SALT I and SALT II offensive arms limits by taking steps on its own to reaffirm these agreements. If the administration does *not* take such action and makes no constructive effort to resolve disputes related to these agreements, the Congress should then consider the imposition of budgetary constraints on U.S. programs that might exceed the SALT limits. Different methods for resolving the outstanding compliance issues should be pursued, depending on the particular nature of the activity in question.

Gray-area issues. In addressing the gray-area issues, the United States should emphasize a problem-solving approach in the SCC, seeking dialogue and compromise with the Soviet Union in order to reach new common understandings. The United States should reopen a number of technical issues with the purpose of obtaining agreement in the SCC. In particular, the United States should work through the SCC to

1. pursue an improved definition of "mobility" for ABM components
2. pursue agreed criteria on exercises that demonstrate reload capabilities for ABM launchers
3. pursue an improved definition of what constitutes a flight trajectory "with characteristics of a strategic ballistic missile," a definition to be revised over time as ballistic-missile technology evolves
4. devise an agreed procedure for bomber conversion, dismantling, and destruction
5. devise a method for the Soviets to demonstrate deactivation of their SS-16 ICBMs
6. devise agreed procedures to verify missile-launcher association
7. devise improved rules governing the use of any "remaining" facilities at sites of dismantled missiles
8. define the area containing ICBM silos that must be visible to NTM and may not be covered by environmental shelters, using specific functional criteria
9. complete the data-base updates mandated by SALT II

Two agreements that involve gray area disputes—the Limited Test Ban Treaty and the Threshold Test Ban Treaty—do not presently fall within the jurisdiction of the SCC. Nonetheless, the United States should pursue a similar problem-solving strategy with regard to disputes involving these two treaties. If, for example, in the course of Soviet underground nuclear-weapon tests, radioactivity is released that crosses Soviet borders, such venting would constitute a violation of the LTBT. The United States could offer technical assistance to the Soviet Union in designing underground nuclear tests that will not vent radioactivity, although this is primarily a matter of more conservative engineering practice on the part of the Soviet Union.

A longer-range measure should be pursued to deal with the dispute concerning adherence to the 150-kiloton yield limit of the TTBT. In early 1987 the president placed the TTBT and the Peaceful Nuclear Explosions Treaty (PNET) before the Senate for ratification, with the stipulation that these treaties be supported by more extensive measures to ensure compliance, including provisions for on-site inspection. Taking into account the statistical uncertainty in measuring underground test yields, there is no persuasive evidence that the Soviet Union is in violation of the TTBT. On-site inspection is not necessary to monitor compliance with either accord, and the Congress should not make U.S.-Soviet agreement on such a provision a prerequisite for ratification.

It is, however, possible to improve confidence in the verifiability of these two treaties through other measures. First, it is possible to narrow the margin of uncertainty about compliance with the TTBT. The TTBT Protocol provides for an exchange of data, for calibration purposes, on the geology of the test sites and on two past tests. To increase confidence in the accuracy of such data, a provision could be added to the TTBT Protocol requiring actual seismographic or other readouts to support the data provided.

Access to data from seismographic and other monitors at the test sites could contribute to confidence in the verifiability of the TTBT. The United States could build on the work of the U.S. Natural Resources Defense Council (NRDC) and the Soviet Academy of Sciences, providing for on-site monitors at both test sites. The United States would need to renegotiate the NRDC/Academy of Sciences agreement to require that the monitoring devices operate during tests, a stipulation not contained in the existing agreement, and to arrive at procedures for validating the data obtained. The data from these monitoring devices could be used over time to create and maintain a data base on test yields.

Second, it is possible to encourage conservatism in design of nuclear tests. The United States and Soviet Union could negotiate a common understanding, pursuant to bringing the TTBT into force, that conservatism in design of test yields is desirable. A similar agreement on conservatism of design for containment would also be useful with regard to the LTBT. Such agreements could contribute to the effective functioning of both treaties.

Third, the United States and Soviet Union could strengthen dispute-resolution mechanisms to resolve disputes over compliance with the two testing agreements. A body paralleling the SCC should be created for resolving disputes related to agreements restricting nuclear tests. The PNET provides for the creation of a Joint Consultative Commission (JCC) to resolve disputes related to provisions of that treaty. TTBT ratification should be accompanied by ratification of the PNET and its protocol, which would bring the JCC into being. The JCC could then be extended to support the TTBT and the LTBT, as well as the PNET. Should the PNET not be ratified, the United States should seek to negotiate an agreement with the Soviet Union to establish a new consultative body to address disputes that arise in connection with existing nuclear-testing agreements.

For now, the new consultative body would deal with questions involving the TTBT, the PNET, and the LTBT. If a data base on test yields were created through on-site monitoring, it could be maintained and updated through the JCC. The JCC could be a forum for each side to raise questions about discrepancies between its remotely measured yields and data from local monitors. It could also prove useful for resolving issues related to compliance with a comprehensive test ban, should such an agreement be negotiated in the future.

Such a body would improve confidence in the functioning of the TTBT and the LTBT. But it would also prove of immediate practical utility. Through this new body, the United States could engage the Soviet Union in the test-data exchange required by the TTBT and could review past estimates of test yields in light of new data and methodologies. Such a step would build on the private and government progress that has been made recently to enhance the verifiability of testing limits.

Questionable compliance. The cases of questionable compliance should be dealt with in different ways, depending on the particular issue, the military significance of the behavior in question, and the feasibility of a technical solution. The general approach should be to neutralize any Soviet advantage gained, but not to mimic or overreact to Soviet behavior through treaty breakout, and to exaggerate neither the certainty of violation nor the importance of the potential transgression. Rather, the provisions of the agreement should be strengthened and loopholes closed. To date the United States has not made constructive proposals for the resolution of these disputes. The following are some elements of an approach the United States might want to pursue in the SCC.

Encryption. As an initial step, the Soviet Union should return to the level of encryption that existed at the time the SALT II agreement was signed. Simultaneously, the United States should pursue a solution to this problem through the SCC. The United States should seek a compromise that meets Soviet concerns about the United States' obtaining valuable intelligence information beyond the parameters specified by the treaty and the U.S. need to verify Soviet compliance with treaty provisions. The United States should review again the sources and methods constraints that have precluded giving the Soviets the parameters (or the channels on which such data are transmitted) that the United States must receive unencrypted to verify SALT II compliance.

Given the ambiguity of the SALT II encryption provision, if the United States wants access to a greater amount of unencrypted Soviet data, the United States must be willing to specify some of the data it needs. The United States should also explore other cooperative measures (for example, limited downrange instrumentation) to compensate for the loss of data through encryption.

SS-25 ICBM. The primary way to neutralize any Soviet advantage resulting from the increased throw-weight of the SS-25 is to keep in place the fractionation limits of SALT II. Through the SCC the United States should also urge Soviet leaders to make available more information on the design and throw-weight of the SS-13 ICBM, to support their contention that the SS-25 is a permitted modernization of the SS-13.

The United States should also pursue a common understanding through the SCC that includes instrumentation as part of the throw-weight of ICBMs, to clarify the meaning of "throw-weight" in the SALT II new-type provision. In general, the United States should seek to add more data requirements to the SALT II agreed data base to better support the SALT II qualitative restrictions.

As part of a general effort to get the dispute-resolution process moving again, the United States might want to seek a strategic arms control agreement with the Soviet Union that would limit the deployment of the SS-25, under the presumption that small, mobile ICBMs should only be deployed under appropriate ceilings and limited to a single-warhead configuration.

Thule, Fylingdales, PAVE PAWS. Since the degree of permitted modernization of existing early-warning radars is not specified by the ABM Treaty, agreement on such a definition should be pursued in the SCC. Such a definition should probably be based on an understanding about the level of modernization that unacceptably increases the ABM potential of such radars. As an initial step, the administration should make the ABM Treaty negotiating record accessible to the SCC and to the appropriate congressional committees, in order to determine the thinking of the negotiators regarding limitations on modernization of existing early-warning radars. Construction of the new U.S. LPAR at Fylingdales should be delayed, pending a review of the program in light of a common U.S.-Soviet understanding regarding the permitted level of modernization of such radars.

It is important to stop the creep of early-warning LPARs away from strict respect for the "on the periphery, oriented outward" restrictions of the ABM Treaty. This is a problem with both Abalakovo and PAVE PAWS. To seek a longer-term solution to the problem of LPARs, the United States and Soviet Union, through the SCC, should carefully review the language of Article VI, with the intent of reducing ambiguity about the definitions of "on the periphery, oriented outward." Also through the SCC, the United States should seek an agreement with the Soviets requiring case-by-case reviews of compliance questions relating to future LPARs for early warning, in light of the more precise definitions reached by the SCC. The SCC should also explore technical means to designate the unsuitability of an LPAR for ABM battle management, such as operating wavelength, lack of site defense, "softness," and limits on infrastructure.

Finally, the United States should seek a common understanding with the Soviet Union about the distinction between radars used for early warning and those used for space tracking and verification. The Soviets have used a loophole in the ABM Treaty—the lack of a definition of those characteristics that distinguish an early-warning radar from a radar for space-tracking/verification—to justify the deployment of the LPAR at Abalakovo. Through the SCC the United States should seek to close this loophole.

SDI. Compliance with the ABM Treaty requires adherence to the traditional, or restrictive, interpretation of that agreement. This interpretation of the treaty clearly prohibits development and testing of technologies based on other physical principles, with the exception of technologies relating to systems operating at fixed sites with the tests carried out at designated locations. According to Senator Sam Nunn, who has exhaustively examined the negotiating record and reported his findings, the reinterpretation of the ABM Treaty promulgated by Judge Abraham Sofaer is not supported by the negotiating history of the ABM Treaty.

Strict compliance with the ABM Treaty leaves ample room for the conduct of vigorous ABM research and for a development and testing program in selected areas. It is gratifying to note that the multiyear SDI program as submitted by the SDIO to the Congress in June 1986 proposed to conduct its research within this interpretation. Thus, the assertion is ill-founded that conduct of the SDI program within the traditional interpretation of the ABM Treaty would "kill SDI."

Programs may be carried out in three categories, and still remain in compliance with the ABM Treaty:

Category 1—conceptual design and laboratory testing. Such tests do not involve field testing or significant releases of energy directly into the atmosphere and presumably are not verifiable by NTM.

Category 2—field testing of devices that are not ABM components or prototypes of ABM components. Some tests in this category presumably can be detected by NTM. The permissibility of specific programs in this category is clearly subject to the details of interpretation of the meaning of "component."

Category 3—field testing of fixed, land-based ABM components. Field testing of such components is permitted, subject to certain treaty restraints. For example, such testing must be carried out at agreed test ranges where the total number of test launchers is limited. Such testing may not involve multiple-warhead interceptors, rapid reload, and so on, as provided in the ABM Treaty.

The SDI activities now in the program can be placed into these categories, although some planned U.S. activities strain compliance in those gray areas that remain, even under the strict interpretation of the treaty. Among such gray areas are the definition of components of an ABM system, questions concerning the boundaries of permitted modernization, and the boundary between research and development. Although the ambiguities within many of these gray areas can be reduced through additional agreed interpretations in the SCC, there is no question that some areas of dispute will remain. We recommend that the SCC undertake a number of such clarifications (as listed earlier in this section), and we also recommend consideration of additional limitations that would go beyond the strict interpretation of the treaty.

The SCC could productively examine the validity of the traditional versus the new, permissive interpretation of ABM Treaty provisions, using the negotiating record and taking into account the mutual interests of both parties. In addition, the SCC could review from a compliance standpoint the planned U.S. SDI tests that could present problems for the treaty over the long term.

Possibly the largest ABM Treaty loophole related to compliance has to do with activities in the antisatellite and ATBM programs of the two countries that have clear ABM applications. We recommend that high priority be given to serious pursuit of separate treaties in both of those areas.

Demonstrated violation: Abalakovo. As a clear violation of the ABM Treaty, the United States must deal with the Abalakovo radar firmly and in a unique fashion. This radar represents Soviet behavior that has no direct U.S. counterpart. The United States could legitimately demand termination of the construction of this radar, or its dismantlement. Short of dismantlement, the radar issue must be dealt with in a way that will give the United States confidence that the radar will be restricted to an early-warning role and that will communicate the message that compliance with the terms of arms control agreements is expected. The following steps should be taken.

First, as part of a balanced resolution of existing compliance issues, the Soviet Union should either dismantle the Abalakovo radar or open it to periodic and extensive on-site inspection to insure that it is configured for permitted space-tracking and/or verification functions. This is the only way the radar issue can be genuinely resolved.

Second, if the Soviets do not dismantle the radar or open it to periodic on-site inspection, the United States should neutralize any Soviet advantage gained through the radar's orientation and placement. The United States should — and presumably already does — exploit the vulnerability of the radar by use of nuclear precursor tactics, penetration aids, or decoys. The United States should also pursue a common understanding in the SCC whereby the Soviet Union would accede to the unilateral U.S. statement, expressed at the time of the signing of the ABM Treaty, that LPARs may not be defended.

Third, General Secretary Gorbachev should be urged to come forward with a full explanation of why the Abalakovo radar was deployed in its present location and with its present orientation, and how the Soviet system permitted such a violation. He should offer recommendations for changes in the Soviet compliance decision-making structure to strengthen the procompliance constituency and to assure the United States that a violation such as Abalakovo will not occur again. Gorbachev's notable announcements regarding the Chernobyl accident provide an encouraging precedent in this regard.

Strengthening Existing Limits; Restoring Dispute Resolution

A more general, but nonetheless important, area for U.S. action lies in improving the environment in U.S.-Soviet relations and in the arms control arena. Toning down the confrontational oratory on compliance issues and restoring the momentum to the arms control process is essential for the ability of the United States and Soviet Union to reinvigorate the process for resolving compliance disputes.

To strengthen arms control, the United States should resume adherence to SALT II and the Interim Agreement. In particular, the verification-enhancing provisions of the agreements are important to preserve: the prohibitions against deliberate concealment, the requirement for prior notification of test launches, and the agreed data-base exchange and updates.

The fractionation limits, which, for instance, restrict the SS-25 to one warhead, are also extremely important. The SS-25 could be a much more significant security problem for the United States without the fractionation limit than if the Soviets are required to comply with the SALT II limits.

It is in the interest of the United States to seek to strengthen and reinforce the limits of the ABM Treaty. A loosening of the treaty's restrictions would permit a number of Soviet activities that the United States should seek to avoid. Pursuant to the Reagan administration's expressed concern about Soviet territorial defense, frequently cited as a rationale for the U.S. SDI program, the United States should seek to restrict the Soviet programs through a further tightening of the ABM Treaty.

The United States and Soviet Union should seek agreement through the SCC to make public the agreed statements and common understandings of the SCC, so that the Congress and the public can properly evaluate the success of that forum in resolving disputes and so that integral parts of existing arms control agreements will not remain secret. The two countries should expand the role of the SCC to foresee potential compliance problems arising from new technology. More attention should be given to the neglected responsibilities in the SCC charter, which call upon the joint body to discuss new elements of arms control agreements made necessary as a result of the U.S.-Soviet compliance experience.

Guidance for New Agreements

It is one of the principal assessments of this report that it is the political process for upholding and reinforcing U.S.-Soviet arms control agreements that has been deficient rather than the accords themselves. Nonetheless, the compliance experience does suggest lessons about how and what to negotiate in future agreements.

In particular, the desire to conclude an agreement sometimes impels the

United States and the Soviet Union to conclude partial qualitative limits on forces or behavior. The experience with compliance suggests, however, that such partial limits should be avoided when possible. Though sometimes better than no provision at all, such limits—the encryption provision of SALT II is the most notable example—have proved susceptible, especially on the Soviet side, to subjective interpretation and to the stretching or the creative reading of treaty language, thus giving rise to instances of questionable compliance.

Uncertainties about compliance would be reduced if the United States and Soviet Union were able to negotiate complete bans on particular types of systems or kinds of behavior. For example, the United States should pursue a complete ban on encryption and encapsulation in any future strategic arms control agreement. The Soviet Union might be willing to accept such a ban in the context of a major new agreement, given their signals about a "new attitude" toward verification. Alternatively, a non–weapon-system–oriented approach to arms control, such as a flight-testing ban, "level of effort" limitations, or other constraints on behavior rather than forces, might be pursued.

Appendix A

U.S. Charges of Soviet Noncompliance

Charge	Issue	Agreement	Source[a]
Circumventions defeating object and purpose of treaty	Use/transfer of chemical weapons in Afghanistan and elsewhere	Geneva Protocol, 1925	WH, GAC
Violation	Continuation of Soviet biological-weapons program despite ban; use and transfer of "yellow rain," 1972 to present	Biological Weapons Convention	WH, GAC
Legal and political violation	Deliberate concealment that impedes verification by NTM	ABM Treaty, XII.3; Interim Agreement V.3; SALT II, XV.3	GAC
Violation	Location and orientation of Abalakovo radar	ABM Treaty, VI(b)	WH
Potential violation	Component mobility; testing of mobile components	ABM Treaty, V.1	WH
Possible violation (insufficient evidence)	ABM capability of SAM systems; upgrade may be part of territorial defense	ABM Treaty, VI	WH
Suspected violation	Concurrent operation of SAM and ABM components	ABM Treaty, VI(a)	WH
Possible violation (ambiguous evidence)	Development of rapid reload for ABM launchers	ABM Treaty, V.2	WH

[a]WH=White House; GAC=General Advisory Committee on Arms Control and Disarmament

Charge	Issue	Agreement	Source
Possible violation	Preparation of territorial defense	ABM Treaty, I	WH
Violation	Development and deployment of mobile radar on Kamchatka Peninsula, 1975; continued development activities	ABM Treaty, V.1, and Common Understanding C	GAC
Defeating object and purpose of agreement	Conversion of launchers for small ICBMs (SS-11) to launchers for heavy ICBMs (SS-17, SS-19) circumvents goal to limit throw-weight	Interim Agreement, II	GAC
Violation	Use of facilities from SS-7 ICBM sites in support of SS-25 deployment and operation	Interim Agreement, II	WH
Violation	Exceeding numerical launcher limits, March 1976–October 1977	Interim Agreement, Protocol	GAC
Probable violation	Production, testing, and deployment of SS-16 mobile ICBMs, 1979–present	SALT II, IV.8, Common Understanding	WH, GAC
Violation	Flight testing and deployment of second new type of ICBM (SS-25)	SALT II, IV.9	WH
Violation	Testing lighter RV than allowed (SS-25)	SALT II, IV.10	WH
Violation	Deliberate concealment of data, excessive telemetry encryption	SALT II, XV.3, Second Common Understanding	WH
Violation	Exceeding limits on SNDVs	SALT II, Memorandum of Understanding	WH

Charge	Issue	Agreement	Source
Activity inconsistent with statement	Production of more than limit of 30 Backfire bombers; Arctic staging	SALT II, Brezhnev Backfire statement	WH
Violation	Concealment of association between missile and its launcher during testing	SALT II, XV	WH
Breach of commitment	Nuclear testing, 1961–62	Unilateral moratorium on nuclear tests	GAC
Violation	Venting radioactive debris beyond Soviet borders, 1965–present	LTBT, I.1(b)	WH, GAC
Likely violation	Testing above 150-kiloton limit	TTBT, I.1	WH, GAC
Violation	Transit of aircraft carriers through Turkish straits	Montreux Convention	GAC
Breach of commitment	Covert shipment of offensive weapons to Cuba and their deployment, 1962	Unilateral commitment not to send offensive weapons to Cuba	GAC
Breach of commitment	Deployment of nuclear submarines in Cuban waters, 1970–74	Unilateral commitment not to send nuclear weapons to Cuba	GAC
Breach of commitment	Deployment of SS-20s	Brezhnev's moratorium on deployment of SS-20s	
Violation	Use of booby-trap mines and incendiaries against civilians, 1981–82	Customary international law and Conventional Weapons Convention	GAC
Violation	Insufficient prior notification of Zapad-81 military exercise	Helsinki Final Act, I	WH, GAC

Appendix B

Soviet Charges of U.S. Noncompliance

Charge	Issue	Agreement
Violation of intent of treaty	Spreading arms race to space by development of antisatellite weapons	ABM Treaty, V.1
Working toward violation	Creation of mobile ABM radar stations	ABM Treaty, V.1, Common Understanding C
Violation	Modification and testing of Minuteman I for antimissile (ABM) purposes	ABM Treaty, VI(a)
Violation	Creation of large-scale ABM defense system: PAVE PAWS radar stations	ABM Treaty, I.2
Violation	Transferring ABM components outside U.S. national territory	ABM Treaty, IX
Working toward violation	Construction of large-scale ABM system, including space basing	ABM Treaty, V.1 and VI(a)
Violation	Testing Shemya radar for ABM purposes	ABM Treaty, I.2 and VI(a)
Violation	Disregard for confidentiality of SCC	ABM Treaty, XIII, SCC Regulations
Violation	Use of shelters to conceal launchers (Minuteman II, Titan II) from NTM verification	Interim Agreement, V; Common Understanding C
Potential violation	Exceeding numerical launcher limits (Minuteman II, Titan II)	Interim Agreement, V.1,2,3; Common Understanding C
Violation	Building additional, fixed, land-based ICBM launchers	Interim Agreement, I
Possible violation	Exceeding sublimit on MIRVed ICBMs through conversion of Minuteman IIs to IIIs	ABM Treaty, V.1

Charge	Issue	Agreement
Violation and undermining treaty's intent	Deployment of SLCMs and GLCMs	SALT II Protocol
Circumvention of treaty's intent	Deployment of Pershing II	SALT II, XII
Violation	Flight testing and accelerated development of more than one new type of ICBM (MX and Midgetman)	SALT II, I and IV.9
Violation	Escape of radioactive substances into atmosphere	LTBT, I.1(b)
Violations	Nuclear explosions in excess of 150-kiloton limit	TTBT, I.1
Violation	Increase of military tension in Europe through Pershing/GLCM deployment	Helsinki Final Act
Undermining treaty's intent	Striving for military superiority; not seriously seeking to constrain nuclear-arms competition	Non-Proliferation Treaty, VI
Undermining arms control process	Nonratification	SALT II, TTBT, PNET
Undermining arms control process	Massive size of NATO military exercises in Europe (conducted with proper prior notification)	None
Undermining arms control process	Modernizing/increasing chemical weapons stockpiles in United States and Europe	None

Appendix C

Estimating the Yields of Underground Nuclear Tests

The magnitude of a seismic event represents the average of the magnitudes obtained at a number of seismic stations distributed under optimum conditions azimuthally around the event. The magnitude is derived from a measurement of the amplitude of the seismic signal at a station and a correction for the distance between the seismic station and the event. The distances in this discussion are called teleseismic and are greater than approximately 2,000 kilometers and less than approximately 10,000 kilometers. Figure C.1 shows the path of the signals.

To estimate the yield of any underground explosion, an empirical yield–magnitude $(Y-m)$ relation is used: $m = a + b(\log Y)$, where m is the observed magnitude, Y is the yield, and a and b are appropriate constants. If m is known, Y can be estimated, or vice versa.

A $Y-m$ relation for a certain region and types of geologic media (in which the explosive is fired) is obtained by relating the accurate yields (as determined by chemical analysis) of a number of explosions with the corresponding magnitudes. Figure C.2 represents the results of such an analysis. Each point represents an event. The line represents a best fit of the $Y-m$ relation to the observed data points. The statistical distribution of data points shows that, if a number of explosions, all of the same yield, were fired in a local region and in the same geologic media, the seismic magnitudes would not be identical. The distribution would reflect unpredictable variations in the physical conditions between the explosion and the measuring station.

Thus, a spread of magnitudes would be predicted from the $Y-m$ relation (as shown in figure C.3). The maximum of the curve corresponds to the magnitude that has been derived from the $Y-m$ relation. Thus, there is an uncertainty in the prediction of the magnitude produced by a given yield, or an uncertainty in the estimate of yield for a given magnitude.

Different local geologic media have different yield–magnitude relations, as shown in figure C.4. Some types of rock do not couple the explosive energy into seismic energy as well as other types of rocks—one speaks of low coupling and high coupling. Generally low-coupling rocks are "soft" (dry and porous), and high-coupling rocks are "hard" (like granite). Thus, the seismic magnitude produced by an explosion in soft rock will be smaller than that produced by the same yield explosion in hard rock. The yield–magnitude relation for one region will not necessarily be the same as for another region. It is important to know the rock type; the difference can be significant.

Part of the purpose of the data exchange in the TTBT Protocol was to allow

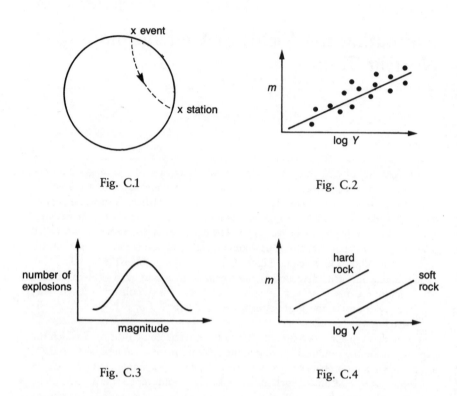

Fig. C.1   Fig. C.2

Fig. C.3   Fig. C.4

identification of the types of rock. On the basis of limited knowledge, it is generally assumed that the Soviet test site consists of high-coupling rock. There is much more variability at the Nevada test site. It is known that the region underlying Nevada absorbs seismic waves to a greater extent than many other regions of the world. A signal from an explosion in Nevada will pass through the region, be diminished by absorption (as indicated in figure C.5), and thus produce a smaller amplitude, corresponding to a smaller magnitude, at the recording station. Figure C.6 represents the difference, or bias, between the Y–m relations for Nevada and Semipalatinsk, a site that has less absorption. In the equation $m = a + b(\log Y)$, the bias relates to the value of a.

Accurate yields for a number of explosions at a site, together with the corresponding seismic magnitudes, provide the best means for determining the Y–m relationship at that site. Because yields are not available for Soviet tests at Semipalatinsk, indirect means must be used to estimate the Y–m relation or the bias. What is known about the geology at the Soviet test site indicates that, as figure C.6 illustrates, detonation of a given yield at Semipalatinsk would generate a larger magnitude than the same yield at Nevada. The estimates of bias that are referred to in the literature on underground tests are based on various indirect means. In addition to the statis-

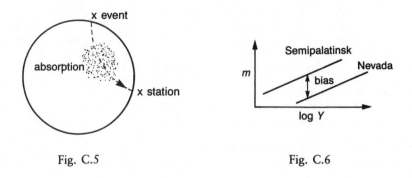

Fig. C.5   Fig. C.6

tical uncertainties mentioned, there are errors associated with the estimates themselves.

The TTBT Protocol calls for providing local geologic information about the test sites. That information would be of value in calculating the effects of the local media on the coupling of the explosive energy to seismic waves but would not in itself determine the bias accurately. For this one would need to measure the seismic signals from explosions of known yields. The TTBT Protocol also calls for calibration shots—that is, underground detonations of known yields. But it provides no independent means for objectively determining the yields of the Soviet explosions, a determination that would be required to settle completely the bias problem.

Because of the statistical uncertainty, approximately half of all yields fired around 150 kilotons will have seismic yield estimates greater than 150 kilotons. There is no way of determining for a single shot that a seismically estimated yield of, say, 225 kilotons was produced by an actual yield of less than 150 kilotons. Given a yield estimate of 225 kilotons and a factor-of-two uncertainty in yield determination, as cited in this report, one can say that, if the true yield were 150 kilotons, the probability of getting a yield estimate as large or larger than 225 kilotons would be 0.125. With that uncertainty one would not ordinarily assert noncompliance. Such a calculation would not prove compliance or noncompliance. All one knows is that, if the hypothesis of compliance is rejected, one would incorrectly reject 12.5 percent of the tests whose true yields were 150 kilotons.

At the time the TTBT was negotiated, it was recognized that one could not determine precise adherence to the 150-kiloton limit. It was believed, though, that one would have adequate assurance that significant violations were not taking place. This report notes that the error or uncertainty in determining yields could be a factor of two. With such a factor of uncertainty, slight unintended breaches would be virtually impossible to determine.

Appendix D

The Standing Consultative Commission

Calendar of Proceedings, Agreements, and Related Events

1969   *November.* During first session of SALT I, United States and Soviet Union agree to concept of SCC. Early drafts of SALT I treaty include articles setting forth SCC functions and responsibilities.

1970–71   SALT I negotiations proceed.

1972   *May.* United States and Soviet Union sign ABM Treaty, Interim Agreement, and Basic Principles of Relations.

1973   *May 30.* **Protocol Establishing Regulations for the Standing Consultative Commission** formally establishes SCC. First session begins.

1974   *Soviet Union reportedly begins encryption of flight-test telemetry.*

              July 3. Pursuant to SCC mandate as specified in ABM Treaty, Article XIII, and Interim Agreement, Article VI, SCC concludes two formal agreements: **Protocol on Procedures for ABM Systems** and **Protocol on Procedures for Strategic Offensive Arms.**

1975   *January 28.* SCC special session convened at U.S. request to discuss Soviet SS-19 ICBM.

              February 13. SCC special session ends. No agreed statement issued.

              June 25. President Ford discusses Soviet compliance at press conference: "I have investigated the allegations that the Soviet Union has violated the SALT agreements. . . . I have found that they have not violated the SALT agreement; they have not used any loopholes."

The SCC held 28 regular semiannual sessions between 1973 and 1986. It also held two special sessions (1975 and 1986) and two ABM Treaty reviews (1977 and 1982). The calendar identifies regular sessions only if it is known that issues were first introduced or specific statements or proposals were made at those sessions.

Sources: U.S. State Department, *A Concise History of the Standing Consultative Commission* (Washington, August 6, 1984); U.S. Congress, Senate Foreign Relations Committee, *SALT II Treaty: Background Documents,* 96th Cong., 1st sess. (1979).

1976   *September 30.* SCC concludes formal agreement: **Protocol on Immediate Notifications.**

October 28. SCC concludes formal agreement: **Supplementary Protocol on ABM Procedures.**

1977   *May 25.* SCC concludes formal agreement: **Agreed Statement Regarding the Protocol of September 30, 1976.**

May 30. SCC concludes formal agreement: **Understanding Relating to the Use of Shelters Over ICBM Silo Launchers.**

November 4. SCC regular fall session ends, and first ABM Treaty review begins.

November 21. ABM Treaty review ends with joint statement affirming both parties' commitment to the treaty and SCC.

December. Former Defense Secretary Laird asserts in *Reader's Digest* that long-withheld evidence "is incontrovertible that the Soviet Union has repeatedly, flagrantly and indeed contemptuously violated the treaties to which [the United States has] adhered."

1978   *February 21.* Secretary Cyrus Vance submits comprehensive report to Senate Committee on Foreign Relations on Soviet compliance with SALT I. Report lists no violations.

July. Soviet Union encrypts more telemetry than ever before during SS-18 flight test.

November 1. SCC concludes formal agreement: **Agreed Statement on ABM Treaty Topics.**

1979   *February 1.* Press reports indicate United States informed Soviet Union that United States would consider levels of Soviet encryption during recent SS-18 flight tests to violate the pending SALT II Treaty.

1980   *Spring.* SCC suspends work on SALT II implementation procedures after SALT II–ratification proceedings are halted in U.S. Senate.

1981   *May 27.* SCC session begins after delay, during which U.S. government debates whether or not to continue utilizing SCC.

October 23. Soviet SCC delegation responds to U.S. concerns about location of Soviet LPARs by stating that their placement took account of "technical and practical considerations."

1982   *September 14 to December 15.* United States asserts in SCC that Soviet SS-16 ICBM is secretly deployed at Plesetsk. Soviets insist that SS-16 is not deployed and is not being produced, and they refuse to inform United States of the whereabouts of SS-16s previously deployed, contending that no provision of SALT II applies to those missiles. The two sides agree to "recess" regular session in deadlock.

October. First flight test of Soviet SS-24 MIRVed ICBM.

November 9 to December 15. SCC convenes ABM Treaty review. Joint communiqué confirms each side's "commitment to the aims and objectives of the ABM Treaty" and to the process of consultation within SCC.

1983 *February.* Soviet Union conducts first flight test of SS-25 ICBM.

March 1. Air Force Chief of Staff Charles Gabriel testifies before Congress, "We do not believe mobile SS-16s are operational at the Plesetsk test range."

April. Senators Hatch and Symms urge President Reagan to publicly announce alleged Soviet cheating.

May. Deputy Secretary of State Kenneth Dam reportedly raises issue of SS-X-25 with Soviet Ambassador Dobrynin.

July. In meeting with Soviet chargé d'affaires Oleg Sokolov, Secretary Shultz requests SCC special session. Soviet Union rejects proposal, arguing that regular session will convene soon.

July 27. New York Post reports existence of Abalakovo radar.

September 22 to December 15. During regular SCC session United States raises issue of Soviet LPAR at Abalakovo. Soviet Union insists radar is for space tracking. United States also raises issue of Soviet SS-X-25 for first time in SCC. Soviet Union contends that, because United States never ratified SALT II, treaty is outside purview of SCC.

October. Senate votes 93–0 to require president to submit report to Congress on Soviet compliance.

December 2. GAC forwards study to president: *A Quarter Century of Soviet Compliance Practices Under Arms Control Agreements: 1958–1983.*

1984 SCC becomes deadlocked on current compliance issues.

January 23. Administration releases first report on Soviet noncompliance. Report includes seven allegations, of activities ranging from violations to probable violations.

October 10. GAC report, sent to Congress in classified and unclassified form, accuses Soviet Union of material breaches and suspected violations of treaties as well as breaches of unilateral commitments.

1985   *February 1.* Administration releases second report on Soviet non-compliance. Report contains 13 allegations, including claims that Soviet Union "may be preparing an ABM defense of its national territory." Some previous charges of probable violations are changed to charges of definite violations; some new charges are added. Charge concerning ABM rapid reload is omitted because it has not yet been discussed with Soviet Union.

February. Lt. Gen. John T. Chain testifies before Senate that, although the Soviet Union has committed some violations, it has "complied with the majority" of arms control treaties.

March 11. Los Angeles Times quotes ACDA Director Kenneth Adelman: "Our security has not yet suffered because of Soviet noncompliance."

Spring. United States for first time in SCC questions Soviet capability to reload and refire ABM launchers in period of time shorter than previously noted.

June 10. Citing Soviet cheating, President Reagan states that there may be no need for United States to continue abiding by SALT II. Status of U.S. no-undercut policy is unclear. Reagan suggests trade-off between U.S. Midgetman and Soviet SS-25.

June 14. SCC concludes two formal agreements: **Agreement Pertaining to the Agreement on Measures to Reduce the Risk of the Outbreak of Nuclear War** and **Agreement to Enhance the Viability of the ABM Treaty.**

November 16. New York Times publishes letter from Secretary of Defense Weinberger to President Reagan urging him to prepare "proportionate and appropriate responses" to Soviet violations and to emphasize Soviet cheating at upcoming summit. Weinberger denounces continued compliance with SALT II and observance of restrictive interpretation of ABM Treaty.

December 23. Administration sends third noncompliance report to Congress. Report cites 18 compliance issues including new charge that Soviet Union conceals association between missiles and their launchers. Other charges of probable violations are changed to charges of definite violations.

1986   *February 1.* ACDA releases report, *Soviet Noncompliance.* Report contains charges of 9 violations, 2 probable, 1 likely, and 2 potential, and 1 breach of political commitment. Report lists 3 cases of ambiguous activity.

May 27. United States announces dismantlement of two Poseidon submarines as eighth Trident submarine begins sea trials. United States remains under SALT II limits but states it will base future decisions on nature and magnitude of Soviet threat rather than "expired SALT agreements unilaterally observed by the United States."

July 22–29. At request of Soviet Union, SCC holds special session to discuss U.S. decision to repudiate SALT II. U.S. officials describe meeting as "very acrimonious and very polemical."

November 28. United States announces deployment of 131st B-52 armed with air-launched cruise missiles, placing United States over SALT II limit of 1320 MIRVed launchers. United States is first country to renounce publicly and deliberately an arms control agreement.

Formal Agreements Reached Through the SCC

Protocol on Procedures for ABM Systems (July 3, 1974)
This protocol establishes procedures for the replacement and dismantlement or destruction of ABM systems. The protocol of October 28, 1976, apparently amplifies this protocol.

Protocol on Procedures for Strategic Offensive Arms (July 3, 1974)
This protocol establishes procedures for the replacement and dismantlement or destruction of strategic offensive weapons as required by the Interim Agreement.

Protocol on Immediate Notifications (September 30, 1976)
Pursuant to the Accident Measures Agreement, this protocol establishes a system of prepositioned messages designed to facilitate notification between the parties in event of emergency situations that might lead to the outbreak of nuclear war.

Supplementary Protocol on ABM Procedures (October 28, 1976)
This protocol amplifies the protocol of July 3, 1974, on procedures for ABM systems. It also provides for the exchange of the one permitted ABM deployment area for another (that is, Grand Forks, N.D., for Washington, D.C.).

Understanding Relating to the Use of Shelters over ICBM Silo Launchers (reflected in four documents dated April 25, May 19, and May 30, 1977)
This understanding records the agreement of the parties to the Interim Agreement to refrain from building, over ICBM silo launchers, shelters that would impede verification of compliance by national technical means.

Agreed Statement Regarding the Protocol of September 30, 1976 (May 25, 1977)
This agreed statement supplements the protocol of September 30, 1976.

Agreed Statement on ABM Treaty Topics (November 1, 1978)

This agreed statement consists of three parts: (1) clarification of the reference in Article IV to current ABM test ranges; (2) clarification of what constitutes testing in an ABM mode (the parties agree to ban concurrent testing of non-ABM and ABM systems or components); (3) clarification of permitted uses of air-defense and other non-ABM radars at ABM test ranges.

Agreement Pertaining to the "Accident Measures" Agreement (June 14, 1985)

This agreement calls for immediate notification in case of use of nuclear devices by terrorists or third countries. According to an ACDA press release, the agreement "records the parties' understanding of their obligations under" the Accident Measures Agreement but does not change or expand the agreement.

Agreement to Enhance the Viability of the ABM Treaty (June 14, 1985)

This agreement prohibits concurrent operation of SAM components and ABM radars co-located at the same test range.

Regulations

1. The Standing Consultative Commission, established by the Memorandum of Understanding between the Government of the United States of America and the Government of the Union of Soviet Socialist Republics Regarding the Establishment of a Standing Consultative Commission of December 21, 1972, shall consist of a U.S. component and Soviet component, each of which shall be headed by a Commissioner.

2. The Commissioners shall alternately preside over the meetings.

3. The Commissioners shall, when possible, inform each other in advance of the matters to be submitted for discussion, but may at a meeting submit for discussion any matter within the competence of the Commission.

4. During intervals between sessions of the Commission, each Commissioner may transmit written or oral communications to the other Commissioner concerning matters within the competence of the Commission.

5. Each component of the Commission may invite such advisers and experts as it deems necessary to participate in a meeting.

6. The Commission may establish working groups to consider and prepare specific matters.

7. The results of the discussion of questions at the meetings of the Commission may, if necessary, be entered into records which shall be in two copies, each in the English and the Russian languages, both texts being equally authentic.

8. The proceedings of the Standing Consultative Commission shall be conducted in private. The Standing Consultative Commission may not make its proceedings public except with the express consent of both Commissioners.

9. Each component of the Commission shall bear the expenses connected with its participation in the Commission.

(Signed and entered into force May 30, 1973)

Abbreviations

ABM	antiballistic missile
ACDA	Arms Control and Disarmament Agency
ALCM	air-launched cruise missile
AOA	airborne optical adjunct
ATBM	antitactical ballistic missile
BMEWS	Ballistic Missile Early Warning System
BWC	Biological Weapons Convention
CIA	Central Intelligence Agency
DARPA	Defense Advanced Research Projects Agency
DOD	Department of Defense
GAC	General Advisory Committee on Arms Control and Disarmament
GBHRG	ground-based hypervelocity rail gun
GLCM	ground-launched cruise missile
HOE	Homing Overlay Experiment
ICBM	intercontinental ballistic missile
INF	intermediate-range nuclear forces
JCC	Joint Consultative Commission
JCS	Joint Chiefs of Staff
LPAR	large phased-array radar
LTBT	Limited Test Ban Treaty
MIRV	multiple independently targetable reentry vehicle
NPT	Non-Proliferation Treaty
NRDC	National Resources Defense Council
NTM	national technical means
PAVE PAWS	Perimeter Acquisition of Vehicle Entry, Phased-Array Warning System
PBV	postboost vehicle
PNET	Peaceful Nuclear Explosions Treaty
RV	reentry vehicle
SALT	Strategic Arms Limitation Talks
SAM	surface-to-air missile
SCC	Standing Consultative Commission
SDI	Strategic Defense Initiative
SDIO	Strategic Defense Initiative Organization
SLBM	submarine-launched ballistic missile
SLCM	sea-launched cruise missile
SNDV	strategic nuclear delivery vehicle
START	strategic arms reduction talks
TEL	transporter-erector-launcher
TTBT	Threshold Test Ban Treaty

Notes

Chapter One

1. U.S. Arms Control and Disarmament Agency, *Arms Control and Disarmament Agreements: Texts and Histories of Negotiations,* 5th ed. (Washington, 1982), is the source for texts of arms control agreements quoted in this report.

2. SALT II, Article XV.3, Second Common Understanding, reads: "Each party is free to use various methods of transmitting telemetric information during testing, including its encryption, except that . . . neither party shall engage in deliberate denial of telemetric information . . . whenever such denial impedes verification of compliance."

3. Phillip R. Trimble, *Soviet Violations of Arms Control Agreements: A Legal Perspective,* working paper no. 53, University of California, Center for International and Strategic Affairs (Los Angeles, 1985), 5.

4. Vienna Convention on the Law of Treaties, United Nations document A/CONF 39127 (New York, 1969), reprinted in *American Journal of International Law* 63 (1969): 875.

5. Leo Sartori, "Will SALT II Survive?" *International Security* 10 (Winter 1985–86): 148–49.

6. The Reagan administration resubmitted the Threshold Test Ban Treaty to the Senate for consideration in late 1986, possibly changing its status to "pending ratification."

7. Trimble, *Soviet Violations,* 13–16.

8. ACDA, *Soviet Noncompliance* (Washington, February 1, 1986), 6.

Chapter Two

1. For an evaluation of the Incidents at Sea Agreement, see Sean Lynn-Jones, "A Quiet Success for Arms Control: Preventing Incidents at Sea," *International Security* 9 (Spring 1985): 154–84.

2. The discussion of SALT I and II compliance draws upon analysis done at the Congressional Research Service; see Charles R. Gellner and Jeanette Voas, *Soviet Compliance with the SALT I and SALT II Agreements on Offensive Arms,* Library of Congress, Congressional Research Service (Washington, June 13, 1985). See also U.S. Defense Department, *Soviet Military Power,* 5th ed. (Washington, March 1986); and Arms Control Association, *Countdown on SALT II: The Case for Preserving SALT II Limits on U.S. and Soviet Strategic Forces* (Washington, 1985).

3. U.S. State Department, *SALT I: Compliance; SALT II: Verification,* selected document no. 7 (Washington, February 1978), 7.

4. Ibid., 8.

5. See M. Elaine Bunn and Charles R. Gellner, *Soviet Compliance with Arms Control Agreements (Excluding SALT II)*, Library of Congress, Congressional Research Service (Washington, October 16, 1978), 5–15.

6. U.S. Congress, House Armed Services Committee, Panel on Arms Control and Disarmament, *Hearings on Verification of a Comprehensive Nuclear Test Ban Treaty, Soviet Compliance with the Threshold Test Ban Treaty, and the Sizes of Soviet Strategic Nuclear Weapons,* testimony by Lynn R. Sykes, 99th Cong., 1st sess. (November 20, 1985), 36.

Chapter Three

1. Ronald Reagan, *Soviet Noncompliance with Arms Control Agreements,* president's reports to Congress, January 23, 1984; February 1, 1985; December 23, 1985; and March 10, 1987.

2. ACDA, GAC, *A Quarter Century of Soviet Compliance Practices Under Arms Control Commitments: 1958–1983* (Washington, October 10, 1984); and Caspar W. Weinberger, Office of the Secretary of Defense, *Responding to Soviet Violations Policy Study,* memorandum to the president, November 13, 1985 (also published in *New York Times,* November 14, 1985).

3. Soviet Foreign Ministry, *The United States Is Violating Its International Commitments,* aide-mémoire from the Soviet Embassy, Washington (in Foreign Broadcast Information Service, *Daily Report: Soviet Union,* January 30, 1984, AA1–AA5).

4. Joint Chiefs of Staff, *United States Military Posture,* FY 1987 (Washington, 1987), 16.

5. Thomas K. Longstreth, John E. Pike, and John B. Rhinelander, *The Impact of U.S. and Soviet Ballistic Missile Defense Programs on the ABM Treaty* (Washington: National Campaign to Save the ABM Treaty, March 1985), 58.

6. Ibid., 57–58.

7. Ibid., 58.

8. Common understandings produced by the SCC are supposedly held confidentially by the United States and Soviet Union. The official ACDA release of June 14, 1985, simply states that the SCC produced "a common understanding intended to further enhance the viability of the ABM Treaty." This specific information on the understanding is from a press leak (see R. Jeffrey Smith, "Arms Agreement Breathes New Life into SCC," *Science* 229 (August 9, 1985): 535.

9. Longstreth et al., *Impact on ABM Treaty,* 60.

10. U.S. State Department, daily press briefing, January 30, 1984, 4.

11. Transcript of working group meeting, July 24, 1986.

12. Joint Chiefs, *Military Posture,* 19; see also Michael R. Gordon, "Joint Chiefs Find No Soviet Cheating," *New York Times,* February 8, 1986.

13. Michael R. Gordon, "U.S. Cites Compliance on Some Arms Disputes," *New York Times,* November 24, 1985.

14. Ibid.

15. Michael R. Gordon, "U.S. Military Intelligence Lowers Estimate of Soviet Bomber," *New York Times,* October 1, 1985.

16. U.S. State Department, *SALT II Agreement,* selected document no. 12B (Washington, 1979), 59.

17. Article IV.9, Second Common Understanding, states that a new type of ICBM is one whose specified parameters differ in value from those of its predecessor by more or less than 5 percent. The determination of whether such a missile is within or outside of the permitted limits is to be made on the basis of the parameters of the missile as of its 25th test launch. The last 12 of these 25 test launches are not permitted to differ from the values of the parameters during the earlier test launches by more than 10 percent. Thus, if SALT II were still in effect, the United States could theoretically have tested the missile up to 25 times without violating the agreement.

18. Soviet Foreign Ministry, *United States Is Violating,* AA2.

19. *President's Statement on Interim Restraint,* White House press release, May 27, 1986, 3.

20. *Report of the President's Commission on Strategic Forces* (Scowcroft Commission) (Washington, April 1983), 23.

21. For an extensive discussion of various viewpoints in this debate, see *Arms Control Today* 16 (September 1986): 8–36.

22. David Dickson, "Soviets Discuss Sverdlovsk," *Science* 234 (October 10, 1986): 144.

23. ACDA, *Soviet Noncompliance,* 15.

24. See Glenn T. Seaborg, *Stemming the Tide: Arms Control in the Johnson Years* (Lexington, Mass.: Lexington Books, 1987), 209–11.

25. See Michael R. Gordon, "Scientists Challenge Method Used to Measure Size of Soviet Atomic Tests," *New York Times,* November 4, 1986.

26. Ibid.

27. Michael R. Gordon, "CIA Changes Way That It Measures Soviet Atom Tests," *New York Times,* April 2, 1986.

28. U.S. Congress, Senate Foreign Relations Committee, *Hearings on the Threshold Test Ban Treaty and the Peaceful Nuclear Explosions Treaty,* testimony by Roger E. Batzel, 100th Cong., 1st sess. (January 15, 1987), 221.

29. Gordon, "Scientists Challenge."

30. KRON-TV, San Francisco, *Target-4,* "Do Soviets Cheat on Nuclear Tests? Pentagon Scientists Say Top Reagan Official Rejects Their Evidence," transcript of interviews of Richard Perle, Lynn Sykes, Charles Archambeau, and Willard Hannon, May 9, 1986.

Chapter Four

1. The 1969 Vienna Convention on the Law of Treaties (Article 62) reflects long-standing law on this point: "A fundamental change of circumstances which has occurred with regard to those existing at the time of the conclusion of a treaty, and which was not foreseen by the parties" may be invoked by the aggrieved party as a ground for terminating a treaty or suspending its operation. This is so if two conditions exist: "(a) the existence of those circumstances constituted an essential basis of the consent of the parties to be bound by any treaty; (b) the effect of the change is radically to transform the extent of obligations still to be performed

under the treaty."

2. Limitations on new types of submarine-launched missiles were also proposed at SALT II, but no mutually acceptable formulation could be found, and the idea was eventually dropped.

3. The "comprehensive proposal" put forward by the Carter administration in March 1977 included an outright ban on new types of ICBMs, which would have required abandoning MX. This was part of a package of very stringent limitations that included a 50 percent reduction in Soviet heavy missiles. The comprehensive proposal was summarily rejected by the Soviets. In 1978 the Soviets themselves, in an attempt to head off MX, proposed a total ban on new types, but this proposal was rejected by the United States. Also rejected was a Soviet proposal to limit the one allowed new type to a single reentry vehicle, which would have likewise ruled out MX.

4. U.S. Congress, Senate Foreign Relations Committee, *Hearings on the SALT II Treaty,* 96th Cong., 1st and 2d sess. (1979), part 4, 482.

5. The parameters dropped from the definition included the "specific impulse" of any of the stages or of the postboost vehicle.

6. Quoted in Strobe Talbott, *Endgame: The Inside Story of Salt II* (New York: Harper and Row, 1979), 191.

7. One expectation on the part of the treaty architects proved to be overly optimistic. They believed the new-types provision would force the Soviets to choose between (1) replacing the MIRVed SS-17 and SS-19 with a new ten-MIRVed ICBM and (2) replacing the SS-11 with a single-warhead ICBM that differed substantially from the SS-11. "They cannot do both," the administration told the Senate Foreign Relations Committee (Senate, *Hearings on SALT II,* committee report, part 1, 375). The possibility that the Soviets might design a new missile around the parameters of the SS-13 was apparently overlooked.

8. See Michael R. Gordon, "Can Reagan Blow the Whistle on the Russians While Saying No on SALT II?" *National Journal* 15 (May 7, 1983): 955.

9. The SS-13 was originally intended to be deployed in a mobile mode; apparently, however, there were problems with the mobile basing, and all the missiles were eventually deployed in silos. See Michael MccGwire, *Military Objectives in Soviet Foreign Policy* (Washington: Brookings Institution, 1987), 239–41.

10. William Drozdiak, "NATO Backs U.S. on Arms Charges," *Washington Post,* October 30, 1985.

11. Quoted in "At the USSR Foreign Ministry Press Center," Foreign Broadcast Information Service, *Daily Report: Soviet Union,* June 6, 1986, AA2.

12. Ironically, the instrumentation package on the SS-25 must include a device for encrypting the telemetry, which is the basis for another major compliance issue.

13. In the view of some U.S. analysts, even subtracting the weight of the instrumentation would not bring the throw-weight of the SS-25 into compliance.

14. Jeanette Voas, *Soviet SALT II Compliance Behavior: The SS-25 and Encryption of Telemetry,* Library of Congress, Congressional Research Service (Washington, June 17, 1986), 4.

15. There is a practical problem here. After the instrumentation package is removed there will be no telemetry, and without telemetry it is very difficult to measure throw-weight accurately (see the discussion in the next section of this chapter).

16. ABC-TV, *This Week with David Brinkley,* March 17, 1985.

17. Bill Gertz, "U.S. Adds Charges of SALT II Cheating," *Washington Times,* April 29, 1985; letter from Senators Jesse Helms, Steve Symms, Chic Hecht, Malcolm Wallop, Jake Garn, Paul Laxalt, Strom Thurmond, and Jeremiah Denton (*Congressional Record,* October 7, 1985, E4466).

18. Mobile missiles were banned in the SALT II Protocol, but the protocol expired in 1981 and no consideration was ever given to extending it.

19. ACDA, *Soviet Noncompliance,* 8.

20. The Soviets obviously assumed their telemetry was being intercepted, or they would not have taken the trouble to encrypt it. But they were at that time not aware of the extent of U.S. collection capabilities. In particular, they were believed to have little knowledge of the capabilities of the Rhyolite signals intelligence satellite, a major U.S. collection asset, until the information was conveyed to them by spies Christopher Boyce and Andrew Daulton Lee in 1975 (Glenn Zorpette, "Monitoring the Tests," *IEEE Spectrum* 23 [July 1986]: 60).

21. Richard Burt, "U.S. Warns Russians to Stop Encoding Missile Data," *New York Times,* February 1, 1979.

22. Talbott, *Endgame,* 200.

23. The verification problem was compounded by the recent loss of the U.S. listening posts in Iran. Because of their proximity to the Soviet launch site at Tyuratam, those posts were especially useful for picking up the telemetry emitted shortly after missile lift-off.

24. Senator Glenn voted against ratification of the treaty in the Foreign Relations Committee, chiefly because of his concern about verification.

25. See, for example, Talbott, *Endgame,* 198–99; and Senate, *Hearings on SALT II,* testimony of General George Seigneous, part 1, 267.

26. See, for example, Senate, *Hearings on SALT II,* testimony of William Perry, part 2, 284.

27. Senator Henry Jackson asked Secretary of Defense Brown whether such practices would be violations; Brown's answer was noncommittal (Senate, *Hearings on SALT II,* part 1, 147).

28. Zorpette, "Monitoring the Tests," 61. Encapsulation is the only means of transmitting data during the reentry phase, when radio transmission is blacked out.

29. U.S. Congress, Senate Foreign Relations Committee, *The SALT II Treaty,* executive report 96-14 (Washington, 1979), 423. Many senators expressed concern over the encryption provision during the committee hearings. In its resolution recommending ratification, the committee unanimously adopted an understanding (proposed by Senator Glenn) that in future agreements all telemetric information should be transmitted in unencrypted and accessible form.

30. Talbott, *Endgame,* 238–39.

31. State Department *SALT II Agreement,* 45.

32. There was a precedent for the discussion of deliberate concealment in the SCC. In 1974 U.S. intelligence noted that the extent of concealment activities associated with Soviet strategic-weapons programs had "increased sub-

stantially." Although the activities in question did not prevent the United States from verifying compliance with SALT I, they were a source of concern. The issue was brought up in the SCC by the Ford administration; no accusation of a treaty violation was made. The Soviets did not admit they were impeding verification, but "careful analysis" in early 1975 led to the conclusion that "there no longer appeared to be an expanding pattern of concealment activities" (State Department, *SALT I: Compliance; SALT II: Verification,* 5).

On this basis the issue was judged to be satisfactorily resolved. The Senate Select Committee on Intelligence, in its report on the treaty, cited this episode as an example of successful operation of the SCC (William C. Potter, ed., *Verification and SALT: The Challenge of Strategic Deception* [Boulder, Colo.: Westview Press, 1980], 238). Critics contend, however, that, since the activities that had generated the original complaint were not halted, the SCC had accomplished little more than legitimizing a Soviet violation.

33. Don Irwin, "Soviet Missile Data Encoded, U.S. Says," *Los Angeles Times,* February 16, 1980.

34. Flight tests of the SS-N-19 sea-launched cruise missile and the SS-20 intermediate-range ballistic missile have also been heavily encrypted. Since those systems are not limited by any treaty, however, encryption of their telemetry is not a compliance issue.

35. See, for example, U.S. Congress, House Foreign Affairs Committee, *Hearings on Continued Compliance with the SALT Agreements,* testimony by Michael Mobbs, 99th Cong., 2d sess. (June 12, 1986), 14.

36. The government does not release official figures on the throw-weights of Soviet missiles. Estimates of nongovernmental analysts are not always reliable. The throw-weight of the SS-N-18, the most modern Soviet SLBM as of 1980, has been estimated as 1,800–2,900 pounds (Jeffrey I. Sands and Robert S. Norris, "A Soviet Trident II?" *Arms Control Today* 15 [September 1985]: 7). *The Military Balance* (London: International Institute for Strategic Studies) cited a figure for SS-N-18 throw-weight of 5,000 pounds until the 1985–86 edition, in which the throw-weight is listed as "not available." The throw-weight of the SS-19 is 7,500–8,000 pounds.

37. Quoted in Miroslav Nincic, "Can the U.S. Trust the U.S.S.R.?" *Scientific American* 254 (April 1986): 38.

38. Don Cook, "Weinberger Uses Photos, Charts to Tell NATO that Soviets Violate Pacts," *Los Angeles Times,* October 30, 1985.

39. Gordon, "Can Reagan Blow the Whistle?"

40. R. Jeffrey Smith, "A New Soviet Missile Angers the White House," *Science* 228 (April 12, 1985): 155–56. It is worth noting that even when telemetry is encrypted it is not totally useless as a source of information. Although the content cannot be deciphered, the so-called telemetry externals can still be used. For example, the Doppler shift of the signal provides information concerning velocity and acceleration.

41. For technical reasons the ratio of RV weight to throw-weight can be determined in a single test with considerably better precision than can the absolute value of either quantity, provided the release of the RV is observed.

42. See note 36.

43. Irwin, "Data Encoded."

44. See Talbott, *Endgame,* 266–67.

45. Debate with Paul Warnke, under the auspices of the Arms Control Association, May 6, 1986.

46. Quoted in "At the USSR Foreign Ministry Press Center," AA3.

47. Ibid.

48. Encryption of telemetry from the SS-18, which has received practically no public attention, probably has the greatest potential strategic significance. The testing of simulated releases, concealed by encryption, could indicate Soviet plans to increase the RV loading of the SS-18. An increase from ten reentry vehicles to fourteen would add more than a thousand accurate ICBM RVs to the Soviet total. This would obviously be a matter of great concern to the United States.

49. ACDA, *Soviet Noncompliance,* 11.

50. Ralph Earle II, "America is Cheating Itself," *Foreign Policy* 64 (Fall 1986): 11.

51. Longstreth et al., *Impact on ABM Treaty,* 39.

52. Gerard C. Smith, *Doubletalk: The Story of the First Strategic Arms Limitation Talks* (New York: Doubleday, 1980), 309.

53. Defense Department, *Soviet Military Power,* 46.

54. Smith, *Doubletalk,* 309–10.

55. Ibid., 313.

56. Gerard C. Smith, chief U.S. delegate to SALT I, remarked that imposing limits on LPARs was "another instance of a twilight zone—where a system, not clearly designed as strategic, could play some strategic role under an arms control regime" (Smith, *Doubletalk,* 310).

57. Leslie H. Gelb, "Moscow Proposes to End a Dispute Over Siberian Radar," *New York Times,* October 29, 1985.

58. Stephen I. Schwartz, *The ABM Treaty: Problems In Compliance,* briefing paper no. 1, University of California, Adlai Stevenson Program on Nuclear Policy (Santa Cruz, August 1986), 4.

59. David C. Morrison, "Radar Diplomacy," *National Journal* 19 (January 3, 1987): 525.

60. Longstreth et al., *Impact on ABM Treaty,* 41.

61. Allan Krass and Catherine Girrier, *American Policy and Alleged Soviet Treaty Violations* (Cambridge, Mass.: Union of Concerned Scientists, 1987), 81.

62. Private communication, July 13, 1987.

63. ACDA, *Soviet Noncompliance,* 1.

64. Longstreth et al., *Impact on ABM Treaty,* 73.

65. Ibid., 40.

66. Soviet Foreign Ministry, *United States Is Violating,* AA3.

67. Michael Getler, "U.S. Dismisses Soviet Charges of Breach of Pact," *Washington Post,* January 31, 1984.

68. Michael R. Gordon, "Soviet Finishes Radar Site In Siberia," *New York Times,* October 11, 1986.

Chapter Five

1. Rowland Evans and Robert Novak, "New Soviet Radar Violates SALT Pact," *New York Post,* July 27, 1983.

2. John Walcott, "U.S. Analysts Find New Soviet Radars, Possibly Complicating Arms Pact Effort," *Wall Street Journal,* August 15, 1986.

3. Longstreth et al., *Impact on ABM Treaty,* 74.

4. ACDA, *Soviet Noncompliance,* 2.

5. Gordon, "Soviet Finishes Radar."

6. Michael R. Gordon, "CIA Is Skeptical That New Soviet Radar Is Part of an ABM System," *National Journal* 17 (March 9, 1985): 526.

7. Longstreth et al., *Impact on ABM Treaty,* 54.

8. ACDA, *Soviet Noncompliance,* 2.

9. Soviet embassy, Washington, press release, April 23, 1985.

10. Starodubov was quoted in the classified version of the U.S. administration's January 1984 noncompliance report (Bill Gertz, *Washington Times,* July 8, 1985).

11. Soviet embassy, press release.

12. Longstreth et al., *Impact on ABM Treaty,* 54.

13. McGeorge Bundy, George F. Kennan, Robert S. McNamara and Gerard C. Smith, "The President's Choice: Star Wars or Arms Control," *Foreign Affairs* 63 (Winter 1984–85): 275.

14. Quoted in Gordon, "CIA Is Skeptical," 526.

15. U.S. Congress, Senate Armed Services and Appropriations Committees, *Joint Hearings on Soviet Strategic Force Developments,* 99th Cong., 1st sess. (June 26, 1985), 59.

16. Quoted in Gordon, "CIA Is Skeptical," 526.

17. Longstreth et al., *Impact on ABM Treaty,* 74.

18. Defense Department, *Soviet Military Power,* 23.

19. Quoted in Jeffrey R. Smith, "U.S. Experts Condemn Soviet Radar," *Science* 227 (March 22, 1985): 1443.

Chapter Six

1. President Reagan's Speech on Defense Spending and Defensive Technology (in *Weekly Compilation of Presidential Documents* 19, no. 12 [March 28, 1983]: 423–66).

2. Department of Defense, Strategic Defense Initiative Organization, *Report to the Congress on the Strategic Defense Initiative* (Washington, 1985), 3.

3. Ibid., 7.

4. Caspar W. Weinberger, *Report of the Secretary of Defense Caspar W. Weinberger to the Congress on the FY 85 Budget, FY 86 Authorization Request and the FY 1985–89 Defense Programs* (Washington, 1984), 193.

5. "Star Wars at the Crossroads," *Time,* June 23, 1986, 16–27.

6. U.S. Congress, Senate Armed Services Committee, *Hearings on Military Implications of the Treaty on the Limitation of Anti-Ballistic Missile Systems and the Interim Agreement on Limitation of Strategic Offensive Arms,* 92d Cong., 2d sess. (June–July 1972), 377.

7. SDIO, *Report to the Congress on the Strategic Defense Initiative* (Washington, 1986), C13.

8. Ibid., C11.

9. Ibid., C12–C13.

10. Ibid., C7.

11. Ibid., C13.

12. Ibid., C14; and Mike Redine (aide to Abrahamson), in news briefing by James Abrahamson, (Director, SDIO) Thursday, September 11, 1986.

13. According to the text of the treaty, each side is allowed two ABM sites, one centered around the national capital, which could include no more than six ABM radar complexes, and one centered on an ICBM field, which could include no more than two large phase-arrayed radars and no more than eighteen additional ABM radars of lesser potential. In the 1974 protocol both sides agreed to reduce the allowed number of sites to one, with the Soviets maintaining their Galosh system around Moscow and the United States retaining the right to an operational site around a missile-silo field. Accordingly, the number of radars permitted under the terms of the treaty is different for the United States and the Soviet Union.

14. U.S. Congress, House Foreign Affairs Committee, Subcommittee on Arms Control, International Security and Science, *Hearing on ABM Treaty Interpretation Dispute,* testimony by Paul H. Nitze and Abraham D. Sofaer, 99th Cong., 1st sess. (October 22, 1985), 2–21.

15. SDIO, *Report,* 1986, C2.

16. See discussion of treaty interpretation in Longstreth et al., *Impact on ABM Treaty,* 23–31.

17. Gerard C. Smith, "How the Administration Amended the ABM Treaty," *New York Times,* October 23, 1985.

18. U.S. Congress, Senate, *Interpretation of the ABM Treaty,* part 1, "The Senate Ratification Proceedings," review by Sam Nunn, *Congressional Record,* 100th Cong., 1st sess. (March 11, 1987), S2967–86.

19. Ibid., part 2, "Subsequent Practice Under the ABM Treaty," S3090–95, and part 3, "The ABM Negotiating Record," S3171–73.

20. Longstreth et al., *Impact on ABM Treaty,* 29.

21. See R. Jeffrey Smith, "Star Wars Tests and the ABM Treaty," *Science* 229 (July 5, 1985): 29–31.

22. Longstreth et al., *Impact on ABM Treaty,* 29.

23. News briefing at the Pentagon, September 11, 1986.

24. Quoted in Richard A. Scribner, Theodore J. Ralston, and William D. Metz, *The Verification Challenge: Problems and Promises of Strategic Nuclear Arms Control Verification* (Boston: Birkhauser, 1985), 131.

25. Quoted in R. Jeffrey Smith, "Soviets Play Tit for Tat," *Science* 229 (July 5, 1985): 30.

26. Quoted in National Campaign to Save the ABM Treaty, *Briefing Book on the ABM Treaty and Related Issues* (Washington, 1986), 9.6.

Chapter Seven

1. Weinberger, *Responding,* 1.

2. ACDA, *Soviet Noncompliance,* ii.

3. During the 1970s, for instance, there was considerable debate within both the Ministry of Defense and the Politburo over the allocation of resources between military and nonmilitary sectors, and within the military sector itself in the Soviet

Union. This internal debate resulted in the strong emphasis on defense spending under the Brezhnev regime and the rapid expansion of Soviet military forces during the 1970s. See Harry Gelman, *The Brezhnev Politburo and the Decline of Détente* (Ithaca: Cornell University Press, 1984), 81.

4. ACDA, *Soviet Noncompliance,* iii.

5. Arthur J. Alexander, *Knowing About Soviet Weapons Acquisition and Strategic Weapons,* (Santa Monica: Rand Corporation, 1986).

6. See Arthur J. Alexander, "Modeling Soviet Defense Decisionmaking," in Jiri Valenta and William Potter, eds., *Soviet Decisionmaking for National Security,* (London: Allen and Unwin, 1984), 9–22.

7. Quoted in Igor S. Glagolev, "The Soviet Decision-Making Process in Arms-Control Negotiations," *Orbis* 21 (Winter 1978): 771–72.

8. Thomas W. Wolfe, *The SALT Experience* (Cambridge: Ballinger, 1979), 74–75.

9. Raymond L. Garthoff, "The Soviet Military and SALT," in Valenta and Potter, *Soviet Decisionmaking,* 144.

10. For instance, during the period of the SALT I and ABM Treaty negotiations, the following high-level Soviet military personnel were involved in the negotiations: Col. Gen. Nikolai Ogarkov (deputy chief of the General Staff), Col. Gen. Nikolai Alekseyev, Lt. Gen. Konstantin Trusov, Lt. Gen. Ivan Beletsky, and Col. Gen. Anatoly Gryzlov. During the SALT II period both Gen. Ogarkov, and Maj. Gen. V. P. Starodubov were involved in the negotiations. In Moscow, defense ministers Grechko and Ustinov both had SALT input and responsibilities. Gen. Mikhail Kozlov, a deputy chief of the General Staff, and Col. Gen. Sergei Akhromeyev, the first deputy chief of staff (now chief of the Soviet General Staff), were both involved in policy-making in Moscow. Other officers were involved as advisers and experts in both SALT I and SALT II, working under senior officers of the General Staff.

11. House, *Hearing on ABM Treaty Interpretation Dispute,* statement by Abraham Sofaer, 4–21. There are exceptions to this rule. During the recent controversy over U.S. treaty compliance, Richard Haddad, DOD general counsel, took a position in general advocating continued U.S. compliance with agreements.

12. Alexander, "Modeling Soviet Defense Decisionmaking," 16–17.

13. MccGwire, *Military Objectives,* 477.

14. Ibid., 239.

15. Raymond L. Garthoff, *Détente and Confrontation* (Washington: Brookings Institution, 1985), 183.

16. See the comments of William Potter in *Explaining Soviet Compliance Behavior,* conference digest, Global Outlook, Palo Alto, Calif., February 14, 1986, 11.

17. Garthoff, *Détente and Confrontation,* 172.

18. Ibid., 173.

19. *Explaining Soviet Compliance Behavior,* 13.

20. "Transcript of the President's News Conference Emphasizing Domestic Matters," *New York Times,* June 23, 1972 (cited in Garthoff, *Détente and Confrontation,* 300).

21. Garthoff, *Détente and Confrontation,* 300.

22. See Raymond L. Garthoff, "Handling the Cienfuegos Crisis," *International Security* 8 (Summer 1983): 46–66.

23. Talbott, *Endgame,* 190–94.

24. Ibid., 194–97.

25. Roland M. Timerbayev, *Verification of Arms Limitation and Disarmament* (translated from *Kontrol' za ogranicheniyem vooruzheniy i razoruzheniyem* [Moscow: Mezhdunarodnyye Otnosheniya, 1983]), Joint Publications Research Service UPS-84-041-L (November 5, 1984), 17–19.

26. Wayne Biddle, "Soviet and U.S. Aides, in Atlanta, Trade Accusations on Arms Talks," *New York Times,* April 14, 1985 (quoting Dobrynin); "At the USSR Foreign Ministry Press Center," 1986, AA8 (quoting Akhromeyev).

27. For a listing and discussion of such Soviet "half-truths," see Robert Axelrod and William Zimmerman, "The Soviet Press on Soviet Foreign Policy: A Usually Reliable Source," *British Journal of Political Science* 2 (1981): 201–25.

28. John Walcott, "U.S. Analysts Find New Soviet Radars, Possibly Complicating Arms-Pact Effort," *Wall Street Journal,* August 15, 1986.

29. Ibid.

30. Gordon, "CIA Is Skeptical," 525.

31. MccGwire, *Military Objectives,* 243–44.

32. Personal correspondence, April 25, 1986.

33. Alexander, "Modeling Soviet Defense Decisionmaking," 16.

34. Gordon, "CIA Is Skeptical," 526.

35. Nikolai Ogarkov, "Guarding Peaceful Labor" (in Russian), *Kommunist* 10 (1981): 80–91.

36. Dmitri Ustinov, "Against the Arms Race and the Threat of War" (in Russian) *Pravda,* July 25, 1981 (translated in Foreign Broadcast Information Service, *Daily Report: Soviet Union,* July 27, 1981, AA1–AA10).

37. ACDA, *Soviet Noncompliance,* 9–15, and previous noncompliance reports dating back to 1984.

38. President Ronald Reagan, message to the U.S. Congress, February 1, 1985 (U.S. State Department, Special Report no. 122, 3).

39. Gelb, "Moscow Proposes to End Dispute."

40. Philip Taubman, "Soviet Diplomacy Given a New Look Under Gorbachev," *New York Times,* August 10, 1986.

41. The Soviet Union has itself emphasized that these initiatives represent a new Soviet approach to verification stressing cooperative measures (see Roland M. Timerbayev, "A Soviet Official on Verification," *Bulletin of the Atomic Scientists* 43 [January–February 1987]: 8–11).

Chapter Eight

1. U.S. Congress, Senate Foreign Relations Committee, "Memorandum of Understanding on the SCC," 61, and "Summary of Miscellaneous Agreements Relating to the Standing Consultative Commission," 79–80, in *SALT II Treaty: Background Documents,* 96th Cong., 1st sess. (1979).

2. Sidney N. Graybeal and Michael Krepon, "Making Better Use of the Standing Consultative Commission," *International Security* 10 (Fall 1985): 186.

3. Carnegie Endowment for International Peace, Panel on U.S. Security and the Future of Arms Control, *Challenges for U.S. National Security* (Washington, 1983), 53.

4. Weinberger, *Responding,* 2, 10.

5. ACDA, *Arms Control and Disarmament Agreements,* 138.

6. U.S. Congress, Senate Armed Services Committee, *Hearings on Soviet Compliance with Certain Provisions of the 1972 SALT I Agreements,* 94th Cong., 1st sess. (1975), 3–4.

7. Talbott, *Endgame,* 198, 200.

8. Melvin R. Laird, "Arms Control: The Soviets Are Cheating!" *Reader's Digest,* December 1977, 98–99.

9. Robert Buchheim, briefing notes, Committee for National Security, June 9, 1983.

10. State Department, *SALT I: Compliance; SALT II: Verification,* 4.

11. Ibid., 8.

12. Robert W. Buchheim and Dan Caldwell, *The U.S.–U.S.S.R. Standing Consultative Commission: Description and Appraisal,* working paper no. 2, Brown University, Center for Foreign Policy Development (Providence, 1983), 9.

13. State Department, *SALT I: Compliance; SALT II: Verification,* 6.

14. Ibid.

15. Senate, "Summary of Miscellaneous Agreements," 80.

16. Strobe Talbott, *Deadly Gambits: The Reagan Administration and the Stalemate in Nuclear Arms Control* (New York: Alfred A. Knopf, 1984), 230.

17. ACDA, *Quarter Century,* 14–15.

18. Talbott, *Deadly Gambits,* 228.

19. Sidney Graybeal, "Negotiating an Accident Prevention Center: The Experience of the Standing Consultative Commission," in John W. Lewis and Coit D. Blacker, eds. *Next Steps in the Creation of an Accidental Nuclear War Prevention Center,* Stanford University, Center for International Security and Arms Control (Stanford, 1983), 29.

20. Stephen S. Rosenfeld, "Clogged Channel," *Washington Post,* February 21, 1983.

21. Ibid.

22. Manfred Eimer (assistant director, ACDA), private discussion, September 12, 1986.

23. Walter Pincus, "Agencies Split on Response to Possible ABM Treaty Violations," *Washington Post,* December 12, 1985.

24. Talbott, *Deadly Gambits,* 319–20.

25. Dan Caldwell, "The Standing Consultative Commission: Past Performance and Future Possibilities," in William C. Potter, ed., *Verification and Arms Control* (Lexington, Mass.: Lexington Books, 1985), 222.

26. ACDA, *Communiqué of the United States–Soviet Union Standing Consultative Commission* (as reported in the *Arms Control Reporter,* no. 2.1 [January 1983]: 603.D.1).

27. ACDA, *Soviet Noncompliance,* 9.

28. Burt, "U.S. Warns Russians."

29. Communication from Isakov (Soviet minister counselor) to Stephen Solarz

(U.S. congressman), April 23, 1985.

30. Means other than telemetry can deny the other side data regarding ICBM test flights. For example, the United States has in the past used low-power telemetry transmissions and encapsulation to prevent the Soviets from gathering information about U.S. missiles during flight tests (see Talbott, *Endgame*, 196).

31. ACDA, *Soviet Noncompliance*, 1–2.

Chapter Nine

1. Weinberger, *Responding*, 9.
2. Graybeal and Krepon, "Making Better Use of the SCC," 193.

Select Bibliography

Alexander, Arthur J. *Knowing About Soviet Weapons Acquisition and Strategic Weapons*. Santa Monica: Rand Corporation, 1986.

Arms Control Association. *Countdown on SALT II: The Case for Preserving SALT II Limits on U.S. and Soviet Strategic Forces*. Washington, 1985.

Axelrod, Robert, and William Zimmerman. "The Soviet Press on Soviet Foreign Policy: A Usually Reliable Source." *British Journal of Political Science* 2 (1981): 210–25.

Buchheim, Robert W., and Dan Caldwell. *The U.S.–U.S.S.R. Standing Consultative Commission: Description and Appraisal*. Providence: Brown University, Center for Foreign Policy Development, May 1983.

Bundy, McGeorge, George F. Kennan, Robert S. McNamara, and Gerard C. Smith. "The President's Choice: Star Wars or Arms Control." *Foreign Affairs* 63 (Winter 1984–85): 264–78.

Bunn, M. Elaine, and Charles R. Gellner. *Soviet Compliance with Arms Control Agreements (Excluding SALT II)*. Washington: Library of Congress, Congressional Research Service, October 16, 1978.

Carnegie Endowment for International Peace. Panel on U.S. Security and the Future of Arms Control. *Challenges for U.S. National Security*. Washington, 1983.

Duffy, Gloria. "Administration Redefines Soviet 'Violations.'" *Bulletin of the Atomic Scientists* 42 (February 1986): 13–17.

Earle, Ralph, II. "America Is Cheating Itself." *Foreign Policy* 64 (Fall 1986): 3–16.

Einhorn, Robert J. "Treaty Compliance." *Foreign Policy* 45 (Winter 1981–82): 29–47.

Garthoff, Raymond L. *Détente and Confrontation*. Washington: Brookings Institution, 1985.

———. "Handling the Cienfuegos Crisis." *International Security* 8 (Summer 1983): 46–66.

Gellner, Charles R., and Judith A. Freedman. *The SALT Process: Reagan Administration Policy*. Washington: Library of Congress, Congressional Research Service, 1981.

Gellner, Charles R., and Jeanette Voas. *Soviet Compliance with the SALT I and II Agreements on Offensive Arms*. Washington: Library of Congress, Congressional Research Service, 1985.

Gelman, Harry. *The Brezhnev Politburo and the Decline of Détente*. New York: Cornell University Press, 1984.

Glagolev, Igor S. "The Soviet Decision-Making Process in Arms-Control Negotiations." *Orbis* 21 (Winter 1978): 767–76.

Glicksman, Alex. "The Soviet Arms Control Compliance Record: Part I." *National Defense* 70 (February 1986): 61–70.

――――. "The Soviet Arms Control Compliance Record: Part II." *National Defense* 70 (March 1986): 43–51.

Gordon, Michael R. "CIA Is Skeptical That New Soviet Radar Is Part of an ABM Defense System." *National Journal* 17 (March 9, 1985): 523–26.

Graybeal, Sidney N. "Negotiating an Accident Prevention Center: The Experience of the Standing Consultative Commission." In *Next Steps in the Creation of an Accidental Nuclear War Prevention Center,* edited by John W. Lewis and Coit D. Blacker. Stanford: Center for International Security and Arms Control, Stanford University, 1983.

Graybeal, Sidney N., and Michael Krepon. "Making Better Use of the Standing Consultative Commission." *International Security* 10 (Fall 1985): 183–99.

――――. "SCC: Neglected Arms Control Tool." *Bulletin of the Atomic Scientists* 41 (November 1985): 30–33.

Krass, Allan, and Catherine Girrier. *American Policy and Alleged Soviet Treaty Violations.* Cambridge, Mass.: Union of Concerned Scientists, 1987.

Krepon, Michael. Arms Control: Verification and Compliance. New York: Foreign Policy Association, 1984.

Laird, Melvin R. "Arms Control: The Russians Are Cheating!" *Reader's Digest,* December 1977, 97–101.

Longstreth, Thomas K. "Report Aims to Sabotage Arms Control." *Bulletin of the Atomic Scientists* 41 (January 1985): 29–34.

Longstreth, Thomas K., John E. Pike, and John B. Rhinelander. *The Impact of U.S. and Soviet Ballistic Missile Defense Programs on the ABM Treaty.* Washington: National Campaign to Save the ABM Treaty, March 1985.

Lowenthall, Mark M. *Possible Means of Improving Congressional Oversight of SALT Verification and Other Arms Control Compliance Issues.* Washington: Library of Congress, Congressional Research Service, 1979.

Lynn-Jones, Sean. "A Quiet Success for Arms Control: Preventing Incidents at Sea." *International Security* 9 (Spring 1985): 154–84.

MccGwire, Michael. *Military Objectives in Soviet Foreign Policy.* Washington: Brookings Institution, 1987.

National Campaign to Save the ABM Treaty. *Briefing Book on the ABM Treaty and Related Issues.* Washington, 1986.

Nincic, Miroslav. "Can the U.S. Trust the U.S.S.R.?" *Scientific American* 254 (April 1986): 33–41.

Potter, William C., ed. *Verification and Arms Control.* Lexington, Mass.: Lexington Books, 1985.

――――. *Verification and SALT: The Challenge of Strategic Deception.* Boulder, Colo.: Westview Press, 1980.

President's Commission on Strategic Forces (Scowcroft Commission). *Report of the President's Commission on Strategic Forces.* Washington, April 1983.

Reagan, Ronald. *Soviet Noncompliance with Arms Control Agreements.* President's reports to Congress. Washington, January 23, 1984; February 1, 1985; December 23, 1985; and March 10, 1987.

Sartori, Leo. "Will SALT II Survive?" *International Security* 10 (Winter 1985–86): 147–74.

Scribner, Richard A., Theodore J. Ralston, and William D. Metz. *The Verification Challenge: Problems and Promises of Strategic Nuclear Arms Control Verification.* Boston: Birkhauser, 1985.

Seaborg, Glenn T. *Stemming the Tide: Arms Control in the Johnson Years.* Lexington, Mass.: Lexington Books, 1987.

Smith, Gerard C. *Doubletalk: The Story of the First Strategic Arms Limitation Talks.* New York: Doubleday, 1980.

Soviet Foreign Ministry. *The United States Is Violating Its International Commitments.* Aide-mémoire from the Soviet Embassy, Washington. (In Foreign Broadcast Information Service, *Daily Report: Soviet Union,* January 30, 1984, AA1–AA5.)

Talbott, Strobe. *Endgame: The Inside Story of Salt II.* New York: Harper and Row, 1979.

———. *Deadly Gambits: The Reagan Administration and the Stalemate in Nuclear Arms Control.* New York: Alfred A. Knopf, 1984.

Timerbayev, Roland M. "A Soviet Official on Verification." *Bulletin of the Atomic Scientists* 43 (January–February 1987): 8–11.

———. *Verification of Arms Limitation and Disarmament.* (Translated from *Kontrol' za ogranicheniyem vooruzheniy i razoruzheniyem.* Moscow: Mezhdunarodnyye Otnosheniya, 1983.) Joint Publications Research Service UPS-84-041-L, November 5, 1984.

Trimble, Phillip R. *Soviet Violations of Arms Control Agreements: A Legal Perspective.* Los Angeles: University of California, Center for International and Strategic Affairs, 1985.

U.S. Arms Control and Disarmament Agency. *Arms Control and Disarmament Agreements: Texts and Histories of Negotiations.* 5th ed. Washington, 1982.

———. *Soviet Noncompliance.* Washington, February 1, 1986.

———. General Advisory Committee on Arms Control and Disarmament. *A Quarter Century of Soviet Compliance Practices Under Arms Control Commitments: 1958–1983.* Washington, October 10, 1984.

U.S. Congress. House. Armed Services Committee. Panel on Arms Control and Disarmament. *Hearings on Verification of a Comprehensive Nuclear Test Ban Treaty, Soviet Compliance with the Threshold Test Ban Treaty, and the Sizes of Soviet Strategic Nuclear Weapons,* Testimony by Lynn R. Sykes, 99th Cong., 1st sess. (November 20, 1985).

———. Foreign Affairs Committee. Subcommittee on Arms Control, International Security and Science. *Fundamentals of Nuclear Arms Control.* Part 4, *Treaty Compliance and Nuclear Arms Control.* Report prepared by Congressional Research Service, 1985.

———. Foreign Affairs Committee. Subcommittee on Arms Control, International Security and Science. *Hearing on ABM Treaty Interpretation Dispute,* 99th Cong., 1st sess. (October 22, 1985), 2–21.

U.S. Congress. Senate. Armed Services Committee. *Hearings on Military Implications of the Treaty on the Limitation of Anti-Ballistic Missile Systems and the Interim Agreement on Limitation of Strategic Offensive Arms.* 92d Cong., 2d sess. (1972).

———. Armed Services Committee. *Hearings on Soviet Compliance with Cer-*

tain *Provisions of the 1972 SALT I Agreements.* 94th Cong., 1st sess. (1975).
———. Armed Services Committee. *Hearings on Soviet Treaty Violations.* 98th Cong., 2d sess. (1984), and 99th Cong., 1st sess. (1985).
———. Foreign Relations Committee. *Hearings on the SALT II Treaty.* 96th Cong., 1st and 2d sess., 1979.
———. Foreign Relations Committee. *SALT II Treaty: Background Documents.* 96th Cong., 1st sess. (1979).
U.S. Defense Department. *Soviet Military Power.* 5th ed. Washington, March 1986.
———. Strategic Defense Initiative Organization. *Report to the Congress on the Strategic Defense Initiative.* Washington, 1985 and 1986.
U.S. Joint Chiefs of Staff. *United States Military Posture, FY 1987.* Washington, 1987.
U.S. State Department. *SALT I: Compliance; SALT II: Verification.* Selected Document no. 7. Washington, Feb. 1978.
———. *SALT II Agreement.* Selected Document no. 12B. Washington, 1979.
Valenta, Jiri, and William Potter, eds. *Soviet Decisionmaking for National Security.* London: Allen and Unwin, 1984.
Voas, Jeanette. "The Arms-Control Compliance Debate." *Survival* 28 (January–February 1986): 8–31.
———. *Soviet SALT II Compliance Behavior: The SS-25 and Encryption of Telemetry.* Washington: Library of Congress, Congressional Research Service, June 17, 1986.
Weinberger, Caspar. *Report of the Secretary of Defense Caspar W. Weinberger to the Congress on the FY 1985 Budget, FY 1986 Authorization Request and the FY 1985–89 Defense Programs.* Washington, 1984.
———. *Responding to Soviet Violations Policy Study.* Memorandum to the President, November 13, 1985. (Also published in *New York Times,* November 14, 1985.)
Wilrich, Mason, and John B. Rhinelander. *SALT I: The Moscow Agreements and Beyond.* New York: Free Press, 1974.
Wolfe, Thomas W. *The SALT Experience.* Cambridge: Ballinger, 1979.

Index